Perfect Husbands
(& Other Fairy Tales)

PERFECT HUSBANDS
(& OTHER FAIRY TALES)

DEMYSTIFYING MARRIAGE,

MEN, and ROMANCE

REGINA BARRECA

HARMONY BOOKS • NEW YORK

Published by Harmony Books, a division of Crown Publishers, Inc., 201 East
50th Street, New York, New York 10022. Member of the Crown Publishing Group.

Random House, Inc.
New York, Toronto, London, Sydney, Auckland

HARMONY and colophon are trademarks of Crown Publishers, Inc.

Manufactured in the United States of America

Library of Congress Cataloging-in-Publication Data
Barreca, Regina.
Perfect husbands (& other fairy tales) : demystifying marriage, men,
and romance / by Regina Barreca.
p.   cm.
Includes bibliographical references.
1. Husbands. 2. Marriage. I. Title.
HQ756.B377 1993
306.81—dc20   93-20328
CIP

ISBN 0-517-59538-9

10 9 8 7 6 5 4 3 2 1

First Edition

I dedicate this book to my husband,
Michael Meyer.

ACKNOWLEDGMENTS

I would thank, by name, the hundreds of husbands who have told me their stories over the years, but since most of them made me swear to protect their anonymity, I can only offer them a general round of applause and promise that I'll never reveal where I heard the story first. To the hundreds of women who told their stories, unconcerned whether they were named or not, I also offer applause; in addition, I offer my nods, howls, and smiles of agreement. To those researchers and writers whose work has supported and guided my own, I owe thanks.

I am deeply grateful to my brilliant, insightful, and supportive editor at Harmony Books, Shaye Areheart. She understood, right from the start, where I wanted the book to go and her direction helped immeasurably. There may not be perfect husbands, but there are perfect editors, and Shaye is one. Her assistant, Kelly Hammond, was terrific, as was my production editor, Kim Hertlein. My gratitude to my agent, Diane Cleaver, extends to preparing and finding a good home for *Perfect Husbands* and far beyond. The Research Foundation at the University of Connecticut was generous in support of this book, and deserves my thanks.

I owe a great debt to my colleagues and friends. Faith Middleton encouraged me to do a show on the subject of "husbands" on her award-winning Connecticut public radio program "Open Air New England," and the program was instrumental in outlining this book; Bob Sullivan and Cindy Adams gave the book detailed, perceptive, and helpful readings; Lary Bloom of *Northeast Magazine* was encouraging from the beginning; Suzy Staubach of the UConn Coop bookstore, and Roxanne Coady of R. J. Julia's bookstore in Madison, Connecticut were invaluable for their suggestions and support; my wonderful research assistants, particularly Allison Hild and Julie Nash, worked diligently and effectively on this project. From the bottom of my heart, Fay Weldon, Rose Quiello, Lee Jacobus, John Glavin, Margaret Higonnet, Sonya Friedman, Dranda Trimble, Bonnie Januszewski, Nancy Lager, Tim Taylor, Pam Katz, Mary Anne Yanulis, Brenda Murphy, Hugo Barreca, Sr., Hugo Barreca, Jr., Wendy Schlemm, Matthew Meyer, Tim Meyer, and many other friends have won my everlasting gratitude for their patient listening, their smart comments, and their remarkable generosity.

To my husband, Michael Meyer, who inspired, infuriated, and enlightened me throughout the writing of this book, I owe only what we give one another freely: respect, admiration, and—astonishingly, consistently—exactly the right kind of love. It is my honor to dedicate this book to Michael, who reaffirms for me, daily, that married life is not a contradiction in terms.

CONTENTS

CHAPTER ONE

WHY A HUSBAND OF ONE'S OWN?

Rights, Rituals, and Relative Happiness

WHY, WHEN A woman has a room of her own in a perfectly good rent-stabilized apartment with her own name on the lease obliging her to pay rent with money of her own—which she makes at a satisfying job—does she still want a husband of her own? What role can a husband possibly play in such a life? I asked myself this question when I was considering marriage for at least the thousandth time—if you count all those names written out in the margins of my notebooks in junior high when I still thought I'd get to be somebody else when I crossed the threshold—or for the second time if you count only those relationships I have formalized with the state.

Since my first marriage did not "work out," as my friends gingerly pointed out, why bother? Why not just keep a nice lover and companion safe from overuse, the way my aunts used to keep the good furniture in the living room safe from what they vaguely referred to as "wear and tear"? If I listened to advice from scores of remarkable women, not least among them Mary Wollstonecraft and Katharine Hepburn, I would follow the maxim that men and women should live near one another and visit occasionally.

But then I am not a remarkable woman. In early childhood, I used to con my mother into buying me "Brides" coloring books over and over again, even after she pointed out that all the outfits were white or black and there was very little to color except the bouquets and bridesmaid dresses (from which arises the tradition dictating lurid colors for all bridesmaid dresses; after all, you were dying to use the "aquamarine" and "magenta" crayons at some point). I dressed as a bride every Halloween, and so did half the other girls in the neighborhood, which probably should have tipped me off to the demographics that would follow those of us born in the late forties, fifties, sixties, and early seventies into our adult years: There were hundreds of little brides out there, but there were no grooms. The only little boys dressed in tuxedo outfits on Halloween were the ones dressed as bums, wearing oversized jackets with torn elbows. Many of the women I know continue to see the world as divided into brides and bums even though they have long abandoned the idea of trick-or-treat.

Then sometime in high school I began to understand that a woman *could* make an impact on the world and I started cultivating ambitions other than matrimony. By the mid-seventies, I was in college and telling the men I dated that I would probably never marry. At that point in my life I decided to be an amalgam of heroines, a cross between the main character from *My Brilliant Career*, Emma Peel from the television program "The Avengers," and Gloria Steinem. At eighteen, I firmly believed that I would rewrite all life's rules and undermine all of its conventions, beginning with my rejection of the idea of marriage. Marriage had been presented to me as one of life's inevitabilities, which made me determined to avoid it. What I wasn't expecting as a sideline to my own decision was the overwhelmingly positive response from the young men I met. They loved this idea of the determinedly *single*-minded woman. I was annoyingly pleased with myself for inadvertently gaining their approval.

At eighteen, you see, my male counterparts at college were also vowing eternal freedom from marriage. When I would announce, "I'm wedded to my independence," the equally self-absorbed young men would fall at my feet. It was the sort of thing perfume commercials promised, but I was shocked that a simple declaration of my intention not to be anyone's "intended" would have the same seductive effect as a heavy dose of Chanel Number 5. The young man of the semester would immediately pledge that we would be tied to one another forever by our shared disdain for the bourgeoisie.

We'd then court like any couple would, but secretly *we* knew we were beyond all the childish rigmarole our lesser compatriots were forced to endure. My friends were pretty much of the same mind, and we were all happy with this arrangement (and nobody saw any irony in the way all of us nonconformists acted alike). We triumphed in the knowledge that independence was sexy as well as ideologically correct. The guys relaxed. They blossomed in the luxury of a relationship that existed without the pressures of anachronistic conventions and rituals.

"THE GIRLS YOU WANT TO DATE ARE NOT THE GIRLS YOU WANT TO MARRY"

Then came the *really* big surprise. When our boyfriends graduated, they coincidentally left to wed "pert-and-perky" cheerleader types. In contrast to the women I knew at college, these girls seemed to have wanted nothing else *but* to be wives. They reminded me of wealthy versions of the older girls in my old neighborhood, the ones who married straight out of high school. But at least *those* girls had made no pretense of ever intending to face the work world (like one of my cousins, who, when her husband suggested that she might get a part-time job, explained in no uncertain terms that "if I wanted to work for a living, I wouldn't have gotten married").

The privileged pert-and-perky girls, however, said they were learning "skills" that they would use in later life. They saw their education as a tool to use in becoming a suitable companion to a man of substance. For them, college was indeed a "finishing school," with all the implications of providing them with an appropriate "ending" in the form of a husband with good prospects. Such young women baked brownies every week and left them outside the guys' doors on a regular basis with cute little notes, very tidily written with a pink Flair. My friends and I were confounded by this. We were struggling to complete the reading assignments and get papers in on time—we hardly had time to eat. How did they find time to *bake?*

The guys would shrug off these attentions, but, thinking back on it, they devoured the offerings without remorse. One or two of the sweethearts of Sigma Nu would go so far as to take a boy's laundry home with her and return it on the next weekend. This was the mid-seventies, remember, not the mid-fifties; washing somebody else's socks for free was not what most of us felt we'd been put on earth to do. Our male friends seemed to have no respect for the young women who were so cloyingly attentive, and we felt smug in our knowledge that the men with whom we shared our time loved us for ourselves alone and not our domestic skills. This sense of self-congratulation was a bad sign. We were foolish to think of ourselves as beyond the pull of the accumulated mythologies of a culture that enshrines the concept of marriage and of appropriate roles within marriage.

Of course, the interesting finale to all of this became a life lesson for the independent. Those brownie-baking young women our male friends didn't date in college turned out to be the girls they wanted to marry once they were out of school. I can now more fully understand the temptation. Someone taking care of you full-time sounds, frankly, like a wonderful idea at first glance. In her collection of essays, *If You Can't Live Without Me, Why Aren't You Dead Yet?* Cynthia Heimel considers the possibility that if she were a man, perhaps she'd also want a traditional wife: "If I were a man, I wouldn't want me. I'd go for a more placid, domestic type in a pretty, flowered dress. A woman who would warm the pot for tea just the way I like it, who would tell the children to shut up because daddy's working, he's on deadline, we mustn't bother him with the petty problems of financial-aid applications and braces." Maybe I, too, would have married a brownie-baking girl if she had offered: Who in their right mind wouldn't want someone to support you emotionally, make all your meals, clean your house, have your children, and through it all believe she was lucky to be granted the privilege? According to the female undergraduates who come to my office wailing and raging against the social system, this still goes on today.

THE PERILS OF GIVING IN—
AND GETTING OUT

I doubt if I could have been a very good full-time wife even if I tried. Instead, I decided to live a conventionally unconventional life. During my twenties, I lived with two men—not at the same time; no New York apartment is big enough—one of whom I eventually married. (The other resides, quite happily I am sure, in a suburb of his own choosing.) My husband-to-be and I lived together for four years, and then decided to marry for very practical reasons—or so I convinced myself. We went down to City Hall three days after his deportation notice arrived, which made it all seem terribly dramatic, as we told ourselves that the choice was made for us by fate (and/or the feds). It also swept away all my residual fears of responsibility: Government bureaucracy seemed to make a wedding imperative. What could we do? We could maintain the fiction, at least briefly, that we were still outside convention.

It wasn't, I told myself, as if I was really giving in. Like the heroine in one of my favorite plays, I vowed that I wasn't going to "by degrees dwindle into a wife." I bought my own wedding ring and bargained it down to a reasonable price; it was going to be a modern marriage. He didn't own me, so why should he be made to put a piece of gold on my finger? The ring I bought did not even look like an ordinary wedding band; I told myself that I was subverting the rituals of matrimony even as I came under their spell.

The trouble was, I didn't see the mechanics of this trick I played on myself: For all my protestations, I still wore a ring on the third finger of my left hand. And I liked the feeling. Amazing transformations occurred, all in my own mind, but they occurred nonetheless. I reverted to the ideas I'd been taught as a child. It took no time at all for me to put away the independence I'd flaunted for ten years. With this wedding ring, I suddenly felt unreasonably safe in the subway, as if no lunatic would bother me now. With this ring, I felt secure in the classroom, believing my students would whisper in relief, "See? You can be a feminist and still get a man." With this ring, I felt confident at my high school reunion: I *was* attractive, and a committed man lived under my roof. It was as if I were surrounded by a kind of marriage-magic that could ward off all unhappiness.

But it was a sham: It was not a magical ring or a magical marriage. What I thought offered safety instead offered captivity. By pretending not to be part of a "real marriage," we could not support the weight of the real concerns of our life together. We buckled under the strain, and the relationship ended after six years.

When the marriage broke up, it was tough to take that ring off, but absolutely necessary to do so. Despite the necessity, I avoided it for weeks. A friend suggested I buy a black stone as a divorce ring. Instead, I wore my wedding ring on my other hand. I wore rings on both hands. I bought inexpensive silver rings and wore them. Taking the gold out of my teeth would not have been more painful than taking off that ring. When I could no longer bear to fool myself, I went ringless. All those ads for gold aside, who notices what jewelry a woman wears unless they intend to mug her, right?

To my surprise and dismay, people noticed. Meeting people as a single woman in my thirties, I was shocked that some of them still kiddingly asked why I wasn't married (in a voice similar to the one used to ask why you don't have children after you *are* married). When I was wearing a wedding ring, nobody had ever asked why I wasn't single. Clearly marriage is still considered the natural state for a woman and, if for no other reason, I decided to avoid it. I relaxed, settling once again with the comfortable idea that I simply was not the marrying kind. The system, I announced cheerfully, just did not work for me. I had tried it, proved to myself it couldn't work, and erased all remaining doubt. I often quoted comedian Lizz Winstead's line "I think, therefore I'm single," and that kept the questioners amused while it also kept them from asking other questions.

Having come out of an unsuccessful marriage, I spent a great deal of time wondering, theoretically and personally, why husbands are still regarded as valuable commodities, so much so that women steal them, barter for them, and stake high claims to keep them when women themselves are no longer looking to be kept. I couldn't imagine wanting to get married again.

GETTING IT RIGHT

Then one day at work a man smiled. I caught a piece of it, smiled back, and we rolled up our sleeves and started a relationship. After some time passed, I worried about my desire to make my new lover into my husband. From what he told me, he was not a very good husband the first time he tried it, but then frankly I was not a good wife. We seemed, for our faults as well as our virtues, to be an inevitable but still unlikely couple.

Where did this leave me? I kept thinking of comedian Joy Behar's declaration: "I want a man in my life, but not in my house. I'm a very busy woman. I want him to come in, hook up the VCR, and leave." I was not sure what space a husband would occupy in my new life, although I had some fantasies both tender and hilarious.

Falling in love in my thirties was very different from my earlier experiences, and I wasn't sure what to expect. I knew from the past that no one else could guarantee safety or happiness, and that the best to hope for was a partner who would represent life's possibilities instead of its limitations. Instead of seeing marriage as a version of "home base" from a children's game where you couldn't get tagged "out" no matter what, I saw marriage as the whole field of play. It would allow us to claim fully whatever victories or defeats we could achieve together; it would provide us a defined but wide arena for our lives. Victorian novelist George Eliot declared that "nothing is as good as it seems beforehand," but I've come to believe that it all depends on *what* you expect beforehand. I thought hard about the idea of marriage, about what it had meant to me and what it now meant to me. The second wedding of my life took place in October of 1991. Some of those earlier fantasies and expectations have played themselves out, and I find myself delighted to be married.

One thing is certain for me: I learned that being single is better than remaining in an unhappy marriage—even a quietly unhappy one.

And I discovered that an authentically good marriage is both possible and enormously valuable. But I have also come to see that, in part, a good marriage depends on developing a clear picture of our own lives, a difficult and painful process for many of us. Too often we pretend that what passes as "good enough" is actually good—telling ourselves we're satisfied when we're not, that we love someone we don't, or that someone loves us when we know deep down inside that he doesn't. We sometimes marry because we want to be safe, cared for, or because we don't want to be regarded as unable to marry. We talk ourselves into relationships that are like an inoculation against life rather than a part of it. This sort of marriage might keep bad things away, but it's just as likely to keep good things away.

Lying to ourselves leads to a kind of violation of our real wishes that is difficult to endure. British novelist Doris Lessing put it this way: "What's terrible is to pretend that the second-rate is first-rate. To pretend that you don't need love when you do; or you like your work when you know quite well you're capable of doing better." To stay in a marriage that is merely "good enough" is not, in fact, good enough for anyone. To spend much of your life telling yourself, "Well, it could be worse" is to forfeit the possibility of it getting better.

Instead of believing that any relationship—however mismatched, unhappy, or destructive—can be made to work if only both partners try hard enough, we should try to evaluate our relationships in light of our needs, our desires, and our expectations. Instead of trying to meet expectations that are out of reach, and thereby teetering daily on the edge of defeat or living in the shadow of inadequacy, we should instead believe that our genuine selves are valuable. Despite generations of advice that counsels a woman to contort herself—physically, emotionally, and spiritually—into whatever shape is demanded of her, we should perhaps consider the dangers of such a covert maneuver. Olive Schreiner, an essayist from the turn of the century, wrote that no human being should have to distort her own personality in order to enter or stay in a relationship. Schreiner argued that "no woman has the right to marry a man if she has to bend herself out of shape for him. She might wish to, but she could never be to him with all her passionate endeavor what [another] could be to him without even

trying. Character will dominate over all and will come out at last."
We cannot, she implies, fool ourselves every minute of every day into
denying our own experience and emotion.

Acting as if you're someone you're not is a weak foundation on
which to build a marriage. Pretending to be shy and quiet when you
have a personality like a brass band is a tough assignment to assume for
the rest of your life; so is pretending to be sassy and adventurous when
what you really want is a quiet and uneventful life. For many of us,
male and female alike, experience is purchased at a dear price and it
should not be relinquished without a struggle. "Why should I want to
hide the lines around my eyes?" asked a friend of mine. "I earned each
and every one of them."

A mature marriage, the old saying goes, represents the triumph of
hope over experience. I prefer to consider a good marriage as a true
coupling of both hope *and* experience—you need both to make it work
and to make it worthwhile. Living only on hope, as we often do when
we're young, or merely reeling in response to experience, as often
happens if we've been wounded badly, permits only the most half-
hearted of lives.

"We should be careful to get out of an experience only the wisdom
that there is in it—and stop there," cautions Mark Twain, "lest we be
like the cat that sits down on a hot stove lid. She will never sit down
on a hot stove lid again—and that is well; but also she will never sit
down on a cold one anymore." That it is difficult to emerge with hope
after an experience full of disappointment and pain is clear, but if we
abandon hope we also risk abandoning experience that will lead to
pleasure, laughter, and joy.

A whole heart depends on both wisdom and the hopes forged out of
that wisdom. I remember driving to my new home for the first time
after giving a talk in another town. I had only recently passed my
driving test, at the age of thirty-three, and found it odd that it was
more difficult to get a driver's license than a marriage license.
(Wouldn't it make sense to *earn* a marriage license? The multiple-
choice and practical tests for a marriage license present intriguing
possibilities. Can you imagine what the equivalent of parallel parking
would be?) I was an especially cautious driver, as first-year drivers
often are. I remember carefully adjusting the rearview mirror before I

started out onto the highway so that I could make sure I knew what was behind me as well as in front of me.

In the bright sun of the late afternoon the gesture made sense on many levels. It certainly reminded me of my married life. I knew that by keeping my eyes on where I was going, as well as by not losing sight of where I had been, I could be safely on my way. I rolled down the windows, switched on the radio, and took the straightest route home.

PLAYING HOUSE VS. PLAYING AGAINST THE HOUSE

To get a clear picture of marriage—our own present, future, or former marriages, our parents' marriages, the marriages of friends—we need to see these within a larger cultural context. All too often what we see as the most eccentric, personal, unrepeatable things in our lives turn out to be those very aspects of life that are general to the human condition. A person might think that she's the only one who still clings to ideas of romance when the rest of the world knows better, or she might think she's the only one who lives alone when the rest of the world seems to be pairing up to get on the Ark.

All of us have grown up with ideas about what love and marriage is and should be like, and often these ideas totally contradict one another, even cancel each other out. Why is this? What do we—both men and women—want? What do we expect? What are the differences between men's and women's beliefs concerning marriage and, specifically, the role played by the husband? This book comes out of my questions about the myths, images, and roles of the husband in contemporary culture.

Marry in haste, repent in leisure.

A good man is hard to find

Marry only for true love.

It's as easy to love a rich man as a poor one.

We hear messages about love and marriage that are so mixed they sound as if they are spoken in code. It's necessary to decipher the iconography in order to make sense of what we hear, and then decide what actually applies to our own lives. Otherwise we carry vestiges of these clichés around our entire lives, bringing them out of mental storage whenever we're at a loss.

Although the social script for marriage has undergone fundamental and irrevocable change over the past two centuries, we nevertheless have an image of what an ideal marriage is "supposed to be," whether or not we have any personal experience of such a relationship. It often seems as if it is imprinted on our genes. In their massive 1983 study *American Couples: Money, Work, Sex*, researchers Philip Blumstein and Pepper Schwartz tell us that "every schoolchild understands what marriage is supposed to be like. Ask a young child to explain marriage and he or she can tell its essential parts: that there are a husband and wife, and eventually a mommy or daddy, that it entails a ceremony, and that the two people live together for the rest of their lives. The child knows just as well as the adult that there are marriages that do not look like this. He may have seen his own parents divorce. But he will not describe real life when he describes marriage—he will describe the 'ideal type.'"

When I read that passage, I thought about what the children around me do when asked to play house. In every instance, the little girls get busy right away doing something inside the playhouse: pretending to clean or to cook. In contrast, the little boys stand around for a minute or so, then pick up an imaginary briefcase or a tool kit or a hunting rifle and leave the house. The boys shout "bye-bye" but the little girls inside the house will probably not notice. The boys then stand outside the house looking confused and not knowing what to do next. Maybe they will even start to make a little trouble once they're outside just to get some attention.

In effect, the only way that boys play house is to leave, because they don't know what else to do. If a boy tries to stay inside the house and play at making dinner or helping with the dolls, the girls will often shoo him away because they're afraid he won't do it "right" or he'll try to do it too aggressively. He might be regarded with suspicion as an apprentice Felix Unger if he starts lining up the pots and pans. This is the way children have play-acted in our culture decade upon decade and it is how most of them still do—the kids I'm describing here come from families where both parents work at least part-time outside of the home.

The images of married life that are formed in childhood remain unwavering even when actual experience might betray them as false. Girls learn to play house; boys learn to play outside of, and even against, the house. They cannot imagine any other possibilities, because we have so seldom offered them examples or even intimations of what the man's role inside the house could be.

THE ROLE OF THE HUSBAND
AS VALIDATED BY
THE ROLE OF THE FATHER

While it is true that over the course of the last few years the image of the husband seems to have undergone some changes—several young actors, for example, have been promoted with publicity shots showing them holding their infants in one arm and cradling their wives in the other—it is also true that in these apparently "new man" poses, wives and babies appear equally dependent on the man in the middle. The husband remains at the center of the shot and the center of the family unit, acting as the infrastructure that supports the economics and emotions of those around him.

When actor Tom Cruise divorced his first wife the articles reporting the breakup made much of the fact that there were no children. Kevin Costner, on the other hand, is a "devoted father and husband," according to a recent celebrity magazine, which emphasizes role rather than chronology in listing the actor's attributes. "It's one thing to be married with no children because then a man still can have one foot out the door. But with children," an aunt of mine used to say, "the door should close."

The perceived responsibility of the husband to his wife is, in other words, greatly overshadowed by the perceived responsibility of a father to his children. A man seems more married when he has children as well as a wife. When the "summer bachelor" husband in the vintage Marilyn Monroe movie *The Seven Year Itch* is asked whether he has any children, he quickly answers, "None." A moment later he slips on a roller skate and backtracks awkwardly, admitting grudgingly, "Well, just one . . ." Being married without children is, apparently, as close as you can get to being single in our society.

It should be recognized that the role of the husband in these instances is validated by the role of the father; once men have children, they are then defined primarily as fathers rather than husbands. The perceived definition of the role of husband gets lost in the large shadow cast by the role of father. A little boy might, in other words, have some idea of what being a dad entails in our society, but being a dad usually means being outside the house making a living, not being at home and part of the everyday family life. No wonder boys prefer to play doctor and find it more rewarding than playing house. It may well be that they behave in much the same way as adults—playing doctor, coming home to eat and sleep, and then leaving again.

Our culture has for the most part extolled the virtues of rough and competitive play for male children, fearful that boys who want to play indoors or play with girls will be labeled "sissies." This is changing, but the change is slow and uncertain. "Family values" as a catchphrase seems to have more to do with making sure that men are out working and bringing home a paycheck to pay for private schooling and that women are baking cookies than it has to do with promoting the idea that every family can invent itself. The typical boy in our society doesn't grow up thinking of himself as someone who will become a husband—it's often the last thing on his mind. He's busy trying to get himself out of the house as quickly as possible and for as long as possible, and his play reflects this. If we regard childhood play even vaguely as a dress rehearsal for later life, we can see the importance of these patterns.

"WHAT EVERY YOUNG WIFE SHOULD KNOW"

A short humorous essay titled "Claustrophobia, or What Every Young Wife Should Know" by cartoonist and author James Thurber supports the observation that there are significant differences between the way girls and boys play house. "The boy of six wants to play outside the house all the time," argues Thurber, who sees this pattern of behavior continuing well into adulthood. "He doesn't even want to come into the house for his meals. On the other hand, little girls like to be in the house as much as they can." The implication, of course, is that little girls often find safety in the indoor world over which they can exercise control, and boys are paradoxically more at home, at least emotionally, when they are running away from the house.

"When dusk falls," observes Thurber, "the little boys are restless under the urge to be several blocks away, playing Go, Sleepy, Go, but the little girls want to be home putting their dolls to bed. Usually at least one of the dolls is ill and needs constant attention. Often it is necessary to force little girls to go outside and get some air and exercise, just as it is frequently necessary to use force to get little boys into the house. And even when girls do go outdoors, they have to be watched like a hawk or they will be playing house in the dog box or under the cellar door." Thurber is far from the only man to assume girls have a craving to play house. Girls are often portrayed as victims of a sort of domestic reflex action; they are under the spell of an uncontrollable urge to play house the way that a gambler will be driven to transform any activity into an opportunity to exercise his habit. Obviously, "playing house" seems like a pretty compulsive activity to Thurber, as he places it in direct contrast to the fugitive nature of the little boys' playfulness.

But Thurber's essay also raises a more complex point, one which interests many contemporary psychologists and sociologists who have written about it in detail: the idea that girls are brought up to remain within a community and family in order to develop their identity, while boys are encouraged to separate, to move away from the family—especially their mother—in order to gain a sense of themselves. "While all children are naturally dependent during certain years, girls are not encouraged to separate and develop in an autonomous manner as boys are," explains psychologist Dr. Alexandra Symonds. "On the contrary, girls are encouraged to maintain their dependent relationships to parents and family, and after marriage transfer them to husband and children." As sociologist Carol Gilligan has described it, where girls learn to seek intimacy, men learn to seek distance in order to develop and strengthen their personalities. In order to develop uniquely "masculine" attributes, boys need to separate themselves from their families. Even after they grow up, the same impulse informs the behavior of many men. They need to get away from women—or one particular woman—in order to "be themselves." This is not to say that all men must spend their lives acting like Tom Hanks in *Big*, living a ten-year-old's life in a thirty-year-old's body, but we ignore these early patterns at our own risk.

STACKING THE DECK

Playing against the house is also a gambling term. To play against the house is to gamble in a particularly risky way. The phrase implies that you are betting against the bank, against the establishment, against the institution. You play against the house when you are particularly confident, when you're feeling adventurous, and when you can afford to lose.

"The house," an expert tells me, "has slightly better odds than the individual player. You join the game knowing that the house has constructed rules that will make it easier for them to win. Put it this way," he instructs, "the house makes the rules, the house stacks the rules agains the individual player, and the house deals the cards, but you play anyway." (My adviser paused here to comment, "You know, it *does* sound like marriage . . .") With the odds stacked against them, I asked, why does anyone play? "Because a gambler thinks he's lucky. Because a gambler believes he's different from other people and that the odds aren't going to apply to him." It is how a number of men feel about playing against the idea of marriage. Wanting to "play against the house" in terms of marriage implies a reluctance to assume the mantle, the responsibilities, of being a husband. Or it means saying in effect, as one acquaintance put it, "I'm not married. But my wife is."

The husband is nevertheless the linchpin in a social system that remains firmly defined and controlled despite changes of attitude, changes of heart, and changes of mind. Only by examining the role of the husband can both men and women come to an understanding of the power, manifest and latent, attached to his position. Only by examining the mechanism of power can it be understood; only when it is understood can it be dealt with effectively.

"LIFE FOR BOTH SEXES . . . CALLS
FOR GIGANTIC COURAGE"

Yet the search for this understanding is only one reason to examine the image and role of the husband in our culture. Another reason lies in the argument raised by Virginia Woolf in *A Room of One's Own*, written more than seventy years ago. Woolf commented on the fact that men write innumerable books about women but that women rarely seem to write about men. (The same holds true today, although there are, of course, notable exceptions.) "Have you any notion how many books are written about women in the course of one year?" Woolf asks her mostly female audience. "Have you any notion how many are written by men? . . . Women do not write books about men . . . Why are women, judging from this [library] catalog, so much more interesting to men than men are to women?" Woolf left the question open, but this book is, in part, a reply.

Men are indeed becoming objects of interest for women who are eager to learn not only of men's inner lives, but to examine men's roles in women's lives. Finally, the larger social scripts given to both men and women need the greatest possible scrutiny because, as Woolf tells us, "Life for both sexes . . . is arduous, difficult, a perpetual struggle. It calls for gigantic courage and strength." Courage and strength are not on the typical list of requirements for a marriage, but perhaps they should be. Perhaps courage, strength, an ability to learn from experience, and a sense of humor should be added to the prenuptial checklist. Examining the relationship of men and women within a larger context will inevitably inform the way we deal with one another on an intimate basis. Once we can see how our most individual actions are informed by forces of which we might not even have been aware, we can make our choices with more insight.

Perfect Husbands (& Other Fairy Tales) examines in detail the representations of the husband as he appears in our hearts and our heads, as well as the ways he appears in literature, film, and popular culture. This leads me back to my original question. Chico Marx used to ask, "Why a duck?" I asked, "Why a husband?" The answer has something to do with how I never felt comfortable with the way my aunts kept those plastic slipcovers, those invisible barriers, over the furniture as if they were afraid of the mess and destruction and markings of life, as if they thought that one day there might be some better reason to unwrap the good stuff than simply the pleasure of settling down into it.

Having something that can be called your own—your own room, your own income, even your own husband—has its advantages. Woolf knew this: In *A Room of One's Own* she implies that only when you can call something or someone your own and have the world acknowledge your right to do so, can you enjoy it without asking for permission or waiting passively for your turn.

Of course, no human being can ever belong to another human being, so no one is ever "one's own" in the most basic sense. Nevertheless, to acknowledge one another as husband and wife connects the worlds of the public and the private, the emotional and the social, and establishes a pattern of priority. A good marriage is a public bringing together of the various elements in our lives so that there is nothing that is secret, furtive, or vague about our affections. At its best, marriage is a visible and recognizable connection between our everyday lives and the person we love.

CHAPTER TWO

GOING TO THE CHAPEL VS.
WEDDING BELL BLUES

*Details on the Feminine Quest
for Romance*

I WAS LOST from infancy to the language of romance. There were stories of my shouting, "Let Me Go, Let Me Go, Let Me Go, Lover" to my overpossessive Sicilian grandmother when I was four, having picked up the terminology from a popular song of the late fifties that was played—*loud*—over all the backyard radios in Brooklyn.

Remembering words to songs from the first moment I heard them probably did me very little good while I was growing up. I was raised to sing along at weddings to Tony Bennett's "Take My Hand, I'm a Stranger in Paradise," wondering whether Paradise was a suburb in New Jersey where the newlyweds were headed and whether it was a good neighborhood. The weddings themselves were amazing events. It was like Lourdes: Women who hadn't walked in years would suddenly get up to dance. We all sang along to "Love and Marriage" and "Here Comes the Bride." I soon graduated to singing along with the entire soundtrack of *The Sound of Music,* batting my seven-year-old's eye-lashes to "I Am Sixteen, Going on Seventeen," a song that no doubt instilled in me the irrevocable belief that a boyfriend should be at least a grade ahead of you.

But all of this was only a prelude; the real business of cultural conditioning started later. I skidded into puberty singing my heart out to such songs as "Tell Him," which was already an "oldie" by the time I heard it. It might have been old, but apparently it is still not yet out of date; it gets significant airtime even today. "Tell Him" contains quite possibly the worst advice ever given to women concerning relationships, despite the fact that the lead introduces the piece by declaring in a genuinely authoritative alto that she knows "something about love," which might raise one's hopes. "Oh good," you think, "here's a woman who will tell me what I want to know!" As it turns out, what she knows about love is simply that you have to want it "bad." This, as we all now know, is an inauspicious beginning. The one thing I already suspected at twelve was that whatever it was, if you wanted it bad, you weren't likely to get it. But the song insists that you should tell "him" that you're always going to love him and that you'll never leave him, no matter what, and urges you to "tell him *now.*"

So I told him, the boy I wanted to marry when I was twelve, and he fled. What did I say? I said something like "I think we should go out." Although I didn't say anything about marriage, underneath it all that was, in fact, my assumption. If he suspected there was something disingenuous about my apparently innocent remark, he won points for perceptiveness if not sensitivity. And if he assumed I was trying to lead him into a relationship that I hoped would continue for the next sixty years, well, he was absolutely right. For many women, the image of ourselves as brides has always been there, from the moment we noticed that the Barbie wedding ensemble was always the biggest feature in the Barbie fashion booklet. (I am convinced that the religious reading of that booklet groomed a generation of women for shopping from the J. Crew and L. L. Bean catalogs.) G.I. Joe, in contrast, had no wedding outfit. There was no G.I. Jill for him to date. There was no implication that G.I. Joe's life was incomplete without a female companion; in contrast, the biggest part of Barbie's day was spent getting herself ready for Ken.

Many of us got little intellectual attention and were given few ambitions apart from marriage and children. The little girls I knew growing up wanted to get married. True, we also vaguely wanted to do something else when we were adults, like be Olympic athletes or work at a department store, or maybe explore the Amazon. Of course, nobody suggested that we get more specific and so we never did. A future in the workplace was something that happened, not something you planned and worked for. In contrast, a romantic life seemed to be something you planned for, not something that just happened. Somehow the two became confused—and confusing.

We fantasized about what kind of husbands the poor little boys sitting next to us would make while they fantasized about monster trucks. We thought about Simon and Garfunkel singing of a dream girl "dressed in organdy" and we just knew they were talking about a wedding. The boys said, with unblinking and earnest finality, that they didn't listen to the words even when they liked the songs. They were content to play air-guitar to the solos. Maybe that was the problem. The guys didn't listen to the lyrics, but the girls kept trying to analyze them. Girls hated long guitar solos; guys loved them.

"ISN'T THAT A BLIMP?"

A reluctance to even acknowledge song lyrics was in keeping with the cool, distanced persona boys cultivated. It was the precursor of their reluctance to discuss emotional issues, a tendency which gradually developed into what I call the "Isn't-That-a-Blimp?" syndrome. It works this way: Women press men to have long and involved discussions analyzing the state of their relationship, and men desperately scan the horizon for any possible diversion, hoping for a natural disaster or at least an unusual airship. "Look, honey," your husband might say, "I don't mean to interrupt the discussion of my lack of ambition, but isn't that the Goodyear blimp? Wow. Amazing. Now what were you talking about?" He'll divert your attention to anything except the subject at hand, saying things like "Yes, of course I'm listening, but look, doesn't the dog seem like he needs to go out?" or "I'll just mute the TV while we talk so I can see when the weather comes on. I *am* paying attention to you, but I need to know what the forecast is for tomorrow, okay?"

"When I tell my husband that I think we should discuss the problems he's been having at work," declares Connie, a thirty-two-year-old accountant married to a thirty-year-old engineer, "he sighs like he's giving in and says, 'Okay, so talk'—like *I* have to do all the talking about the problems *he's* having." Connie's frustration is not uncommon. Even something as simple as talking has different functions for men and women. As linguist Deborah Tannen explains, "For women, talk creates intimacy. Marriage is an orgy of closeness: You can tell your feelings and thoughts, and still be loved. [Women's] greatest fear is being pushed away. But men live in a hierarchical world, where talk maintains independence and status. They are on guard to protect themselves from being put down and pushed around." Jean Kerr, playwright and author of *Please Don't Eat the Daisies*, comments that "women speak because they wish to speak, whereas a man speaks only when he is driven to speech by something outside himself—like, for instance, he can't find any clean socks." Or when he invents a useful blimp.

All these diversionary comments are the grown-up equivalent of the sixth-grade comments made by boys after you casually asked if they were planning to go to the party on Friday night. "Look at Jimmy's fake rubber eyeballs, aren't they gross? Now what did you ask me? Did you do the math homework? Can I copy?" All the signposts were there, from the moment they said they never listened to the words to songs. If we ignored the signposts, it was at our own peril.

UNSEEN BUT POWERFUL PRESSURES

Most of us learned not to say it out loud, but the idea of marriage was like the air around us: unseen, full of pressures, exerting influences we couldn't chart and therefore didn't question. I concede that mine was a working-class, perhaps even anachronistic, family. Nevertheless, when women say they grew up *never* thinking about marriage I am suspicious. Even today there are virtually no mature unmarried heroines in sitcoms who are not romantically involved or perpetually searching for a relationship. Looking back several decades, there were no unmarried women on TV at all, unless you count Rosemarie on "The Dick Van Dyke Show," who was both the prototype for the unattractive spinster and, perhaps not coincidentally, the only female character who was known for her sense of humor. How could we escape the influence of culture's emphasis on marriage for every woman? Wasn't it the romantic equivalent of a chicken in every pot? I believe there was no way to evade these images, even if we decided to reject them.

I'm not arguing that it was a good thing to be subject to pressures to marry from age six onward, but I am making a case for recognizing that no matter what your particular upbringing, the profound attempts at cultural conditioning were unavoidable.

So even if only a few of us wanted to get married to the exclusion of any other activity by the time we were in college, we nevertheless came of age in a culture where a woman was defined by her marital status. The forms we all seem compelled to fill out daily, for example, offer "Mr." for a man, while offering "Miss," "Mrs.," and, in recent years, "Ms." for women. A man is never identified by his marital status. "Mr." implies neither married nor single. Seldom is "Ms." the only option for a woman to check. So how can anyone avoid thinking about the impact of marriage when a woman has not only to check of the box indicating her sex, but then indirectly has to comment on whether she's making use of that sex in lawful matrimony?

"HOW LOVELY TO BE A WOMAN"

Where did we learn the social script that dictated that girls should look forward to weddings? Perhaps from one of the billions of high school productions of *Bye-Bye Birdie*. (I was recently told that one of the most elite prep schools in New England chose *Gypsy* as their school play last year, so that interested female students had to audition for parts as strippers. Didn't someone suggest that maybe this wasn't a terrific idea?) As a kid, I used to love to watch Ann-Margret in the movie of *Bye-Bye Birdie*, playing another sixteen-going-on-seventeen girl (although unlike her *Sound of Music* counterpart, Ann-Margret looked like a discount hooker), and singing her immortal version of "How Lovely to Be a Woman."

For those whose high schools were doing authentically Jacobean productions of *Edward the Third* instead of musicals, the lyrics can be summed up as follows: "It's lovely to be a woman and have only one thing in mind, which is to pick out a suitable guy and make him into the man you want." You're supposed to do this while you're still in high school, of course, so that you won't have to worry about finding a date, or heaven forbid, a vocation, in college. Finding Boy Right (he isn't old enough to be called "mister" yet) meant you could spend your high school years pouring over bridal magazines instead of reading Emily Dickinson. Ann-Margret hugs herself and prides herself on the loveliness of being a woman "like me."

Was any woman really able to escape the hipper influences of Bob Dylan, Bob Segar, or Mick Jagger? (I learned by freshman year never to mention Tony Bennett.) I had replaced my earlier fondness for a smooth voice with the scratchy insistence of Dylan's "Lay, Lady, Lay." Romance overcame any problems I had with the refrain as an English major, since changing the words to "Lie, Lady, Lie" would be changing the sense, and replacing what was romantic with what was only accurate. No one needed to convince us that the grammatical and emotional change just wouldn't be right. We secretly wondered what kind of woman Frank Zappa and Jerry Garcia had married, even if we didn't want to ask.

"WE'VE GOT TONIGHT" VS. "WILL YOU STILL LOVE ME TOMORROW?"

In song as in romance, women were caught between Bob Segar's "We've Got Tonight" and Carole King's "Will You Still Love Me Tomorrow?" Segar insists that we've got tonight and asks, "Why don't you stay?" The promise of tomorrow is in his voice and he knows it, even if he ignores it. King answered Segar's apparently rhetorical question when she asked whether the affair upon which she was ready to embark would be a "lasting treasure" or if it was only a "moment's pleasure?" Is there any wonder where the confusion started?

So the answer to "Why don't you stay?" is "Will you still love me tomorrow?" Women learned to answer a question with a question. The old joke goes, so why shouldn't we answer a question with a question? But there were good reasons for someone to come up with an answer, it was just hard to find one. Instead many of us avoided declarative sentences for as long as possible. That meant subjecting oneself to lengthy exchanges during which vital items of clothing were removed or replaced. These exchanges went something like "Can we spend the night together" answered by "Do you really love me?" answered by "Can't you tell?" answered by "Can't you tell me in words?" answered by "Why do you need to hear that all the time? Isn't it enough that I'm here?" answered by "Why is it so difficult for you to make a commitment?" *ad infinitum.*

But of course the musical questions about love and commitment didn't start with the baby boomers and subsequent generations. Consider Cole Porter's lyrics, or Ira Gershwin's, or the songs sung to our mothers by Frank Sinatra. Tea for two was supposed to be sufficient, and the small hotel was nestled in the woods waiting for a honeymoon couple. If you weren't making whoopee, you might suggest beginning the Beguine so that some enchanted evening a stranger from across the room will take all of you (why not take all of you?). If it wasn't love and marriage going together like a horse and carriage, then it was just one of those things, unless of course you got somebody under your skin. Just one of those things would leave you playing solitaire, or leave you sitting in a dive bar somewhere with smoke getting in your eyes, having one for your baby and one more for the road.

But we thought we were tougher than our mothers. By our teens and twenties, we jeered at John Denver's "Annie's Song," which declared everlasting love for his wife (from whom the singer was subsequently divorced). But we sang along with the Beach Boys despite ourselves when they wished in their later albums for a "peaceful life" complete with a "forever wife" and children. But where were the women's songs? As adults, men could sing with a straight face about wanting or loving a wife even as they also sang about the importance of traveling fast and alone. You could have a "goodhearted" woman waiting at home for you and still keep your reputation as a "good timing man" intact. Were there equal but opposite replies from the other side, the woman's side?

No. None, at least, that I heard. And I was listening carefully, turning to the radio the way you'd turn to a Oujia board to figure out what to do. It was the mid-to-late seventies and men and women were reassessing their positions. Yet Linda Ronstadt was reaffirming that "Love Has No Pride" and we believed her, despite the fact that we were in college and planning ambitious careers in medicine and business that had replaced our ambitions to chart the Amazon. Janis Ian sang about how "love was meant for beauty queens," and we all felt like she was singing to each of us. Joni Mitchell told us that she was alone and traveling, but she sang about picking up a lover in a Bleecker Street café and cast it straight into romance: She's found someone "to love" in this temporary adventure. We knew she was always "blue" anytime she was alone anyway, despite her admirable independence. As an antidote to such doting, we went to see a new kind of musical in a small Greenwich Village theater. It was called "I'm Getting My Act Together and Taking It on the Road," and featured women musically renouncing relationships with men, singing their "Strong Woman Number" and leaving home. We sang along, since it was a smarter version of "I Am Woman, Hear Me Roar," which was just too absurd (and talk about ungrammatical!) to be politically correct even before anyone had heard of the term.

DOES LOVE HAVE TO END IN MARRIAGE?

But where were the songs that suggested we were allowed to return to our fantasies of relationships that outlasted the night? I stopped listening for them. I started graduate school, started writing and teaching, I married, and thought of myself as beyond the pull of romance. "Why do we talk about a relationship *ending* in marriage?" teased a freshman in one of my classes. "Shouldn't it *start* there?" We all laughed good-naturedly, but his words stayed with me. It was a better question in retrospect than he gave himself credit for asking.

In the early eighties, when they were selling bands like the Pet

Shop Boys instead of the Beach Boys, there was an astonishingly over-produced song called something like "I Need a Hero." This number had everything except fog horns and sirens, and for all I know, maybe they were there, too. But I heard it once on the Manhattan country station, which, for some reason, I played continuously while writing my doctoral dissertation. I'd pretty much stopped obsessing about song lyrics (although country music could always be counted on for some great titles, such as "Drop Kick Me Jesus, Through the Goalposts of Life" or "If I Said You Have a Beautiful Body, Would You Hold It Against Me?" and, one of the best songs about divorce, "She Got the Goldmine, I Got the Shaft"). But hearing Bonnie Tyler belt out "I Need a Hero," hearing her voice tear the heart out of the radio, yelling about how she wasn't going to compromise on romance, I was stunned.

I shoved my paperwork out of the way after hearing the first line. The song lit into me, firing up the emotional kindling that had remained hidden but crisp. The singer is holding out for a hero (despite the fact that, as both playwright Alice Childress and psychologist Sonya Friedman have told us in the very titles of their respective books—two books published at different times and with different audiences in mind—"a hero ain't nothing but a sandwich"). Tyler sings about holding out for a man who has to be strong, brave, and "fresh from the fight." And when I heard the last bit—"fresh from the fight"—I thought in an instant of every romantic character I had ever imagined. I thought of the sexy, doomed boys in the planetarium scene from *Rebel Without a Cause,* and I thought of Heathcliff in *Wuthering Heights.* I thought of Gilbert Osmond from *Portrait of a Lady*, and I thought of Rodolphe from *Madame Bovary.* I thought of Robert De Niro, David Bowie, Jimmy Dean, and Sid Vicious. And then I thought how crazy I was to be thinking about these Bad Boys, and how wrong I was to be hooked by a poorly arranged pop song.

EMOTIONAL PORNOGRAPHY

And I secretly bought the 45. I hadn't bought a 45 since I was about fourteen, but I went out and bought that record like I was buying pornography, hiding it in a plain paper bag, listening to it when I was alone, taping it so I could play it on my Walkman as I took the long ride to Queens College to teach evening classes in psychology and literature. It was pornography, in a way, but only insofar as sexual romance becomes fetishistic for women. Women look to romance instead of to relationships the way a shoe fetishist will cling to footwear instead of a woman; women cling to and adore a different kind of heel, perhaps. But romance can become as fetishistic and, as Louise Kaplan has termed it, as "perverse" as any other misdirected sexual and emotional energy. Ellen Moers, in her brilliant 1976 work, *Literary Women*, made very much the same point when she declared that what had been considered the "female eccentricities" of romantic obsession "must be called by a stronger name: perversities."

It seems, then, if you want only a *piece* of someone but not the whole person you, too, are a fetishist. If men want only golden tresses, then they are hair fetishists. But then are women who want a man taller than themselves fetishizing height? (Unlike golden tresses, I suppose, you can't actually possess a man's height, unless you're going to walk away with his thighbone in your pocket, so even the fetishizing of height includes in some way an acknowledgment of the whole person.) Do women have a fetish about the idea of romance, perhaps, even at the expense of a relationship? For many of us, I knew the answer was yes. Like Molly Bloom in James Joyce's *Ulysses*, I thought about my younger days and remembered the luxury of unmarried bliss. In my dreams I repeated Molly's words, "Yes I said yes I will Yes." I dreamt of men who would speak quietly but still seductively about the impossibility of love. I wanted to hear sentences that began with a barely suppressed sigh, "If only . . ." I thought about men who had a swaggering but melancholy attitude, the ones who looked as if they had secrets, passions, harrowing griefs, and adventures. I knew better than to put my relationship with my husband in danger, but it was danger I hungered to be near.

Why did I long for another man when I already had a "perfectly good husband," as I described him? I wanted something else. I fantasized about the kind of man who would probably not be a "perfectly good" husband but would remain the Outsider, the authentic Other. I was not alone in these dreams. When I aired these contraband thoughts with other young married women, they echoed my very phrases. I came to realize that this was what everyone had always hinted at: This was the hitch in getting hitched. I thought this sense of disillusionment just happened to men, but I was wrong. Did a woman need two men in her life?

MILD-MANNERED HEROES?

Do you need two men to make up one "real" man, one hero? It is as if a man can be only one thing at a time; even Superman and Clark Kent have to take turns appearing in the same room. Michael Keaton and Batman show up on the screen one at a time. In effect, no one can be a mild-mannered hero because the two cancel each other out. Even if the character possesses two distinct personalities, only one can be revealed at any given moment. (In response to this idea, a colleague of mine dryly commented that the men she meets are more likely to have their personalities split, not along the lines of Clark Kent and Superman, but rather along the lines of Norman Bates and his mom in *Psycho*.) It is as if you had to mix the two kinds of men into one compound, finding their essential elements and then kneading them together, starting from scratch.

A MAN AND TWO (OR MORE) WOMEN

For generations, men were given permission to have a mistress as well as a wife. In Italian, there is a word for the woman you "see" on the sly on a Friday night (but, as another disgruntled Italian wife once suggested to me, there should also be words for the women they see on Tuesday morning, Thursday afternoon, and so on . . .). Indeed, we have been encouraged to tolerate adultery in every man, from our kings, to our presidents, to our ministers. There is a long history of men believing that since they cannot have everything they want in one woman, they are entitled to have as many women as they want. They may be interested in a sunny blond but also in a sultry brunette. A vibrant redhead shouldn't be ignored either, and since no woman

can be expected to color her hair three times a week, they feel justified
in finding somebody else.

Albert Ellis argues in a psychological study titled "Healthy and
Disturbed Reasons for Having an Extramarital Affair" that the average
man "lusts after innumerable women besides his wife, particularly
those who are younger and prettier than she is; he quite often en-
hances his marital sex enjoyment by thinking about these other
women when copulating with his spouse; he enjoys mild or heavy
petting with other females at office parties, social gatherings, and
other suitable occasions."

"Suitable occasions," I thought when I read this, is that what their
female partners are considering these episodes? Can you imagine a
woman thinking, "Oh, this is dandy. Here's a suitable occasion to
have a meaningless grope with a married man who is part of my
everyday life. I suppose I simply cannot pass it up"? And yet in a book
called *The Executive's Wife,* author and "executive wife" Ninki Hart
Burger tells a story more illustrative of the heartbreak of marriage for
many women than the lighthearted "this-sort-of-thing-happens-all-
the-time" attitude the writer would have us believe she is presenting.
She describes seeing her husband at a party in a huddle with an attractive young woman: "I noticed her in a corner, holding hands
with my husband. I don't mind that sort of thing at luncheon. You've
got to go along with some of that. Then you can turn a blind eye to
it . . . I was so annoyed and felt that it was time this little girl
knew she was misbehaving. My husband thought I was an utter
spoilsport."

Spoilsport? Let me get this straight: *He's* mad at his *wife* for not
letting him hold hands with the boss's daughter? He thinks he has a
right to be angry? Has this man never read *Medea?* The thought of
normalizing this sort of behavior is clearly acceptable for some men,
but the thought of normalizing it for women has always seemed to be
out of the question. I would like to emphasize the difference between
the way our culture views men's appetites and the way it views the
appetites of women. Is there anyone who can imagine a faithful
husband being expected to turn a blind eye to his wife's flirtations and
extramarital affairs?

REAL MEN EAT ANYTHING

Ellis goes on to claim, in his essay about "good and bad" reasons for affairs, that the man who "resides in a large urban area and who never once, during thirty or more years of married life, is sorely tempted to engage in adultery for purposes of sexual variety is to be suspected of being indeed biologically and/or psychologically abnormal; and he who frequently has such desires and who occasionally and unobtrusively carries them into practice is well within the normal healthy range." Ellis is arguing that if nobody gets hurt then the situation is healthy.

So the non–adultery-minded man is sort of abnormal, according to these theories. Indeed, the good man may not be hard to find, but the question is: Would you want him after you found him if he was so grievously lacking in what seem to be the normal range of hormonal reactions? Apparently, if we're going to cast it in terms of appetites, it is not that real men don't eat quiche, but that real men will eat *anything*.

SO, DO YOU NEED TWO MISTER RIGHTS?

For women who choose to abide by the strictures of conventional society, there has always been a different set of rules. Women were supposed to fulfill all their dreams by marrying Mr. Right. Mr. Right, in turn, had to be whoever it was that you married—it was a sort of "de facto" arrangement. There's an old saying that goes, a woman just happens to choose the man who chooses her—implying that all women would be happy to marry almost any man by simple virtue of his willingness to marry. Despite the modern woman's right to choose, this is the caliber of thinking that kept a stranglehold on the minds of young women from the 1940s, throughout the 1950s and into the early sixties when the pressure to marry young finally began to ebb.

Consider, for example, the wisdom offered in an article from a 1953 issue of *Good Housekeeping*, one of the most widely read "ladies' magazines" both then and now. In a piece entitled "This Is Why," justifying very early marriages, the author suggests that "being an older unmarried girl"—of twenty-five or twenty-six, for example—has its "problems as well as its superficial advantages." Among these "problems" is the thought that you might be forced to support yourself instead of having a man who will provide for you. "As a career girl in your late twenties, you have been most probably able to surround yourself with certain material assets . . . to which you shortly become accustomed. Will you then be eager to marry a man who cannot keep you in your customary supply of worldly goods?" Warns the author Lee Tidball, who married quite young, "It's a big comedown from a Bahama cruise to dirty diapers." So is it better, then, never to have been on a cruise since you might not get to go on one again? Is it better never to have developed your own talents since the expectation is that you'll never use them? Is it better never to have been happy because you might not be happy one day? That's like saying you should be born old, since one day you'll be old.

Clearly, the thought that a woman could keep working after getting married and thereby raise her spouse to her standard of living was out of the question since the unchallenged assumption was that a woman takes on her husband's status in life. Tidball goes on to prompt the unmarried woman to take the plunge as quickly as possible because "in the shuffle of weekends, pay raises and new hats," the unmarried woman might lose sight of the fact that her "independence can often be frightening" to men, since an independent woman "seems to be so completely sure of [her]self as self-sufficient." Tidball then warns that "if . . . you balk your natural urges time after time, they become confused and twisted."

What, exactly, might happen? Obviously, the self-sufficient career girl might well put on her new hat, bought with her pay raise, and take off for a week in the Bahamas. Does that sound so bad to you? Clearly Lee Tidball's intention in 1953 was to put the fear of God into any young woman foolish enough to choose independence over dependence because, obviously, independence can be dangerously habit-forming. To make the subtext more explicit: If you find that you can live alone, why would you ever marry? It sounds, in fact, as if Tidball's estimation of marriage is pretty low if it collapses under the weight of any comparison with unmarried life.

Is such advice to women completely outdated? Consider the speech delivered by Marilyn Quayle at the Republican convention in August

1992. "Women do not wish to be liberated from their essential natures as women," she announced, speaking in her capacity as Vice-Wife (or Second-Lady?). She went on to illustrate the "essential nature" of woman as a dependent creature when she explained that it would damage society for men to no longer have to "take care" of women and children. "To liberate men from their obligations as husbands and fathers" was a devastating idea to Quayle, and it is clear that she means to keep men and women in the roles prescribed by the 1953 issue of *Good Housekeeping.* If a man doesn't have to look after you, the argument would seem to run, then he's going to find some other woman to look after, and you'll lose him. When asked whether his wife was involved in any causes, Dan Quayle is quoted as replying, "She has a very major cause and a very major interest that is a very complex and consuming issue with her. And that's me."

No wonder women are caught between a longing for independence and the fear that once they achieve independence they will be considered unlovable. And yet, many men argue that it is the perpetual weight of a woman's dependence that alienates them once they enter into a committed relationship, eventually driving them away, often into the arms of a partner who has maintained her autonomy.

"MARRY YOUR DAUGHTER WHEN YOU CAN"

"Marry your son when you choose," advises an unromantic shibboleth, "but marry your daughter when you can." So again the traditional definition of Mr. Right devolved into almost anybody who wanted to marry you. Resisting a suitor was often viewed as antisocial behavior. Let's say there was no outstanding reason not to marry a particular man. "Outstanding reasons" included another women to whom he was still legally wed and with whom he still slept, another man with whom he still slept, a history of parole violations, and very little else. (One currently popular postcard depicts a young woman saying, "No, Mom, I haven't met Mr. Right yet. But I have met Mr. Rude, Mr. Cheap, and Mr. Married.") Better to marry than to burn, wrote St. Paul in another backhanded compliment to wedded bliss. Better, too, to marry than to be forced into frigidity. For generations, women who did not marry have been considered outcasts, secondhand goods, or bitter spinsters. The images we saw of these women chilled us into relationships just so that we could get out of the cold. (Shelley Winters once described a hotel room in Philadelphia as being "so cold, I almost got married.")

Remember, for example, the Donna Reed character in the film *It's a Wonderful Life?* She is the chronically cheerful wife of suicidal Jimmy Stewart. During the part of the movie where the Stewart character gets to see what the world would have been like if he'd never been born, he witnesses all sorts of tragedies that his very existence prevented: the death of his beloved brother, the alcoholism and ruin of his boss, and—misery of miseries—the spinsterhood of his wife. It is one of the climaxes of the movie: Jimmy Stewart realizing with mounting horror that, had he never been born, this woman would now be not only single but—gasp!—a librarian! He, therefore, decides that his life has been meaningful, if only because he saved people from death, ruin, spinsterhood, and the horrors of librarianship.

No wonder many of us grew up thinking it was better to marry than to remain single, and best to marry as soon as a good candidate showed up. By contrast our brothers were counseled (usually by haggard male relatives) to stay single as long as possible. As Barbara Ehrenreich has established, the man who "postpones marriage even into the middle age, who avoids women who are likely to become dependents, who is dedicated to his own pleasures, is likely to be found not suspiciously deviant, but 'healthy.' " A man was perceived as more likely to be successful, interesting, and "masculine" if he stayed single by choice. The "by choice" factor should not be discounted, of course, but as long as a man was not positively inhuman, *he* could be considered single "by choice." Given the popularity of both the syndicated television series and the cartoon movie of "Beauty and the Beast," being inhuman might not be a real drawback for a male, so long as he dresses in stylish Armani suits and discreetly encases his paws in Ferragamo shoes.

Ehrenreich sounds very much like her predecessor, Simone de Beauvoir, author of the ground-breaking book *The Second Sex*, first published in 1948. De Beauvoir offered some insight into the way in which the institution of marriage differed for men and women, and her comments are as valid today as they were nearly fifty years ago.

While she argues that "for both parties marriage is at the same time a burden and a benefit," the French philosopher declares that "there is not symmetry in the situations of the two sexes; for girls marriage is the only means of integration in the community, and if they remain unwanted, they are, socially viewed, so much wastage. This is why mothers have always eagerly sought to arrange marriage for them." Life as a wife was supposed to be easier than life as a "single girl," whereas life as a husband was supposed to be more difficult than life as a bachelor.

It is interesting to note that a man could be simply unmarried, but an unmarried woman was a single "girl" or a career "girl." "By 1965, the only possible answer to the question 'Are you a career girl?' " said my older friend Gerry, "was 'Yes. Are you a career boy?' " Gerry also commented that if she was asked whether she was a "single girl" back in the fifties, she used to answer, "No, I'm a lady who drinks doubles. Wrong on both counts." Traditionally an unmarried woman has been thought of as both vulnerable and dangerous, perhaps even volatile. Certainly single women were considered a threat to the stability of married couples. It was thought that by her mere presence, the single woman would send the average husband into a paroxysm of adulterous longing. A "gay divorcée" was even worse, since she was a sexual initiate. But in whatever state of sexual experience, the unmarried woman was made to feel unwelcome in the company of married couples and families, while also being chastised for going out alone or with a male companion unless she was chaperoned. A woman knew it was her job, her duty, and her destiny to marry as soon—and as well—as possible.

"A GIRL MUST, A MAN MAY"

Edith Wharton, whose *House of Mirth* is a classic American novel, has her heroine Lily Bart spell out the dynamics at work in society when a male friend suggests to Lily that marriage is her vocation. Lily agrees and explains that in terms of marrying, "a girl must, a man may if he chooses," thereby echoing the points made by Ehrenreich and De Beauvoir. Lily illustrates her point by observing that "your coat's a little shabby—but who cares? It doesn't keep people from asking you to dine. If I were shabby no one would have me: a woman is asked out as much for her clothes as for herself. The clothes are the background, the frame, if you like: they don't make success, but they are a part of it. Who wants a dingy woman? We are expected to be pretty and well-dressed till we drop—and if we can't keep it up alone, we have to go into partnership." The "partnership" offered to a woman in terms of marriage is an unequal arrangement, given that women "must" marry when they can offer their assets at their most valuable: when they are young and beautiful.

For Lily, and other women at the turn of the century, few options other than marriage offered themselves if a woman was to remain in the middle or upper classes. Lily, in her late twenties, is seen as running out of time. She considers her situation with a certain amount of cynicism, as when she is trying to snag the attention of Percy Gryce. Gryce has come into a fortune "which the late Mr. Gryce has made out of a patent device for excluding fresh air from hotels." At one point, Lily had "been bored all the afternoon by Percy Gryce—the mere thought seemed to waken an echo of his droning voice—but she could not ignore him on the morrow." Lily knew that she must "follow up her success, must submit to more boredom, must be ready with fresh compliances and adaptabilities, and all on the bare chance that he might ultimately decide to do her the honor of boring her for life." Wharton is ruthless in exposing the mechanism behind the setup that would harness the energetic, intelligent, and witty Lily to the droning, airless heir, Gryce.

But, tragically, Lily knows that she mustn't risk rejecting Gryce if she wants to remain within her chosen social circles. Important for Lily, marriage would offer her a way into the community from which, as a single woman with little money, she would otherwise be excluded. That marriage offers such immediate acceptance has always been one of its largest draws. As Maxine Hong Kingston writes in *The Woman Warrior*, "Marriage promises to turn strangers into friendly relatives." A woman like Lily, without immediate family and with no network of relatives at work for her, needs marriage in order to be offered the instant, solid support of a community.

Indeed, anthropologists argue that the combining of communities was the origin of marriage rites in nearly evey culture. Even Tidball's article in *Good Housekeeping* promises this instant community as part and parcel of marriage when she writes that the married woman inevitably will have "an added number of friends in all age groups, married and single, with whom you share your free moments when you're not doing something just for two." Marriage meant that you crossed the threshold of acceptability—you joined the club. The "old maid" was a terrifying specter, as we've seen, characterized by a woman standing exiled from a room filled with noise, warmth, and gaiety. Women are assumed by many people, even today, to have wasted their lives if they do not marry, or at the very least, as having wasted their youth if they marry late. One female comic jokes that "I've never been married, but I say I'm divorced so people won't think there's something wrong with me."

For men, in contrast, there seemed to be a win/win situation: happily unmarried, happily married, or even unhappily married with, therefore, the perfect excuse to find an extramarital partner with whom to be happy.

GOING DOWN THE AISLE VS. GOING DOWN

Even today many women feel as if marriage alone can secure their happiness. Nora Ephron's heroine in *Heartburn* eyes a policeman who takes her statement about a crime and "wondered whether Detective Nolan was single. He wasn't exactly my type, but look where my type had gotten me. Then I wondered if I could be happily married to a policeman. Then I wondered why I was so hopelessly bourgeois that I couldn't even have a fantasy about a man without moving onto marriage." Ephron's heroine has a lot in common with Erica Jong's heroine in *Fear of Flying*, who declares that "all my fantasies included marriage. No sooner did I imagine myself running away from one man than I envisioned myself tying up with another. I was like a boat that always had to have a port of call. I simply couldn't imagine myself without a man."

According to a recent article in *New Woman* magazine, women's romantic and erotic daydreams inevitably end in the fantasy of "the lover" becoming "the husband." It is hard to imagine a similar survey of men conducted in *Esquire* or *Playboy* reaching the conclusion that men's erotic daydreams end in the fantasy of the lover becoming the wife. Putting it more directly, women seem to have fantasies about somebody going down the aisle where men just have fantasies about somebody going down.

THE OVERVALUATION OF LOVE

Women whose primary goal in life is to marry fit into the pattern described by psychologist Karen Horney in her work on "The Overvaluation of Love." Horney reports that in her clinical work she repeatedly met women who, although ambitious, independent, and capable, focused their emotional lives so completely on the pursuit of men that they were in a constant state of emotional devastation. "These women were as though possessed by the single thought," Horney writes, telling themselves, " 'I must have a man'—obsessed with an idea overvalued to the point of absorbing every other thought, so that by comparison all the rest of life seemed stale, flat and unprofitable. The capabilities and interests which most of them possessed either had no meaning at all for them or had lost it all." Horney wrote those words in 1933.

My friend Gail is, self-admittedly, one such woman. "I was really happy when they started naming hurricanes after men," she remarked rather wryly. "It made national disasters sound even more like my emotional life. 'Brian Wrecks All' could be a headline from my journal."

By 1976, according to psychologist Alexandra Symonds, very little had changed. "These women feel they have no value unless desired by a man," writes Symonds of her case studies. "From childhood on, this patient's entire life was oriented toward having a boyfriend and getting married. Higher education and profession were entered into mainly to make herself more valuable to men, and now it seemed a handicap because some men were threatened by it." Symonds refers to such women as "casualties" of the cultural pressures transmitted through generations of women who were told that they could not "function unless attached to a man," and who therefore use all their talents to achieve that end, "only to find that no man lives up to . . . unrealistic expectations." But many women continue to believe that marrying the right man will completely and forever change their lives for the better.

Some of us wait for rescue, wait for excitement, even wait for life to show up on our doorsteps—as if we could order our destiny take out–style and have it delivered while we keep our feet up. We place unrealistic pressures on men ("Will you make me incredibly happy for the next sixty years?" "Will you provide emotional, physical, and financial support without making demands that will interfere with my career/child-raising/bridge game?") and then we wonder why men are skittish when the question of marriage comes up, why they feel as if marriage is a game played at their expense. We should wonder, rather, what men think of marriage from their own perspective.

CHAPTER THREE

WHY DO HUSBANDS HATE SUNDAYS?

Men's Uneasy Domesticity

"I NEVER FEEL more married than I do on a Sunday, and I never like it less," says my friend Mark. A high school teacher in his early forties, Mark has been what I would call "happily married" for a little more than ten years. But on Sundays, he says, he is often overwhelmed by a sense of life's having passed him by. He is antsy, unsettled, and uneasy. He reports becoming wistful, sentimental, and prone to bouts of regrets. "I love my wife," he explains, "but sometimes I wonder whether there's another woman out there whom I would have loved even more. Living my kind of ordinary life, I guess I'd never meet this Mythical Woman—I picture her living in Bangkok or Rio—but maybe she would have been so fabulous that she would have made *me* into somebody extraordinary."

Mark smiles sheepishly and suggests, "Maybe Sundays are still the days of reckoning, whether you're a churchgoer or not. Maybe it's the

time when you reflect on your life and are bound to think that maybe
it comes up short, and one easy target for blame is your marriage." In
the habit of many men, Mark believes himself to be representative in
his response to the world and was the first to suggest to me that I
should "ask most men who have been married more than five years.
Husbands hate Sundays."

What kind of day is Sunday? Some people think, "Ah, perfect, the
day is stretched out in front of me like a cat in the sun, relaxed and
calm," while others think some version of "Escape, how can I escape?
How can I make the day go faster?" How we feel about Sundays is a
pretty good barometer of how we feel about our personal lives in
general. If you love Sundays, terrific, you feel comfortable in your own
home and inside your own head.

Sundays seemed to take forever when I was a kid. After the aunts
got back from church and after the uncles finished washing the cars
(treating God as if he were a relative on the wife's side of the family
that only she had to visit), my big Italian family would sit down to
what seemed like a seventy-three-course meal in the middle of the
afternoon. They talked and ate and talked until it was time for Ed
Sullivan to come on TV. The conversation was boring and endless
for us kids. All my cousins and I wanted to do was get out from under
that itchy, woolly, grown-up talk and head outside, away from their
droning voices and the stuffiness of a day unmarked by the usual
routine of school and cartoons. It was like trying to write on unlined
paper or to figure out what time of day it was without a clock—the
lack of specific demarcations made Sunday a tough day to get
through.

But I hadn't remembered these feelings in years until I began testing
Mark's theory about married men and Sundays. Apparently many
grown-up men still experience that fugitive, need-to-run-away feeling
on Sundays, as if the boy in every man wants to flee the parlor for the
wildness of the backyard and alleyway, leaving the tedium of ritualized
conversation and behavior far behind.

Sundays are a time when many married men long for the their
bachelor days. Single men can do what they please without anyone
looking askance. They can get up and properly nurse a hangover so
that they are ready to eat nachos out of the bag while watching the

football game. Or they can get up at six, run ten miles, meet friends for brunch, and work on their novel all afternoon without being disturbed. Both these scenarios depend heavily on one thing: not being disturbed. As one pal put it, "I have tremendous memories of generally reckless, ill-advised, unproductive but vastly entertaining adventures from my premarriage days."

The early days of a relationship are also roped off from the usual Sunday pattern. "When we were lovers," explained one thirty-year-old doctor, "Sundays meant spending the day in bed. That even lasted into the first couple of years of marriage. I can't remember when it happened, but at some point it seemed like spending the day in bed—drinking coffee, reading the paper, and making love all afternoon—was a waste of time. Now, it seems like we talk about our relationship instead of enjoying our relationship." Another thirty-something friend agrees, adding that "it's no surprise to me that 'Sixty Minutes' is the most popular program on television. You want a diversion by the end of the evening, something else to focus on besides your relationship. Even stories of fraud, dishonesty, and corruption are preferable to always having to talk about 'us.' "

"WILL I LOOK AS GOOD AS TINA TURNER WHEN I'M FIFTY?"

As an independent, funny friend from my old neighborhood describes it, his wife usually picks Sundays to ask winning questions such as "If I died suddenly, what kind of woman would you marry?" "When she asks a question like that, I just kiss the whole day good-bye. That's it for the afternoon and most of the evening. It took me three years of hearing questions like that to understand that what I was supposed to say was some fool thing like 'I'd never look at another woman, even with you dead.' That's what she wants to hear. Last week I wanted to say in a voice like Ralph Kramden from "The Honeymooners" would use, 'You ask me that one more time and we'll find out sooner rather than later what kind of woman I'll marry after you're gone . . .' but I'm too nice a guy to say that even for a joke."

He paused and then in an earnest and low voice pleaded, "Why the hell do women ask questions like that? Don't they have enough to think about?"

Another friend added his favorite example to this list: "My wife asks if she'll look as good as Tina Turner when she's fifty. I tell her she didn't look as good as Tina Turner when she was nineteen. She gave me a look that would have melted glass."

So we can see that for many married men, Sundays are days of great disturbance, a time when a husband (and father, when that applies) is "on call" emotionally the way he rarely is during the rest of the overscheduled, strictly plotted workweek. He can't call his wife back as he can when he's in the office because now she's standing in front of him. He can't beg off an activity by conjuring up the usual excuses: I have a meeting, I have to write a memo, I have another call coming in. Since the usual escape routes of the workday are abruptly closed off, this can cause a small sense of panic. This quiet Sunday panic was mentioned to me repeatedly by the men I interviewed for this book, and I stumbled across reference after reference in literature.

In John Updike's "A Month of Sundays," for example, one character describes a Sunday at home as the time "when marriages closed in upon themselves like flowers from which the sun is withdrawn, an evening giving a smeared window on Monday." One male friend bets a hundred bucks to any comer that most relationships end late on a Sunday afternoon and believes that no married couple should spend the day together alone unless they are willing to risk it.

John O'Hara's book *Butterfield 8* was the first novel that tipped me off to the Sunday syndrome. *Butterfield 8* contains what I initially thought was a rather incidental line: "When Sunday morning came Paul Farley never liked to be alone with his wife, nor did Nancy Farley like to be alone with Paul." I was struck by the passages concerning married men because they uncannily presented sentiments similar to the voices I hear when talking to men today. I'd seen the 1960 film version of *Butterfield 8* with Elizabeth Taylor and Laurence Harvey, but I was reading the 1935 book for the first time, and I marked the passage with red ink so that I could consider it in further detail. I moved on to novels by other writers, and the red ink marking the Sunday sections began to suggest a connect-the-dots pattern: There seemed to be at least one scathing reference to the married man's Sunday in innumerable works of fiction by male authors.

John Cheever's 1970 story "The Fourth Alarm" begins with a disappointed husband telling us, "I sit in the sun drinking gin. It is ten in the morning. Sunday . . . It is autumn." Autumn apparently increases this husband's sense of purposelessness. "The leaves have turned. The morning is windless, but the leaves fall by the hundreds. . . . I seem to miss some part of the morning as if the hour had a threshold or series of thresholds that I cannot cross. Passing a football might do it, but Peter is too young and my only football-playing neighbor goes to church." In Philip Roth's 1974 novel *My Life as a Man,* a character tells us that "to watch the cycle of disaster repeating itself was as chilling as watching an electrocution, the burning up of . . . life, seemed to me to be taking place before my eyes Sunday after Sunday. . . . I thought: 'What am I doing with these people?' And thinking that, could see no choice for myself but to stay."

Over and over again, I stumbled over the same modest detail: Sundays seemed to be a terrifying time of the week for many husbands. When I started talking to men from around the country about their married lives and about their perspectives on being husbands, I came across—with startling regularity—the fact that many husbands regard Sundays as one of the most difficult times of the week.

FEAR OF "SHARING"

"Ever wonder why Sunday papers are so incredibly long?" asked one of my colleagues, who, tellingly enough, asked not to be identified. "Reading the paper is one of the few things I'm permitted to do alone on a Sunday morning. Even if we get up early, reading the paper lets me off the hook until at least lunchtime. Everything else," he sighed, "we're supposed to share." He involuntarily shuddered at the last word. "And to top it off, when she reads a section of the paper first, it looks like it's been stuffed into somebody's shoes." This has not gone unnoticed by women, by the way. In Dorothy Parker's short story "Too Bad," a wife in an unsatisfying marriage ponders this phenomena: "She wondered how Ernest could get so much enjoyment out of a newspaper. He could occupy himself with one for almost an hour, and then pick up another and go through the same news with unabated interest." Clearly, writers believed the habit of scouring the Sunday papers to be problematic. On Sundays, husbands feel slightly out of control, off their own turf, and skittish about what will be demanded of them. Often they hide behind the newspaper as a paper fort erected against the onslaught of a woman who might have her *own* news to discuss.

Even men with rigorous, stressful, or physically demanding jobs often longed for the weekday routine by four o'clock on a Sunday afternoon. "If I can't watch football or baseball, I leave the house," declared one maintenance worker without hesitation. These husbands seemed to drum their collective fingers on their collective dining room tables. I must admit that I had expected to hear that men looked forward to the weekends, given that they were free from the pressures of the workplace. This turned out not to be the case, and the arguments made against Sunday seemed to reflect much larger issues of men's discontent with their role in a marriage.

Men seem to talk lovingly of Saturdays, it should be noted, focusing on car washing, trips to the hardware store (one man had such passionate attachment to using double- and triple-coupons at the local megasupermarket that I was slightly worried), going out in the evening, or renting a movie. They often looked forward to spending time with their children and wives, although the best of these times seemed to rely on some sort of structured activity.

"I prefer when we—I suppose I should more accurately say 'she,' since my wife is the one to do this sort of thing—arrange to meet another couple and do something in town," said forty-three-year-old Ben. "I don't like it when we're at a loss or when we just stay at home and wonder whether we're missing out. When we just stay at home I feel we've become an 'old couple' but if we dress up and go out, go to a nice restaurant or a show, I feel pretty damn good about myself." Saturday nights hold the promise of fun, of a diversion away from "normal" time, and offer the possibility of a sense of renewal. Sunday mornings, in contrast, seem to offer only an emotional hangover of sorts, a realization of the suspicions of entrapment felt by many men.

One financial analyst told me that he arranged to play tennis every

Sunday, summer or winter, rain or shine, just so that he had a built-in excuse to get out of the house. "By the end of the day," he explains, "I feel like my wife has already breathed up all the air in the house. Everything is exhausting—it's like there's not enough oxygen in the room. I really understand when people talk about needing 'a breath of fresh air.'" He reminds me of a character from D. H. Lawrence's *Sons and Lovers,* who, "sitting there, quite alone, and having nothing to think about" in his own home, would nonetheless "be feeling vaguely uncomfortable. His soul would reach out in its blind way to [his wife] and find her gone. He felt a sort of emptiness, almost like a vacuum in his soul. He was unsettled and restless. Soon he could not live in that atmosphere, and he affected his wife. Both felt an oppression on their breathing when they were left together for some time."

Clearly men do not hold the patent on these emotions and responses; I've met plenty of women who share them and understand them. Nevertheless, the pattern remains interesting. One of the husbands discussed by psychologists Richard Meth and Robert Pasick in *Men in Therapy* is quoted as complaining that "I deal with problems and pressure and conflict all day long. When I come home I just want things to be easy. So, when Jan brought family problems to my attention that needed to be talked about, I didn't want to hear it and the more she pushed, the angrier I got and the more I withdrew." He was particularly frustrated because "even when I do talk with her about what I feel or think, she tells me I'm not letting her know what's really inside of me. It's frustrating, because no matter what I do, it's not enough."

A successful and charming engineer told me that he looked forward to spending time with his children, but felt like his wife was "all over him" to "spend time together." "Enough already with the togetherness business," he said with what I thought of as uncharacteristic impatience; I knew he was part of a long and what I considered happy marriage. "We've been married nineteen years," he continued, "what does she want me to do? Remove my internal organs so that she can get to know what's really going on inside of me? Sometimes I want to say, 'Here's my liver, honey. This is the real me. Now let me watch television in peace, okay?'" This man quoted an old line, a standard used by comics and greeting-card writers for decades: "I never knew what real happiness was until I got married. And by then it was too late."

"EVERY WOMAN SHOULD MARRY,
AND NO MAN"

This same man quotes Benjamin Disraeli, a prime minister and novelist, and declares, "I respect the institution of marriage—I have always thought that every woman should marry, and no man." Although he treats his situation with a certain bitter humor, the underlying guilt and anger is not unusual.

In part, the belief that "no man should marry" comes from the belief that greatness—intellectual as well as physical—is a profoundly unmarried state. The way that football players are told that sleeping with women before a big game will "weaken the legs," so are preprofessional and professional young men told that marrying will dilute their abilities to be great. A professor of sociology at Vassar College wrote an essay which ran in *The Saturday Evening Post* under the title "Why Get Married?" It is not surprising that this should have run in the *The Saturday Evening Post,* priming men's discontent with Sundays; the male half of the audience was primed to hear this tirade against marriage. Professor Leslie Koempel reported that the faculty at Princeton University had once named the ten biggest contributors to the advancement of human knowledge. While it perhaps goes without saying that Dr. Koempel's list included only white men, what bears consideration is the fact that it was argued—however tongue in cheek—that a causal relationship existed between the contributions made by these figures and their relatively wife-free states.

"Of the ten," Koempel maintains, "Plato, Newton, and Leonardo da Vinci never married; Socrates couldn't make a go of it; Aristotle and Darwin married long enough after embarking on their work; and domesticity does not seem to have made many demands on Galileo, Shakespeare, Pasteur, or Einstein. Similarly, Michelangelo and Keats never married. Milton, Lincoln, Edgar Allan Poe, and Shelley were 'failures' at marriage." This tidy summation of the best that has been thought and felt in the world is an intellectual slight of hand. Of all the men on the list, only three were actually unmarried.

But the attack on marriage remains formidable because it draws its strength, not from examples or facts, but from a sense of limitation felt by many married men. "If I'd stayed single," such a man might think,

"I could have been a world-traveling, internationally recognized leader in my field. Instead," he'll sigh, "I got married." That he might not have become a leader among men no matter what his marital status doesn't get figured into this mindset; he mistakenly identifies his suspicions of personal inadequacy as the limitations imposed on him by the role of husband.

"LIFE IS GOOD . . . BUT NOT FOR ME"

Al Bundy in the popular television series "Married With Children" dreams of his success as a high school football star and compares those glory days with his time as a husband. "Life is good," says Al, "but not for me." Once "trapped" into marriage by Peg, his "red-haired monster" of a wife ("Crosses, sunlight—nothing works on you anymore, does it, Peg?"), he works as a shoe salesman. His domestic life is less than ideal, causing him to say things like "Feed me, Peg, or feed me *to* something—I just want to be part of the food chain." In his own mind, Al has forfeited the right to succeed by marrying straight out of high school. Less than supportive, Peg tells him that he should lead the "failure pride parade" on a float made of shoes. He has forfeited everything, it seems, except his right to complain and seek minor forms of revenge on those who are more successful, such as his nerdy neighbor, Steve. Whereas Steve was a "tap-dancing geek" in school, in comparison to Al's record-breaking football career, Steve now owns a Mercedes and works as a loan officer. But Al got married because, we assume, he and Peg had sex and pregnancy forced them into a quick and early marriage (there are many references to their eldest daughter's appearance quite soon after their wedding) instead of a profitable career. Trading success for sex, Al feels trapped by his marriage. He also feels a great sense of fellowship with other "losers," men married with children and with low-status jobs. He's also angered and defeated by what he sees as the larger cage of culturally sanctioned man-hating. When Al tunes into a late-afternoon "woman's talk show," he hears a coming attraction for the day's topic "Men: Round Them Up, Shoot Them All."

While Al Bundy is hardly representative of many husbands, he is an interesting character because he seems to have a perpetual sense of having missed out on the best things in life. Do a significant number of husbands feel as if they've missed out? In short, yes. Al Bundy and all his frustrated and angry male kin come from a long and rich tradition of male anger at women.

In one of the best-sellers of the 1940s and 1950s, A *Generation of Vipers* by Philip Wylie, marriage was described as a trap for men set by the character of "Cinderella," the all-American girl described by Wylie as "the shining-haired, the starry-eyed, the ruby-lipped virgo aeternis, of which there is presumably one, and only one, or a one-and-only for each male, whose dream is fixed upon her deflowerment and subsequent perpetual possession. This act is a sacrament in all churches and a civil affair in our society. The collective aspects of marriage are thus largely compressed into the rituals and social perquisites of one day."

Wylie then describes "the transition of Cinderella into Mom" with special emphasis on childbearing. For example, he sees the rigors of labor as merely a sort of rumor put forth by manipulative females that "the bearing of children was such an unnatural and hideous ordeal that the mere act entitled women to respite from all other physical and social responsibility. Woman has capitalized heavily on that theory ever since Cinderellaism and chivalry allowed her to conceive of it. She does so still, in spite of the fact that modern medical practice is able to turn most childbearing into no more of a hardship than, say, a few months of benign tumor plus a couple of hours in a dental chair."

It is a difficult passage to read. Clearly, the author is disgusted by the physical aspect of women and terrified by what he perceives as her manipulative "wiles." It must have been a dangerous passage to encounter as a young man in the post–World War II world of changing and shifting values and systems. Wylie's rhetoric was powerful and no doubt effective. Young men looking for a scapegoat found her in the role of Cinderella, Mom, and She, the evil female triumvirate wheeled out by Wylie. Clearly, Wylie's fury poisons any possibly rational response. He's of the league that defines a wife as a sort of gadget, "something you screw on the bed to get the housework done."

Wylie tapped into a great if unspoken vein of confused anger felt by some men after marriage, when they experience what they consider to be the transformation of their wives into their mothers. "Once she was this wild, funny, adventurous woman, and now she's yelling at me if I don't eat my vegetables," complains Frank, a commercial photographer. "She gets mad if I'm late for dinner, and wants to know where I am every minute of the day. Hell, if I wanted to live like this I would have stayed at home with my mother. Then at least I could have dated other women." Frank is bothered by the pattern he sees in his four-year marriage where his wife seems increasingly concerned with domestic matters. "I fell in love with her because she was absolutely cool about the fact that I was more interested in keeping my darkroom organized than I was in keeping the apartment clean. That's changed, and she's changed."

Desiring a woman who would meet his fantasy of the nondomestic type, he married a cosmetician who was ambitious and admired in her field. May saw herself as a party girl and a tireless worker; she certainly didn't see herself as anybody's "mom." But over the years, she became concerned with having a more stable and steady home life than she'd had in her early twenties. She wanted Frank to pay as much attention to their home as she was. The house and its well-being became the physical symbol of the health of their marriage. May continues to see herself as simply giving more to the relationship, and expecting Frank to do the same.

Frank sees it differently. "I realize that I'm selfish and all that," he says as if he doesn't really believe it, "but I want my sexy girlfriend back. This lady I'm living with is very nice but she's not the girl I married." He feels that he's under his wife's thumb, and unmanned by the arrangement. "I very deliberately went out of my way to find a female who was as different from my mother as possible—even though I love my mom and all that—but I ended up with the girl who married dear old Dad. And I didn't *want* that—I'm really not turned on by it."

This story reminds me of a character from a nineteenth-century novel by Thomas Hardy. In it an elderly husband finds that marriage has cooled his passions. Although he couldn't have wished for a handsomer woman, he couldn't help his "wicked heart wandering" because this handsome woman just wasn't as attractive once she was "ticketed as my lawful wife." He cured his problem by making her remove her wedding ring, calling her by her maiden name, and fantasizing that she was not married to him at all. "And as soon as he could thoroughly fancy he was doing wrong and committing the seventh, he got to like her as well as ever, and they lived on a perfect picture of mutual love." Hardy is drawing our attention to a sort of "incest taboo" that haunts long relationships, in which it becomes increasingly difficult to call forth sexual feelings for someone who is, by this point, "family." In *Men in Therapy,* the researchers tell us that "the most common representations by husbands of their wives were mother figures." Thinking of your wife as your mother—even if such a thought is unconscious—makes thinking of her as your lover difficult. The more a wife mothers, the less desirable she becomes.

Of course, we must remember that marriage involves *two* people. If a woman becomes more like her husband's mother than his girlfriend, then it is probable that he is acting more like somebody's son than like her husband. If, for example, he becomes reliant on his wife to perform domestic tasks, then he can hardly expect her not to assume some domesticity. If, like a teenage, he wants to come home to find a snack waiting and his clothes clean, then he can hardly object to the process that ensures these matters are taken care of—but he does object. "I hate feeling like she's willing to dump all the responsibility on me in some areas—like taking care of money issues—and then not allowing me any sense of competence in others," Frank sums up. "I want somebody to trust me enough to know that I'll eat when I'm hungry, sleep when I'm tired, and buy new clothes when I think I need them. As it is now, she nags me to do this stuff as if I can't make reasonable judgments for myself. I'm afraid that I'm going to have to 'leave home' the way I did when I was eighteen in order to feel like I can live as an independent adult."

The association of the mother with the wife, to the detriment of a marriage, is not surprising, but it bears repeating. We all too often discount the influences of our inherited ideas about the roles and institutions of our society. It is also important to draw attention to the way that the legacies left by bitter and insecure men with a public forum, such as Wylie, continue to influence everyday relationships.

A foundation of misogyny was laid down centuries ago by the likes of Aristotle. One of the founding fathers of philosophy, Aristotle declared that "although there may be exceptions to the order of nature, the male is by nature fitter for command than the female . . . The relation of the male to the female is of this kind, but there the inequality is permanent." Not one to allow for exceptions, Aristotle helped to build contempt for women into our culture as if contempt were factory-issued. But many others, such as Wylie, have not only added on the accessories of modern misogyny, but made the original blueprints accessible for others to follow. Is this sort of "ragging" on women still going on today? Haven't we left this all behind?

Consider, for example, the remarks of wildly popular radio personality Rush Limbaugh, whose *Undeniable Truths of Life* hang in pride of place at the ABC studios in New York. Truth number 24 is a classic: "Feminism was established so that unattractive women could have easier access to the mainstream of society." Clearly, Limbaugh wants his fans to believe that feminists are homely, unable to catch a man, and possibly trying to avoid a career as a librarian by secretly organizing corporate takeovers.

This narrow and mean-spirited definition of "feminist" is more than misleading; it is a harmful lie. Feminists are women and men who consider the lives of women to be of equal value to the lives of men. Feminists work in offices and they work at home (as my friend Bonnie reminds me, "The phrase 'working mother' is redundant"). Feminists can be vegetarians and wear flat shoes, but they can also wear mascara and red-spiked heels, and love barbecue. A feminist might like to dance, might delight in the company of men, and might well marry one of them. Feminists are certainly flooding the mainstream of society since, in my definition, any woman who regards her life as her own and who doesn't want someone else to make her decisions for her (on either a personal or a political level) is a feminist. We have to steal back the word *feminist* from men such as Limbaugh so that we can continue to have a name we're proud of to call ourselves.

Limbaugh's Truth 24 is followed, cleverly, by Truth number 25. In this truth, we hear that "love is the only human emotion which cannot be controlled. You either do or don't. You cannot fake it (except women—and thank God they can)." Obviously "you" are a man, since this universal axiom doesn't apply to women. Women are addressed as if they are not in the room, or else can't read. Maybe

Limbaugh is concerned that women are, in growing numbers, realizing that they shouldn't fake love any more than they should fake orgasms or disguise their intelligence.

THE HUSBAND AS VICTIM

Perhaps you might protest that no one but Rush Limbaugh and the sixty-eight million people who listen to him every day think along those lines? Certainly, at least, no one who can read without moving his lips? Then consider the remarks made by contemporary best-selling journalist and author P. J. O'Rourke. O'Rourke counsels his fellow men to "stay away from girls who cry a lot or who look like they get pregnant easily or have careers," thereby bringing together a delightful assortment of possibilities and suggesting in his own way that men should find cheerful, infertile, homebound women exceedingly attractive. Neither Limbaugh nor O'Rourke is alone in his sentiments. Many men feel like they are the suckers of a system set up by women.

Men, even those who consider themselves happily married, are often haunted by the idea of what they have missed. But the ones who consider themselves less than happily married appear to be absolutely furious. The proverbial anger of a woman scorned pales to nothingness in comparison to the unleashed and uncensored anger of a man who suspects that he's become a victim.

"Male chauvinist pigs who neglect their wives, underpay their women employees, and rule the world—are literally slaves," declares one man in "In Harness, the Male Condition." He claims that men are "out there . . . working fifty hours a week to support themselves and the plantation, only then to come back to the house to do another twenty hours a week rinsing dishes, toting trash bags, writing checks, and acting as butlers at the parties." Despite the fact that, as a friend of mine put it, husbands often act "like they're at a party at somebody else's house" when they're the host, the anger behind this man's statement is undeniable. He feels like he's been sold a bill of goods, like he's on the short end of a very bad deal.

Are many men actually in the position of having to take on "two jobs"—worker and domestic—in the modern world? Arlie Hochschild and Anne Machung argue in *Second Shift,* a 1989 book about the division of domestic labor in the homes of working couples, that "men married to working women spent only three-quarters of an hour longer each week with their kindergarten-aged children than did men married to housewives." Despite these statistics, many men believe that they now have the worst of both worlds. If they are angry but unwilling to admit to their anger, a number of other behaviors will attest to it.

The passive-aggressive man, for example, will appear to want to help his wife when asked, but will be so inept, so slow, or so dependent on her instructions that she learns not to bother asking. When Dagwood from the cartoon strip "Blondie" quits his job to work for his wife's catering business, she fires him after a short period of time because he literally "eats up the profits." The passive-aggressive husband is a staple of cartoons, comedy routines, and sitcoms. Male characters are often put in a situation where they are asked to help their wife clean the house, for example. They don an apron and get to work—only to break the vacuum cleaner, put wool sweaters in the dryer, and burn dinner. The wife throws up her hands, declares her husband "impossible," and resumes her usual chores. The last shot will show the husband with his feet up, reading the paper, and winking at the camera as if to say, "See how clever I am? I acted dumb to manipulate her back into doing it all herself. Ha, ha."

When Ralph Kramden decides he can do housework better than Alice, or when Lucy and Ethel trade places with Ricky and Fred, the men are presented as unable to perform the simplest household task. Part of the problem here is that men and women then seem fixed in their gender-specific roles naturally and forever. Lucy and Ethel can't keep up with the conveyor belt at the candy factory and so need to return to their own kitchen. "The boys" can't manage at home, so they should return, of course, to work. The lesson seems to be that any gender role change is unnatural, and that we're better off staying in our assigned places. The husband in such a situation realizes, consciously or unconsciously, that he gets what he wants by holding back. Therefore, by not doing what his wife wants him to do, he becomes exempt from being called upon to do it again. Withholding help, intimacy, or attention can have a profound effect on a relationship.

THE WITHHOLDING MAN

Another way in which anger can manifest itself is through a man's withholding of his own needs and desires in order to punish the wife who won't be able to meet them—unless, of course, she can guess what they are. A man may neglect to tell the woman in his life what he wants and needs, for fear of appearing too dependent. He might sulk or tune out for days at a time until she "wheedles" information out of him. One husband of a friend used to have an almost comically exaggerated gesture of looking out from underneath bushy eyebrows until someone asked him what was wrong. Invariably, he'd say, "Nothing," until everyone around him was trying to figure out—without his help—how to cheer him up. He became the center of attention by default, until his wife decided not to participate in that game any longer. "When you want to tell me what's disturbing you, I promise I'll be happy to listen. But I'm not going to beg you to talk to me anymore." He kept looking up from under those eyebrows for a few months, but eventually he did learn to speak, as his wife put it, "in actual words."

Victor Seidler explains that "it was as if [men] had got used to women interpreting our needs, desires and feelings for us in their emotional realm, so that we never had to find words and a language of desire and needs for ourselves." Mothers did not want to embarrass their sons by forcing them to explain their moods and so men were, in many cases, not encouraged to speak about emotional matters. Their mothers, however, often intuited what they needed and supplied whatever it was without their sons having to ask, whether it was slipping them an extra five-dollar bill, making their favorite meal, or running interference with their fathers. Many men learned to depend on this elaborate unspoken vocabulary. "This was a way we could have our emotional needs met without really having to show our vulnerability and need." When a woman asks her adult husband, usually in great frustration, "What did you expect me to do, read your mind?" the real answer might well be "Yes." His mother knew how to make things better, so why can't his wife do the same? Why does she need to humiliate him by forcing him to tell her what he needs?

"I don't think women understand the vulnerability of most men—

women are deceived by the stereotyped 'masculinity' roles and attitudes attributed to the male population; a little more understanding and compassion would be helpful," says a respondent quoted by Anthony Pietropinto, M.D., and Jacqueline Simenauer in *Beyond the Male Myth*. Other answers strike similar chords: "Men are more fragile than women. Men need the ego boost a woman can give . . . Many 'liberated' women emasculate men badly." A man might well fear appearing dependent on a woman since he has cultivated an image of himself as completely invulnerable. When he desires something, he often depends on her anticipation of his needs. In many cases a man will count on the fact that his wife will "insist" that they discuss problems, or "insist" that he tell her what's bothering him. It would appear, too, that men fear appearing too dependent because they themselves are fearful of being needed by someone else. It is clear that all of us, men and women alike, would be pleased by the idea that our desires and needs could be met automatically, but it simply doesn't work that way. Women should not be expected to read men's minds any more than men should be expected to read women's minds; often we don't know exactly what we want until we are able to ask for it.

When we ask for something, we are also indicating a willingness to admit and accept responsibility for our desire. Let's say I want to go out for Chinese food. When asked what I'd like to do, however, I simply say, "I don't care," and yet I secretly harbor a grudge if my husband doesn't suggest we go for Chinese food. In this case, I have only myself to blame if the evening turns sour instead of sweet. But, on the other hand, since I made no suggestion, I can't be blamed if the evening doesn't turn out well or if the food isn't any good. Certainly it's a game two can play, but one in which nobody wins. Men might be tempted to do this even more often than women, especially if they were brought up expecting a woman to decode their secret signals.

LOOKING FOR "AN EIGHTEEN-YEAR-OLD VIRGIN NYMPHOMANIAC"

Pietropinto and Simenauer supply another man's definition of the perfect woman: "An 18-year-old virgin nymphomaniac whose father owns a liquor store." But once faced with the "perfect woman," a man risks sexual failure for a number of reasons, according to these researchers.

To put it mildly, such men regard women as "Other," as not-like-them, as objects or numbers or pieces on a game board, not as complete human beings. "Misogyny has deep cultural roots," explains Victor Seidler in *Rediscovering Masculinity*. "This is the reason we can so easily despise women we have sexual relations with. Because the very existence of our sexual feelings proves our own unworthiness, we can despise any woman who wants to have sexual relations with us. We can withdraw from them as soon as we have had sexual contact. This used to be a very familiar feeling for me, as I felt unable to stay the night in the same bed with a woman I had made love with. I felt a sense of unease, even disgust, after orgasm."

Women are, in such cases, seen only as possessors of sexual apparatus, not as complete human beings. It is important to note that the men involved cannot for the most part prevent themselves from surrendering to this feeling about women; Seidler makes it clear that he does not respect his own response, and yet cannot contain it. It is no wonder that women remain foreign objects, slightly distasteful and certainly threatening in such circumstances.

The authors of *Beyond the Male Myth* apparently concur with such findings. They seem to be countering the assumption that, as one friend of mine put it, it is easier for men to go for therapy these days because when they're asked to return to their childhood, most of them are already there. "Men seem less complex only because most of the time nothing is coming out," claim Pietropinto and Simenauer. In reality, they say, "the therapeutic work is infinitely slower because men are not only reluctant to talk about sex, but actually fail to confront their feelings about it. Many of them regard their genitals as detached objects, independent of their thoughts and emotions, and their sexual partners become the equally detached targets of their genitals."

Simone de Beauvoir gives the definitive definition of the concept of the "Other" in *The Second Sex* when she argues that a woman, especially in the eyes of the sort of man whose testimony we have just heard, is "a womb, an ovary; she is a female—this word is sufficient to define her. In the mouth of a man the epithet 'female' has the sound of an insult, yet he is not ashamed of his animal nature; on the contrary, he is proud if someone says of him: 'He is a male!' The term 'female' is derogatory not because it emphasizes woman's animality, but because it imprisons her in her sex." The Otherness of women here means that all the emphasis is placed on her as a sexual being and involves the fetishization of her sexuality. Even as the Otherness of the heterosexual partner is frightening, it is also usually the center of attraction. Clearly there is bound to be trouble. Dorothy Parker's story "Dusk Before Fireworks" illustrates, in part, the point that the implication of "female" is derogatory in the following exchange between two lovers: "Oh, good Lord, what's the matter with women, anyway?" asks a handsome young man. "Please don't call me 'woman,' " snaps his paramour, to which he wryly replies, "I'm sorry darling. I didn't mean to use bad words." In general, to be told that one is acting "just like a woman" is rarely a compliment, especially when the comment is made by a man.

What happens to this sort of man if and when he does marry? Perhaps the most accurate and disturbing insight into this phenomenon is offered once again by De Beauvoir when she argues that "Man has succeeded in enslaving woman; but in the same degree he has deprived her of what made her possession desirable. With woman integrated in the family and in society, her magic is dissipated rather than transformed; reduced to the condition of servant, she is no longer that unconquered prey incarnating all the treasures of nature. Since the rise of chivalric love it is a commonplace that marriage kills love. Scorned too much, respected too much, too much an everyday matter, the wife ceases to have erotic attraction."

The man might feel as if he is contracted into a relationship with declining returns, and feel as if "he is taken in the snare set by nature: because he desired a fresh young girl, he has to support a heavy matron or a desiccated hag for life." He has to pay the price for his wife throughout his life. As one rather callous man of my acquaintance put it, "It's like making payments on a car you don't even want to drive anymore."

THE AGING WIFE

Such men might see their thoughts reflected in Sherman McCoy's interior monologues from *Bonfire of the Vanities* by Tom Wolfe. Early on in the novel, Sherman calls his own number rather than his mistress's from a phone booth, mistakes his wife's voice for his lover's, and calls his wife by the wrong name, which, not surprisingly, causes his wife to doubt his fidelity. Rather than question his own judgment, inwardly he wonders about the restrictions imposed by the unnatural institution of marriage. "Why couldn't he (being a Master of the Universe) simply explain it to her?" Sherman asks himself. Instead of having to lie and cheat, he would like to be straightforward and explain why his role as a husband is simply too confining. What he would like to say is "Look, Judy, I still love you and I love our daughter and I love our home and I love our life, and I don't want to change any of it—it's just that I, a Master of the Universe, a young man still in the season of the rising sap, deserve more from time to time, when the spirit moves me . . ."

Sherman also finds himself returning to the question of his wife's age. Being a mere thirty-eight years old compared to his wife's advanced age of forty, Sherman feels justified in having a younger mistress to meet his sexual needs, not to mention the requirements of his vanity. "Still a very good-looking woman, my wife . . . But she's forty years old! . . . Not her fault . . . But not mine, either! He deserved better. She was two years older than he was, and his mother had said such things could matter—which, the way she said it, meant it would matter." The number of years is clearly insignificant. What is significant, however, is Sherman's perception of his wife's decline in her sexual market value (Sherman works with stocks and is very conscious of such matters). As she ages she "loses points" because she becomes, in his eyes and in the eyes of those around him, less valuable. She was in her prime in her twenties and thirties when she was most sexually desirable, whereas Sherman is hitting his prime in his middle age because his attractiveness depends not solely on his physical condition but on his financial and social standing as well. Obviously such a system of perceptions is not only grossly unfair but is also unnervingly ruthless. It works this way: As Sherman's wife ages, she spoils, like milk left out too long in the heat; as Sherman ages, he matures, like wine left in a cool cellar to reach its full flavor.

This reminds me of a man I met who presented the whole issue of age in marriage in rather basic terms. "When you think about a woman's age as compared to a man's, you have to do some arithmetic. It's like a woman of forty is a very different age from a man of forty. You'll excuse me if I put it this way," he hesitated, and then explained, with eyes averted, that "it's like when you figure how old a dog or a cat is in human years. The cat may be ten years old, but in human years she's sixty. A woman might be no older than a man on paper, but she seems older than he does. You have to count 'women years' differently from how you count 'men years.'" He could tell that I was disturbed by his theory, but I congratulated him on his candor. And then I came across a mildly terrifying passage from Sigmund Freud, which I am fairly sure did not inform my acquaintance's theory, but nonetheless upheld his position.

In *New Introductory Lectures on Psychoanalysis*, Freud writes that "a man of about thirty strikes us as a youthful, somewhat unformed individual, whom we expect to make powerful use of the possibilities for development opened up to him by analysis. A woman of the same age, however, often frightens us by her psychical rigidity and unchangeability." While I believe that today very few people would agree with Freud and consider a woman washed up by thirty, emotionally petrified into one psychical position, they might well think, like Sherman, that a man is still basically a "kid" at forty where a woman is past her best by the same age. Freud continues his argument by claiming that at thirty, a woman's "libido has taken up final positions and seems incapable of exchanging them for others. There are no paths open to further development; it is as though the whole process had already run its course and remains thenceforward insusceptible to influence—as though, indeed, the difficult development to femininity had exhausted the possibilities of the person concerned." It is as if life stops at thirty for a woman, in Freud's estimation, since she cannot accommodate any new emotional information after that age. Conveniently, then, a woman's mind becomes rigid at just about the time the rest of her gets a little soft. Therefore men will be publicly justified when seeking out younger women for the suppleness of mind as well as the firmness of thighs.

We hear in *Men and Marriage*, by Heather Jenner and Muriel Segal, that "whatever they may say to the contrary, men still prefer to marry a girl younger than themselves. Aristotle advised men of thirty-seven to marry girls of eighteen, and there is an old adage that a man should marry a woman half his own age plus seven. This is going a bit far and must have been thought up by some elderly widower: It works out that he is sixty-two when she is still only thirty-eight." (Winner of the "going a bit far" sweepstakes: actor and director Woody Allen, who at age fifty-seven began dating the twenty-one-year-old daughter of his longtime companion Mia Farrow, thereby breaking not only some fairly significant taboos, but also forgoing his right to be taken seriously when discussing relationships between adult men and women.)

In the comedy *City Slickers*, the character played by Billy Crystal asks an age-obsessed pal, "Have you noticed that the older you get, the younger your girlfriends get? Pretty soon you'll be dating sperm." What is spotlighted by this punchline is the idea that the drive to find an ever-younger woman is basically unhealthy. If the best thing offered by a woman is that she was born the year the guy got his first car, then the relationship doesn't look very promising. The fetishization of age for its own sake is particularly damaging because age is one thing that is bound to change over time.

The idea that the cute girl loses her cuteness after a few years of connubial bliss is not a new one. The much-married woman has few champions of her desirability, although in 1745 Benjamin Franklin wrote to a friend that since "a single Man has not nearly the Value he would have in the State of Union" (if he were married) and because the single man is an incomplete animal, resembling "the odd Half of a Pair of Scissors," the friend should marry an experienced and older woman. Why? Franklin explains that "when Women cease to be handsome they study to be good. To maintain their Influence over Men, they supply the diminution of Beauty by an Augmentation of Utility. They learn to do 1,000 Services small and great." For this reason (and because "They are so grateful!!" according to the statesman), men should seek them out. But such praise, even such dubious praise, is scarce.

Almost any wife over forty appears in many novels, plays, and films to be a sexless creature, a woman beyond her prime. "She had become so dully habituated to married life that in her full matronliness she was as sexless as an anemic nun," writes Sinclair Lewis of Babbitt's wife. "She was a good woman, a kind woman, a diligent woman, but no one, save perhaps Tinka, her ten-year-old, was at all interested in her or entirely aware that she was alive." The wife in Wolfe's *Bonfire* has grown too thin, becoming a "social X-ray"; the wife in *Presumed Innocent* has grown too self-absorbed, "largely a willing captive within the walls of her own home, flawlessly keeping our house, tending our child, and toiling endlessly with her formulae and computer algorithms"; the wife in *Babbitt* is good enough, but no better: "She made him what is known as a Good Wife. She was loyal, industrious, and at rare times merry. She passed from a feeble disgust at their closer relations into what promised to be ardent affection, but it drooped into bored routine."

Leggitt's wife in *Butterfield 8* has become so polished a surface that she can only reflect her surroundings: "All her life Emily had been looking at nice things, nice houses, cars, pictures, grounds, clothes, people. Things that were easy to look at, and people that were easy to look at; with healthy complexions and good teeth, people who had had pasteurized milk to drink and proper food all their lives from the time they were infants; people who lived in houses that were kept clean, and painted when paint was needed, who took care of their cars and their furniture and their bodies, and by doing so their minds were taken care of; and they got the look that Emily . . . had." The husband's contempt for what he sees as the simplicity and luxury of his wife's life encourages him to vent his resentment by having an affair with a woman whose wild life is completely different. He builds up innumerable reasons why he should leave his wife, but it comes as no surprise that age has something to do with it. His wife is his age; his mistress is twenty years younger, the age of his eldest daughter.

Mystery writer Agatha Christie offers one solution for women who are concerned with these horrifying visions of aging. Christie declares that "an archaeologist is the best husband any woman can have; the older she gets, the more interested he is in her." The other strategy for dealing with these issues is to examine them in light of the larger sense of crisis experienced by these men who probably know better than to respect their own responses and actions in such situations.

THE IMPORTANCE OF CRISIS

The husbands presented by the novelists mentioned above rarely evaluate their own circumstances until a crisis appears. But the importance of a crisis, whatever its occasion, cannot be underestimated. A crisis often leads to change, and change will lead to movement and growth. "To precipitate a crisis takes courage," but, Doctors Joan Wexler and John Steidl remind us, "the precipitator may feel tremendous guilt as well as fear for making the first move . . ."

A moment of crisis, a crossroads or a turning point in life, can encompass everything from a fortieth birthday to confronting alcoholism, from the birth of a child, to meeting a son's first girlfriend—both major and minor events can create a state of crisis. Even at these most memorable and focused moments, however, men often cannot answer the questions put before them: What do they think about this event? Perhaps more important, how do they feel?

Over and over again we hear that men in mid-life cannot define their own lives with any accuracy or legitimacy. Their most frequent response appears to be confusion and doubt. "I don't even know if I'm unhappily married," cries Leggitt from *Butterfield 8*. "I don't know anything about myself. I must be happy, because whenever I've looked back and remembered times when I was happy, I always find that I didn't know I was happy when I was."

When men do attempt to define themselves, they come up against their own inner voices, voices which make them question the most fundamental aspects of their lives. "I am a good man," insists the hero from Sloan Wilson's *The Man in the Gray Flannel Suit*. "I have never done anything of which I am truly ashamed." This declaration defies any doubts on the part of the speaker, yet, even as he positions himself as a "good man," Sloan tells us that "curiously" he "seemed to be mimicking himself . . . A gust of ghostly and derisive laughter seemed to ring out in reply." The inner voice acts the way a schoolyard bully would act—nasty, taunting, teasing, and full of contempt for any assertion of self.

Similarly, George Babbitt's protective environment is pierced by the realization that he does not actually know the purpose of his life. "It was coming to him that perhaps all life as he knew it and vigorously practiced it was futile." Lewis shows Babbitt worrying "that heaven . . . was neither probable nor very interesting; that he hadn't much pleasure out of making money; that it was of doubtful worth to rear children merely that they might rear children who would rear children. What was it all about? What did he want?" *Babbitt* was one of the most influential and important books of its day in part because George Babbitt's plight reflected the depressions and pitfalls into which an ordinary man could fall. Not very much has changed in that perilous landscape during the last sixty years.

Babbitt's soul-searching can easily be compared to what writers like John Updike are scripting for their middle-class, middle-aged, and middle-of-the-road characters a half-century after Sinclair Lewis's novel was published. "I'm dying," laments one of Updike's men in *Couples*, "I'm a thirty-four-year-old fly-by-night contractor. I have no sons, my wife snubs me, my employees despise me, my friends are all my wife's friends, I'm an orphan, a pariah." The sense of isolation and the lack of intimacy not only from others but from one's own self is the key characteristic of such men.

"These husbands are lost souls," as one of my young male students said, and they are terrified of the high, endless, blank wall of their own fears. For many husbands, marriage offers merely a mirage of intimacy, an intimacy which, like a mirage, gradually disappears just when they thought they were saved. They retreat behind the Sunday newspapers, silently questioning how they ended up where they are, sitting like their fathers once sat, feeling not quite as if they are in their own homes.

CHAPTER FOUR

WHOSE DEAL
IS IT ANYWAY?

*Why Men Think Women Control the
Dating and Newlywed Games*

IT IS CLEAR that men are faced with unique problems. They are having
to unlearn how to be the men they were brought up to be as well as
learning to be the men they would like to be. They have gone from
regarding sex as being "as fun as tennis—a little volleying, some
baseline strokes and then the big slam at the net," according to
essayist Skip Hollandsworth, to seeing it as a game that's "as complicated as chess and as dangerous as Russian roulette. Almost every
man under the age of 40 learned about sex in an era when the subject
was most visibly addressed by a crowd of happy hookers and Dr.
Feelgoods and swinging couples and the Playboy Man. Today, sex is
discussed by representatives from the Centers of Disease Control and
by various legal scholars hired by the networks to comment on rape
trials. Suddenly, for a man, being single and unattached is more of a
burden than being married." Men who were taught to evade domestic

responsibility for as long as possible might now be facing a dread of being single that once confronted only their female counterparts.

UNLEARNING THE ROPES

There are other problems as well. Hollandsworth continues his article by defining what he terms "the Frigid Male": "Today's Frigid Male sees a woman who's as powerful as he is at work and at the gym. He sees a woman who is proud of her own sexual nature, who wears breathtakingly sexy outfits—yet who will not put up with any leering, sexist male attitude. She will turn against him over an indiscretion; she will not sit passively by if she feels wronged. The Frigid Male isn't sure how to talk to this kind of woman, let alone how to seduce one. So he becomes more passive, more sexually withdrawn, uncertain how to display his own erotic nature."

John, a good friend of mine at Georgetown University, tells me that the Catholic Church grants most of its annulments to Americans based on male "psychological impotence," an inability to form intimate emotional bonds. "It's known as the American Impediment," says John. We've seen some of the reasons why men in our culture are raised to think it necessary to keep themselves emotionally separate from women in order to retain their masculine integrity. But there are other manifestations of the tensions underlying these issues.

Pietropinto and Simenauer give some insight into literal as well as metaphorical impotence when they find in their research that "it is not uncommon to encounter cases of impotence when a man confronts a woman he deems himself unworthy of: one with superior intelligence, a more successful career, a great deal of sexual experience, or even a particularly voluptuous figure. Neurotic men may have difficulty with maternal or cultured women, feeling that a sexual act would debase these madonnas." In part, these men are acting out a pattern of behavior described by Freud in a 1914 essay titled "The Most Prevalent Form of Degradation in Erotic Life." Freud describes men who, because of their early upbringing, divide women into two distinct categories: the lovable and the desirable. "Where these men desire," explains Freud, "they cannot love. Where they love, they cannot desire." If such a man is sexually interested in a woman, he resists finding out anything about her as a person—his interest depends on seeing her solely as a sexual object. If, in contrast, he has tender, compassionate, or affectionate feelings toward a woman, he is unlikely to be able to imagine her as a sexual partner. He will think of her as "too good" for his sexuality, denying her even the option of refusal.

"YOU KEEP ME HANGING ON"

Such a dynamic informs many of the relationships that keep women "hanging on." A woman may well wonder why a male friend, for whom she might harbor romantic feelings, will date a series of floozies for whom he has no respect instead of considering *her* as a potential partner. He doesn't even seem to think of upgrading *their* relationship to a sexual one. In such a man's mind, of course, he is not *upgrading* a friendship to make it sexual—he is *degrading* it. And while he is probably unconscious of these responses, they nevertheless inevitably affect the relationships he has with women.

Not only are men afraid of debasing the women they see as "madonnas"; in many cases, they seem to be afraid of women generally. Women represent the fearful unknown and unknowable. They are creatures of mystery—and that isn't a compliment. In John Updike's 1992 story "Baby's First Steps," the central character becomes involved with a woman only to be "confronted . . . with that female openness and depth of interrogation which remind men of the dark, of the ocean, of the night sky, of everything swallowing and frightening." Women are presented the same way in contemporary fiction as they were presented three hundred years ago, when sin enters the Edenic garden of Milton's paradise in female form. Their sexuality, in particular, is threatening because it appears secretive and hidden. Men's sexual apparatus is out there for the world to see—like the safety implied by an unconcealed weapon—whereas women's sex appears covered, hidden, even invisible. "What's it like once you're in there?" I remember hearing a seventh-grade boy ask, in all candor, in sex-education class. The penis-as-Christopher-Columbus, heading off into virgin territory (or at least into the unknown . . .), makes the boy's body seem like a vehicle of discovery, a way of plunging into a new environment, the tool by which a new world is conquered. In one of the most enthusiastic love poems in English literature, seventeenth-century poet John Donne sings the praises of his lover's preparation for bed. During the climax of the poem he looks at her and calls her, in all exuberance, "Oh my America! my new found land!" He is about to explore her as a scout might explore a new, unmapped landscape ("Licence my roaming hands, and let them go/Before, behind, between, above, below"), with curiosity as well as with an awareness of how foreign the place can be—how dangerous, and how unknown.

The images of women as unknowable and insatiable appear over and over again: Men describe women in terms of cavernous, mysterious, unmappable, and unknowable terrains. Freudians would argue that men are afraid of being absorbed back into the womb, metaphorically if not literally. They fear what they see as the unfulfill-able need women have for intimacy; they want to flee from the undifferentiated layers of emotion and sexuality. Women seem to be insatiable; the fearful image behind the cliché of the frigid woman is the woman who can never have enough. She is the real Medusa here, the female who will strip a man of his masculinity by asking for more once he has given everything he has.

This sense of being insatiable can manifest itself in small as well as large ways. I sat diagonally across from a couple in their thirties while traveling on an overcrowded Amtrack train at the beginning of one holiday weekend not long ago. The husband across from me had brought several old New Yorker magazines, and seemed settled in for the trip. Once into the journey, the wife asked her husband if she could read one of the magazines, and he seemed delighted to give her one. They smiled at one another, and he resumed reading. For the next twenty minutes, she proceeded to interrupt him at five-minute intervals to show him every one of the cartoons and waited for him to react. At the first few, he laughed and nodded. Then his responses became more strained. I could see him close his eyes briefly when she once again repeated, "Just look at this one," and it was clear that she wanted much more attention than he was prepared to give. Finally he said in a low voice, "Please, I thought you were going to read. I don't want to see every cartoon; I'll read them myself when I get to them. Can't I finish this story?" She colored immediately; he looked both angry and embarrassed. He tried to give her what she needed by listening and laughing, but I'm sure he felt like she was never going to be satisfied until he gave her every ounce of his attention. By trying to engage him more and more closely, she managed only to push him away.

In D. H. Lawrence's *Sons and Lovers*, we hear the central character, Paul, berate his girlfriend Miriam for what he sees as her infinite need. He was enraged when "she bent and breathed a flower," because "it was as if she and the flower were loving each other. Paul hated her for it. There seemed a sort of exposure about the action, something too intimate." He is terrified by what he regards as a sort of emotional black hole in her personality. "You don't want to love—your eternal and abnormal craving is to be loved," he asserts. "You aren't positive, you're negative. You absorb, absorb, as if you must fill yourself up with love, because you've got a shortage somewhere." It is not surprising, then, that men have designed the emotional machinery to lift them out of the slough of need and desire they see as the province of the female. Such emotional machinery has at its center the mechanisms of authority and control.

In many cases, the assumption of authority and control by men can be a learned adaptive maneuver and can become an inexpert attempt to convince themselves that they have some say in the running of their lives—otherwise, they would be "used up" by women. A former student of mine, in his early twenties and recently married, is disgruntled by what he regards as the "lie" that men "run the world." "I can't believe that I'm considered privileged," he says, incredulous. "What are these rights I supposedly have? The right to scramble for a mediocre job so that I can support my family when the time comes, buy a house with a fat mortgage, send my kids to college, and die of a stress-related heart attack fifteen years before my wife? Boy," he pauses, and then says without emotion, "what a lucky guy."

Philip Roth questions the "growing body of opinion which maintains that by and large marriages, affairs, and sexual arrangements generally are made by masters in search of slaves: there are the dominant and the submissive, the brutish and the compliant, the exploiters and the exploited. What this formula fails to explain, along with a million other things, is why so many of the 'masters' appear themselves to be in bondage, often times to their 'slaves.' " Yet the man's most potent asset in a marriage is his right to categorize, name, and assign positions to the players. It is he who chooses the rules of the game. The "slave" is "master" only to the extent that the master permits it. The "rule" of the slave is superficial at best; the slave is subject to the definition offered by the master, but powerless to change it. That the balance between feelings of powerlessness and the need to control one's own environment is precarious will come as no surprise to women.

Men are confused by the push and pull of the expectations handed them in childhood and adolescence, worried by their sexual longings, and concerned about their definitions of appropriate masculine and feminine spheres and behaviors. Because of these relevant insecurities, the institution of marriage itself, like city hall, is a difficult one to fight. Researchers Blumstein and Schwartz argue convincingly that "an institution is a way of life that is very resistant to change. People know about it; they can describe it; and they have spent a lifetime learning how to react to it. The idea of marriage is larger than any individual marriage. The role of husband or wife is greater than any individual who takes on that role." Yet many people might feel as Mae West did when asked her opinion of marriage: "Marriage is a great institution. But I'm not ready for an institution yet."

Who governs the "institution" of marriage? Who administrates it? Who has control, who makes the rules, who sets the limits? Whom do we cheat if we try to look after our own interests? Who walks away with the big prize made at the expense of the individual loser?

At our worst moments, each sex believes it is the other who runs the show and reaps all the rewards. Like an optical illusion where we can see only one image at a time, we sometimes believe that our spouse is seeing only half the picture—and seeing the wrong half, at that. For example, the viewer sees either two profiles on the periphery of the picture, or a vase in the center—the viewer cannot simultaneously see both images. One picture both defines and cancels out the other.

Consider the following experiment as a sort of "audial illusion" along the same lines as an optical illusion. Read the passage and imagine the speaker: "I'm fed up with doing everything your way. We always do everything you want to do. You decide how we spend our time—in fact, you decide when we should spend time together and then demand that we do it at that moment, no matter what I'm involved with or what sort of mood I'm in. You badger me about money and unless it involves spending money on what you want to do or spending on something you think 'we' should have, you always make me feel like there isn't enough money to go around. You control everything around here."

Who said those words? Chances are that each partner hears it in the other's voice. Many husbands feel as if their wives complain constantly, no matter what they do or how much effort they make—and many wives feel that husbands do exactly the same. Women often believe that men control all the money in the house, and men often believe that women tie the purse strings on to their apron strings. Everyone believes and fears that he or she will lose ground and end up being the "sucker" in a bad deal. This is one speech that is not gender specific. In many cases, each spouse regards the other as unfairly in control. In many cases, each feels the other is something of a bully, and each feels like something of a victim.

"HIS AND HER MARRIAGES"

It seems to be the same in terms of marriage—there are two versions. As a number of psychologists and sociologists have argued, there are "two marriages" in every marriage—his and hers. Jessie Bernard makes this point most explicitly in her major work, *The Future of Marriage*, when she states that "there is by now a very considerable body of well-authenticated research to show that there really are two marriages in every marital union, and that they do not always coincide." In fact, research shows that although "there is usually agreement on the number of children they have and a few other such verifiable items," there is little agreement on, for example, the "length of premarital acquaintance and of engagement, on age at marriage and interval between marriage and birth of first child." So, too, is there a belief that the other partner has all the control and is running the game, which is to say that each partner might well believe the other is getting a kickback from the system, getting paid under the table. How else could this other person have taken over so completely?

IN AND OUT OF CONTROL

It is clear that for a group who are regarded as being in control of the power structure, many men often feel out of control in their own emotional lives. These men see themselves as doubly restricted: They feel that they can neither wield unlimited power nor admit to their powerlessness. They are caught between understanding that their responses and reactions are important while simultaneously believing that if they admit to feelings of worry, fears of inadequacy, or lack of ambition, they will be penalized. "My wife wants me to share my feelings with her," complains one anguished friend. "But then she resents or picks apart everything I say. My wife means well, but she gets on my nerves when I admit that something's bothering me. As soon as a problem is out of my mouth, she's all over me for details when I just want to be left alone, and then I'm sorry that I ever said anything. In the end, I worry about her being worried. It's easier to keep it to myself."

In a 1989 article about the popular television series "thirtysomething," writer Stephen Fried quotes those involved in the creation of the male characters. The producers explain that "there are still real dangers in expressing feelings . . . the world is still an emotionally dangerous place, especially for men . . . There is still a real danger if a man is considered weak in this society, and there are still lots of people who will take honest expression of feeling as expression of weakness." The issue here concerns a man's sense of vulnerability, a sense that he is making himself a victim of circumstances rather than someone who masters circumstances. According to the "thirtysomething" group, "A man in that position stands to lose, in his work and at home. What if, by being honest, he makes his wife frightened that he can't support the family? That's going to put up barriers in the relationship." The belief that honesty will add to the burdens of a marriage rather than relieve them is a trait that can be most associated with a traditionally masculine privileging of repression over expression of emotion.

A man feels he cannot afford to let the other player know what cards he holds. The essential lesson learned by many men early on is the art of the bluff. Bluffing is an essential strategy in playing poker, for example. One of the essential truths of the game is that a good player never lets anyone else see a flicker of reaction—either positive or negative—to a hand that he's been dealt. Four natural aces will never raise an eyebrow in surprise; a pair of twos will not provoke a frown. You can win the pot with that pair of twos if everyone else at the table believes you have a great hand—if they "fold" in surrender at your bluff.

A winner, by the way, is under absolutely no obligation in such a situation to show his hand once he wins. No one will ever know whether he had a royal flush—or nothing at all. All that matters is that everyone thought he was a winner, and so awarded him that position by refusing to challenge him and run the risk of being a loser.

According to this way of looking at the world, you keep your distance, keep your feelings to yourself, and you'll win. Anyone close to you can both damage you and be damaged by you. Which may be why, as one male friend from college once told me, some men are so reluctant to say "I love you" to a woman. "I'll never tell a woman that I love her," said Jim, "because then I will never have to risk hearing myself say, 'I don't love you anymore.' "

Many men believe they must pretend that everything is just fine, no matter how they feel. Victor Seidler, in *Rediscovering Masculinity*, agrees, pointing out that "as boys, we are brought up to distance ourselves from fear. We learn that we have constantly to prove our masculinity, we can never take it for granted. This builds enormous tension into contemporary conceptions of masculinity. Fear is defined as an unacceptable emotion, but in disowning our fear and learning to put a brave face to the world, we learn to despise all forms of weakness." Clearly this leads to the discounting of everyone else's weakness as well; someone who has not learned self-control is regarded as feeble, perhaps even contemptible. Women are often seen, by such men, as less than equal because they cannot master their emotions sufficiently; that women should value the expression of weakness or fear is dismissed as unimaginable. "Strength is identified with a stiff upper lip, as we learn systematically to discount any feelings of fear," explains Seidler. "We learn not to show our feelings to others, since this is an immediate sign of weakness." Therefore, a man's sense of masculinity derives from his ability to estrange himself from any sense of vulnerability.

This is one reason men are often accused of seeming cocky and arrogant: They are trained to bury any other versions of themselves. This leads to the sort of comment made by one woman who, when asked if her husband was religious, replied, "Yes. He thinks he's God."

"From an early age we learn to dismiss what girls are involved with," such as caretaking or expression of intimacy, Seidler argues. He underlines the significance of the fact that boys are trained very differently from girls in terms of what is of value, especially when it comes to relationships with women. "[Men] grow up with a very different sense of what is important. We can find it hard to give significance to and put our time and attention into relationships. Since we have often learnt to be independent and self-sufficient ourselves, through suppressing our own neediness, it is hard to credit the needs that others express. It is in forsaking our own needs that we prove we have the self-control that makes our masculinity secure." Since they are taught to trivialize their own fears and needs, it is clear that the fears and needs expressed by others will often seem childish and self-indulgent. Even when they "know better" than to try to disregard the misinformation they were given as children, it is no easier for men to erase those early lessons than it is for women.

"Stop whining," a man might snap at his wife, who is deeply hurt by what she reads as his curt dismissal of her genuine worries. "You're hysterical," a husband might sneer at his wife when she cannot stop weeping during a traumatic argument. "We can't talk about anything because you always turn everything into a crisis," says a husband as he walks out the door after a difficult discussion about money that leaves his wife asking question after question about the security of their future.

If a girl's greatest and most secret fear is that no one will ever ask her to marry him because she is too plain or unattractive, then a boy's fear is that he will be considered a "loser," someone voted "least likely to succeed" in high school. If a girl is supposed to be cute enough to impress her boyfriend's buddies, he's supposed to be able to reel off a list of ambitions when her father meets him at the door and asks him about his plans for the future. In a popular board game called *Heart-Throb*, which is marketed to "Girls of All Ages Who Like Boys," photo-cards of possible boyfriends are handed out along with cards that list their ambitions. As a player, you can choose, for example, between a young man who "Hopes to Become a Fighter Pilot," one who "Wants to Be an Aerobics Instructor in a Woman's Health Club," one who "Wants to Win the Oscar for 'Best Actor,' " one who "Wants to Live Off the Land in the Wilderness," or even between one who "Would Like to Become President of the United States" and one who "Plans to Start His Own Religion." (Given the political climate of the last decade, it would be difficult even to *separate* these final two, let alone choose between them.) Presumably different little girls have differing fantasies, although I have yet to personally meet a seven-year-old who has her eye on an aerobics instructor in a woman's health club. The point here, however, is that the girls—of all ages—are encouraged not to choose just by looking at the cute photographs but by seeing whether the boys will go on to be "successful."

FEAR OF FAILURE

There can be no doubt that men are reeling from the information they received as boys and teenagers in much the same way that women are still experiencing the aftershocks of youth. What were men hearing? According to a book titled *Men: The Variety and Meaning of Their Sexual Experience* (edited by A. M. Krich and published in 1954 with an introduction by Margaret Mead), they were instructed that "a man's social status has a sexual value [and] his business or professional success is therefore a means of sexual attraction. Money, like glory, is the practical expression of that success. Therefore the influence which a large fortune, like that of social position, exercises upon a woman seeking a mate may be adjudged a legitimate biologic means of attraction." The authors state explicitly and repeatedly that "economic equilibrium, then, becomes a point of sexual attraction. And in general, this equilibrium is reached only in postjuvenile years, when the chronologic field of masculine sexual suggestion is considerably widened. This inclination of young women toward mature men at times finds a corresponding phase in the attraction which young women have for many men who have reached the age of sexual subsidence." So where did men learn to think of failure like a disease? How did they come to consider themselves "success objects," and where, simultaneously, did they learn that if they "made it" in financial terms, then they could have any woman they wanted? They learned it from a society that places too much value on success, on *what* men are rather than on *who* they are.

In their 1983 comprehensive study, *American Couples*, Blumstein and Schwartz found that "fewer than a quarter of the wives felt it was not important for their husbands to furnish them with financial security." One woman I knew several years back decided to quit her fast-paced and demanding job. She had a ready-made excuse: She wanted to stay home with her children full-time. Now, there are certainly a great many women who make the choice to give their time to their children, and the argument is compelling. My acquaintance put forth this position publicly, and in part, of course, it was undeniably true; she really did enjoy being home with her children. What was also true, however, is what she told only her female companions: She was tired of her profession. She was fed up with the bureaucracy and anxious to find another way to spend her time. When she spoke most candidly, she admitted that "it's tough out there. It takes everything out of you to face the world every day when you're not sure you'll ever be rewarded for anything you do. Ambition is lonely." Still, my female friend could have it both ways; she could be in the marketplace or she could be a full-time homemaker. She felt as if she had the option to withdraw from the professional world while still saving face.

Not many men feel as if they have the same option. Most men have internalized the lesson that the world must be faced no matter what, that it's a do-or-die battle every day, with hundreds of prisoners taken by the hour. Many men envy what they regard as women's choices and options. They feel as if they will never be able to step off the treadmill, because if they do, they will risk losing their place in the lockstep of the corporate march. Trained as they are from boyhood onward to identify themselves by what they do for a living, many men today are jealous of what they see as a woman's chance to "have it all."

WHY MEN SEE WOMEN AS IN CONTROL

Men receive conflicting messages about marriage. They are told to remain single and be successful. But they are also encouraged to marry and "settle down." Many men, for example, believe that mothers, daughters, sisters, and friends conspire in order to force them into the role of the husband. They regard themselves as victims of the wedding game, as prey marked for capture by women who want to be wives. They are sometimes made to feel that their sexuality will be questioned if they remain single, or that they need marriage to provide a maturity they cannot manage on their own.

In contrast to what they might hear from their friends, the benefits of taking a wife are usually recited to men in detail by parents, churches, schools, and other institutionalized authorities. In *Marriage and Personal Development*, Rubin Blanck and Gertrude Blanck summarize the received wisdom heard by the marriageable man: "Marriage is sometimes advised in the hope it will constitute a cure for some of the incomplete integration of . . . adolescence. 'It will help him settle down.' 'It will make a man of him.' 'He needs the steadying influence of a good woman.' There is also the thought that a regular outlet for sexual urges will be stabilizing." These psychologists go on to illustrate the problems inherent in this form of advice, however, by pointing out that "one would not suggest that the eight-month-old infant who cries at the sight of a stranger be sent to school so that he can get used to strangers."

Of course, an unmarried man might not wished to be "saved" from his fate any more than an independent unmarried woman wants to be saved from hers. The single man might well want to "wallow" in the supposed depths from which marriage is destined to save him. Men, however, are less likely to have internalized the image of marriage-as-rescue-and-redemption than women because marriage is not supposed to change their lives in the same drastic manner as women's lives. After all, a man can expect to keep the same name, same job, same social status, same standard of living, and, often, the same dwelling after he marries. Traditional marriage ceremonies pronounce the couple "man" and "wife." He is a man, presumably, even before the ceremony, otherwise she wouldn't be tempted to marry him; he *stays* a man, she *becomes* a wife. He will also expect, not surprisingly, to be able to keep his personality, habits, and customs. It is said that troubles arise after the wedding because a woman marries a man expecting him to change and is disappointed when he doesn't, and that a man marries expecting a woman not to change, and she does.

Very likely, a man who is unsteady, immature, and selfish will not be transformed into a terrific husband just because he has signed off on the wedding contract. Many men feel as if they can hold on to their deepest wishes and greatest freedoms only if they remain single because entering into marriage assumes that they will become dutiful, responsible—and fettered. An unmarried man might view himself as a rebel with a cause, a heroic figure who is holding out against convention in order to preserve his integrity. He might agree with Ralph Waldo Emerson that "society everywhere is in conspiracy against the manhood of every one of its members," and so regard himself as holding out against one of society's most debilitating conspiracies.

"WHEN I WAS TWENTY, I WANTED TO BE THIRTY-FIVE . . ."

Young men might well internalize social pressures, and push themselves into marriage in order to feel the way they are "supposed" to feel. Novelist and essayist A. Alvarez writes of his first, early marriage that "I had this terrible lust for premature maturity, this irresponsible desire for responsibility, before I had any idea what maturity involved or had ever tasted the pleasures of youthful irresponsibility." Like many, Alvarez seems to have regarded a marriage license as a passport into maturity. Frequently young men want to put distance between themselves and their youth—put the things of childhood away—and getting a wife is one of the more obvious manifestations of manhood.

It isn't even so much that they necessarily want to marry a particular woman as it is that they want to be regarded as fully adult by their families or coworkers. It is a feeling, apparently, that lasts only a limited length of time. As one male friend told me, "When I was twenty, I wanted to be thirty-five. Now at thirty-five, I want to be twenty." When he was a youth, he longed for maturity; as a mature man, he is wistful about his all-too-brief youth.

But some men act as if the pressures to become a husband are applied exclusively by the world around them, not from within themselves. Such men often feel as if they have been both lured by women and pushed by society into the matrimonial cage. "Marriage is worse than being mugged," one recently divorced male friend bitterly complained. "At least a mugger gives you a choice between your money or your life. Your wife takes both." At their worst, wives are regarded as greedy, demanding, and intolerant. Many unhappy men regard themselves as escapees from the tyrannical guardianship of their wives, and see any action against their marriage as justified sedition.

"TAKE MY WIFE, PLEASE"

Where did marriage get such a bad reputation among men? From, perhaps, the likes of Henny Youngman, of "take-my-wife-please fame," who was given to such witticisms as "Do you know what it means to come home at night to a woman who'll give you a little love, a little affection, a little tenderness? It means you're in the wrong house, that's what it means"? Or perhaps from Norman Mailer, who, in his book *The Prisoner of Sex,* names—without much wit—married men "P.O.W.s," meaning "prisoners of wedlock." Perhaps they heard the joke that asks the immortal question: "What's the difference between your wife and your job?—After five years, your job still sucks."

"DIFFERENT AIMS, SAME METHODS"

Traditionally, we were led to think of marriage as a simple exchange, as a system of barter where men and women exchange what is most important to them. What do they barter? Men offer their commitment for sexual favors; women offer sexual favors to secure men's commitment. "It appears that ordinary men take wives because possession is not possible without marriage, and that ordinary women accept husbands because marriage is not possible without possession; with totally differing aims the method is the same on both sides," writes Thomas Hardy in *Far From the Madding Crowd*.

In *Why Men Are the Way They Are*, published in 1986, Walter Farrell discusses at length the idea that was presented by Hardy at the turn of the century—that women seek emotional and financial security from strong men while men seek erotic relationships with sexually attractice women. Farrell goes into detail about what he sees as a system whereby men can be seduced by those females who, in my old neighborhood, we charmingly called "C.T.s"—shorthand for girls who appeared to promise more than they offered. Farrell sees men as the victims of women's sexual bait, creatures who are strung along by the promises of sexual satisfaction until they give into marriage.

He sees marriage as women's "primary fantasy," whereas men's "primary fantasy" is to have sex with as many beautiful women as possible (echoing the idea of "going down the aisle" in opposition to "going down"). For Farrell, then, a man's "willingness to give up a lifetime's stimuli of beautiful women . . . to commit to sex with one woman exclusively, and less of it than he wants," is "the most unappreciated adaptation in all human behavior. And almost as unappreciated is what his willingness to adapt implies about men's desire for intimacy and love." Clearly from this point of view, men are the losers in marriage. Clearly, too, Farrell is underscoring the idea that men are suckered into marriage by the false promise of sex. It's as if Farrell is thinking along the lines of Joan Rivers's comment that "all a woman needs is a pretty face and a trick pelvis and she's home and dry."

My fiftyish friend Jack agrees with Farrell. Jack cites the fact that male superstars get to sleep with as many anonymous female partners as possible ("See Wilt Chamberlain's autobiography," he says), where female superstars get to marry as many male partners as possible ("See Elizabeth Taylor's spread-sheets, so to speak").

Even if we ignore the statistics that indicate women feel more deprived of sex in marriage than their husbands, it remains interesting that men are portrayed by Farrell exclusively as the ones who desire sex with as many attractive partners as possible—as if women wouldn't want the same thing if there were no adverse consequences. Imagine sleeping with dozens of Mel Gibsons, Charlie Sheens, Michael Douglases, Denzel Washingtons, Jimmy Smits, and Clint Eastwoods . . . and then having them disappear back into their haze of sexy handsomeness, no questions asked, the way that centerfold girls collapse neatly into thirds once the magazine is put away. I bet a good many women would consider *that* a pretty primary fantasy.

Women are often bullied into marriage for sexual reasons as well. For example, Florence King, author of *Lump It or Leave It,* presents the idea that women marry for "regular sex" just as much as men do when she declares that "the only thing about marriage that appealed to me was sex without scandal: Husbands could be counted on not to ask, 'How come you let me go all the way?' "

"What was I supposed to do for fun?" questions my fifty-five-year-old friend, Marie. "When we were kids a nice guy could sleep with a 'bad girl' and he wouldn't then become a 'bad boy' by association. But if I had slept with a *saint* and somebody had found out, I would have been considered a tramp. If the secret got out, the girl was labeled a slut, and the boy got all sorts of 'oh-you-sly-dog' backslapping. Sam and I married at sixteen. I thought that at least I could sleep with him without getting run out of town."

SAYING NO, SAYING YES

Women have been on the losing side of the sex game for hundreds of years. Many women, especially before the advent of readily available and reliable birth control, risked unwanted pregnancy and social disgrace by entering into sexual relationships with men who promised marriage as they unzipped their flies, only to change their minds once the encounter was over. Endless versions of the same stories appear in both great and trashy literature from time immemorial to the present day—the girl who gives up her virginity to the man who falsely promises her security. " 'Don't worry, darling. I'm going to marry you,' " begins a story in a 1939 issue of *True Confessions* magazine.

"Then with a half shamed, boyish chuckle—'I just can't wait for the whole world to know that you belong to me alone. I'm sinfully proud.' I lay quite still in his arms, thinking ahead. Oh—I wasn't afraid that Grant wouldn't do the right thing . . . His eyes were loyal and clean—if you understand," explains the gullible narrator. We anticipate her fate the way that audiences in movie theaters anticipate the fate of curious out-of-towners who decide to buy the gloomy, empty mansion. "Oh-oh," we grimace as somebody heads up the flight of stairs to the bedroom, "now she's really in trouble."

It is a familiar story: Think of the fallen heroines from Ophelia to Hester in *The Scarlet Letter,* to Hetty from *Adam Bede,* to Tess from *Tess of the D'Urbervilles.* These heroines give their all for love, only to be exiled or executed. But it is true that there are also hundreds of tales of men trapped by women: Dreiser's *An American Tragedy,* Joyce's "The Boarding House," and Inge's *Come Back Little Sheba* to name a few. These heroes are portrayed as the pathetic victims of the female mafia, who come to "collect" once a man sleeps with a woman.

WHY IS GOD A BACHELOR?

Some men's views of marriage are based on thoughts along the lines put forth by essayist and songwriter Allan Sherman in his book titled *The Rape of the APE* (APE being "The American Puritanical Ethic"). Sherman wonders whether eventually "those who insist on believing that God invented marriage will have to write long papers explaining why He remains a bachelor. Or why He would invent marriage solely for human beings and no other creatures on earth. Or, is marriage God's little joke on people?"

Sherman suggests that men are stuck in their old illusions and unable to move out of the uncomfortable rigidity of their inherited roles. "We American males are accustomed to our illusions—that we are sweeping girls off their feet, overwhelming them, that any girl who goes to bed with us belongs to us alone, body and soul, and has had no other sexual experience." He then cautions his fellow men about retaining that fantasy, since "it's nice work if you can get it, but you can't get it anymore."

CARNAL KNOWLEDGE

That tragedies—great and small—await men who live an unexamined emotional life is the subject of the 1971 film *Carnal Knowledge*, in which Jack Nicholson and Art Garfunkel grow from college boys into middle-aged men. The portrait of their burgeoning manhood is less than flattering, but strikingly convincing. It is both scary and worrying for any man or woman to watch one socially prescribed self-deception pile upon another. Screenwriter Jules Feiffer's dialogue cuts with the precision of a surgeon's knife searching out the illnesses of a hypocritical society. When the boys are about to start their freshman year at Amherst, they discuss what they really want in a woman. The Nicholson character sensitively claims that "she should be very understanding. We start the same sentences together," and then pauses before he adds the real requirement: "Big tits."

The Garfunkel character is equally blind to the contradictions betrayed by his own fantasy of marriage to a woman who is "a companion," because, after all, "the other stuff I can get on the outside." Nicholson's character had earlier rejected a girl not because she was a C.T. but because she wasn't: "I was starting to fall in love with her but then she let me feel her up on the first date. Turned me right off." Obviously he wants to fall in love with a lady. (The division of girls into "tramps" and "ladies," however, is fraught with perils both seen and unseen. Essayist Fran Lebowitz cautions men, "Should one of you boys happen upon a girl who doesn't put out, do not jump to the conclusion that you have found a lady. What you have probably found is a lesbian.")

Nicholson's scheming, overconfident, and misogynist character is destined for unhappiness. He bitterly concludes, after ten years of working as a lawyer in New York, that "the women today are hung better than the men." In contrasting but equal unhappiness, Garfunkel spends his youth playing the "obedient son game, the good student game, and the good father game," and marries a woman who is "a very good homemaker. Everything is in its place when I get home." Not surprisingly, he is stunningly bored and concludes about sex that "maybe it's just not meant to be enjoyable with people you love."

NOT SO LOVELY TO BE A WOMAN . . .

Nicholson's character, still unmarried, hooks up with a twenty-nine-year-old woman named Bobbi, played, ironically enough, by Ann-Margret. It turns out that it's not so lovely to be a woman after all (no matter what she sang in *Bye-Bye Birdie*). An actress who plays a stewardess in a television commercial, Bobbi becomes increasingly dependent on live-in lover Nicholson, especially after he tells her to quit her job. "I want you right here where you belong," Nicholson tells her. When she dares to ask, "And you?" he replies gruffly, "When I'm here, I'm here."

Immediately after this curt reply, he creates a perfect "isn't-that-a-blimp" moment, yelling, "Where the hell is my shoehorn? This place is a mess!" and then accusing her of not being able to just "leave us alone" without questioning their relationship and thereby ruining it. Having called his bluff by requiring him to examine their relationship, Bobbi has made Nicholson suddenly and painfully aware of his emotional shortcomings. He must then punish Bobbi for some sort of shortcoming of her own.

Frustrated by her demands on him after several months, Nicholson reverses his earlier demand and tells her she *should* "get a job." Ann-Margret, now almost completely debilitated by the pointlessness of her life, wails, "I don't want a job, I want *you!*" She's changed the focus of the full beam of her attention from herself to the man in her life. Nicholson, trying to free himself from her neediness, heart-rendingly screams, "But *I'm* already taken—by *me!*" Needing to separate himself from the dependent, emotionally draining woman, Nicholson becomes the paradigm of the boy who wants to escape the house in order to keep his own life intact.

He then accuses her of exercising the worst possible judgment by staying with him. "Why do you let yourself in for this abuse?" he asks, pleadingly. "Please leave me. I'd almost marry you if you'd leave me." Restoration playwright William Congreve had a character say very much the same thing in a play performed in 1693. "I could find it in my heart to marry thee, purely to be rid of thee," wails one character. Things do not seem to have changed much between 1693, 1963, or even 1993.

We might well grimace in wry recognition of this impulse; few of us have made it past a couple of serious relationships without thinking the same thing about someone. (One of my favorite Rodney Dangerfield routines insists, "We sleep in separate rooms, we have dinner apart, we take separate vacations—we're doing everything we can to keep our marriage together.") It is a common phenomenon, apparently, and especially prevalent among men. According to Herb Goldberg, author of the psychological study *The New Male*, when a lover "is suddenly faced with the realization that his woman is . . . serious about leaving, his 'love' for her and even his once flagging libido are reignited. In fact, there seems to be no more powerful aphrodisiac for a man than to be told by his woman that she wants out or is involved with somebody else. Perhaps the freedom created by a safe emotional distance and the excitement of the renewed challenge bring about a rebirth of his feelings of caring and sexual desire."

Some men can only love you as you wave good-bye. I came across this phenomenon when I dated a man who liked me best when I was threatening to leave him. It became what in retrospect seems like an almost comic routine—I'd be packing my toothbrush and swearing I wouldn't even return his phone calls, and he'd begin rattling off all the endearments I'd been longing to hear. I'd throw my keys to his apartment on the bureau, and he'd call my name in a soft, sweet, pained voice and I'd turn to see him with tears in his eyes and I'd lose all resolve. Things would be fine until the very moment I'd silently tell myself, "This time it'll work," at which point his secret radar would kick into gear and he'd become distant and aloof. The more I needed, the less he was able to give, and we'd circle around one another like a couple of fighter planes. When I'd take off in my own direction, he'd follow—but otherwise we were stuck in a pattern. He couldn't bear to have me leave, or more accurately, he couldn't take responsibility for leaving himself. Instead he behaved in such an inconsiderate manner that, essentially, he "forced" me to leave him even as he pleaded for me not to go. It was a great relief, not surprisingly, to sign off on that relationship.

One of Feiffer's great moments in *Carnal Knowledge* concerns exactly this push-pull dynamic between Nicholson's character and his girlfriend Bobbi: By exposing the double-bind that insists on separation as the paradoxical basis for intimacy, Feiffer spotlights the collision of need, desire, fantasy, and reality. We balance the risk of intimacy with our own need to retain our own separateness. We try to get close, only to rebound when the closeness threatens to overwhelm us. I always think of the toy I had as a kid: a pair of magnets shaped like little Scotty dogs. One was black and one was white, and when they were placed a certain way they were inseparable; when they were placed another way, they repelled one another and nothing could bring them together. Relationships sometimes mimic this pattern of extreme attraction coupled with repulsion. Try as we might, we often end up aware of our own separateness even as we strive for togetherness. As Lily Tomlin said in *The Search for Signs of Intelligent Life in the Universe*, "We're all in this together—alone."

"STAYING WITH THE HAND YOU'RE DEALT"

One representative husband discussed by Goldberg in *The New Male* "became particularly uncomfortable" when he thought about the circumstances of his marriage. This respondent offered the following assessment of his marriage, according to Goldberg: "I was really bored with Joanna after the first month of dating but I couldn't admit it to myself because I thought I had a great thing going. I married her because I figured if I didn't one of the other guys would. I couldn't let that happen." Believing that he would regret *not* having married this woman more than he would regret *having* married her, Goldberg's subject is playing a poor hand. He is battling fear rather than going for happiness. He is drawn to the idea of the relationship more than he is to the actual woman. This is territoriality and rights of possession, and all of it is a far cry from love.

Love rarely enters into the discussion of many men's reasons for marrying—unless we hear that in retrospect men recognize it by its absence. We hear from the protagonist of John O'Hara's novel *Butterfield 8* that, in middle age, "it was just beginning to dawn on him that he never had loved [his wife]. He was so flattered by what she felt for him before they were married that he had been blinded to his true feeling about her . . . There had been nothing but the habit of marriage." Rereading his youthful affection for his wife through the lens of their married life together, the hero can see nothing but his boredom and lack of love. The earlier attraction for one another by O'Hara's central couple has been eclipsed by the years of feigned enjoyment, scripted passion, and tedious exchanges of "intimacy" that do not even merit such a name. A man like O'Hara's hero might well think that he's making the best of a bad situation by "at least" staying married to a woman whose main attraction was that she liked him when he was unsure of himself as a youth. His contempt for his wife will inevitably color his relationships with all women, whether he meets them in a personal or professional setting. Bad marriages seep, like a sort of creeping damp, into the infrastructure of society.

PLEASE, MR. POSTMAN

We saw that the territory traveled by our society in respect to the position of women between Lee Tidball's article in 1953 and Marilyn Quayle's remarks in 1992 has not added up to as significant a distance as women might have imagined. "What we've gained on the back roads we lost in the straightaway," as Jesse, an older activist friend, put it. "I thought that we women would have made greater and steadier advances by this point, but I see young women starting out from the same old place I began in 1942." Is it any different for our male counterparts? Have things changed significantly for men in the last fifty years?

Consider the remarks by essayist Andrew Postman in a 1992 issue of *Glamour*. Postman declares that "men in their twenties hang on to their college lovers after graduation in an absentminded, distracted way. Without paying much attention, they find they've made a commitment and then are too cowardly to break it. 'They panic,' says Peter, a former Berkeley student. 'They realize that what seemed transitory in college might become permanent. Many of my buddies suddenly felt trapped. They were dealt a hand in college and for some reason they're still holding it. End of Quest!' "

Staying with the hand you are dealt is obviously a way of seeing yourself as a victim of fate rather than as an inexpert, foolish, or inexperienced player. One man I know said that he wishes arranged marriages still existed since "no matter who you marry you always end up married to somebody else anyway. Might as well have somebody else take the blame." Certainly many men seem to feel a need to justify marrying by suggesting that it was not really their idea, that they were "bullied" or "trapped" into marriage. Jack Tanner from George Bernard Shaw's play *Man and Superman* sums up the fears of many men when he proclaims to the heroine that "we do the world's will, not our own. I have a frightful feeling that I shall let myself be married because it is the world's will that you should have a husband." It is convenient, of course, to believe that you are free from free will. Then you can behave as if you were pressed into service against your inclination and so justify all selfish behavior. "I married you, didn't I?" such a man might say to his wife. "What more do you want from me?"

"WILL YOU LOVE ME TILL THE END OF TIME?"

Having a drink at a local pub that boasted the phenomenon of Karaoke, I was surprised to hear the same song played twice and chosen both times by guys in their early twenties. They picked a number that I'd heard back in college, from an album entitled *Bat Out of Hell* sung by Meat Loaf. The song apparently has the same appeal now that it had fifteen years ago. (I should mention here that there *are* a few favorite songs chosen by young men, which of course I regard as the exceptions proving my earlier rule saying men skip the words and go for the bass line.) The song is a riff on the old idea of the girl's saying "Will you love me tomorrow?" along the lines of what we heard from Carole King. But the twist offered by Meat Loaf is his focus on the guy's text. Meat Loaf sings about a couple who are "barely seventeen and barely dressed" necking and finding "paradise by the dashboard lights."

Before the boy can get to "home base" (there is even a baseball play-by-play by Phil Rizutto heard dimly in the background), however, the girl says he has to promise to make her happy for the rest of her life, make her his wife, and love her "till the end of time." The male voice shouts out that he was "crazed" by all the pregame activity and "couldn't take it any longer" and so "started swearing to my God and on my mother's grave" that he would love her until the end of time.

What happens? The baseball game on the car radio reaches a crescendo, we hear their heavy breathing, and the girl threatens, "I can wait all night . . ." through her staccato gasps. The song then changes completely. There is a second's break, and then we hear him sing that he's now "praying for the end of time" to hurry up and arrive because if he has to spend another minute with her, he doesn't think he can survive. This last description of why a man might marry is representative of a whole school of thought devoted to the justification of marriage which, in retrospect, seems like a youthful—but grave—error. Errors count in a ballgame, and they count when making a marriage.

Psychologists such as Dr. Theodore Rubin assert that marriage offers "no great virtues or rewards" for men. So why do men marry? Traditional wisdom has it that a woman pursues a man until he catches her. Everything from personal anecdotes to the plots of best-selling novels focus on the way men are "coerced" into marriage against their better judgment. In this way, of course, the male characters at the center of these stories can disavow any responsibility for their own actions. "I didn't marry her," insists one physician. "She and my mother decided that she would marry me. She was the same religion, our mothers approved, and she skied. Now neither of us practices our religion, our mothers have both died, and I have to bribe her to go near a slope. But I feel like we have to stay together because I'm afraid that if I leave I'll lose my kids and I'll probably have to move my practice. I married," he says with finality, "for all the wrong reasons."

CHAPTER FIVE

LEARNING THE ROPES AND TYING THE KNOT

Men's Lessons in Love and Marriage

ARE THERE ANY "right" reasons to marry? "Why did *you* marry?" I asked dozens of men of various ages and various professions. Those few occasions when no response was forthcoming (and when I felt like I should do a mirror test to make sure that they were still breathing), I suggested that perhaps they wanted "to set up house?" Men often responded like the character from the Thurber essay mentioned earlier who admits that a fellow doesn't really want the pressure of making a "home," *per se,* although he "likes to be able to say where he lives when he goes to vote, and things like that." Such a man might like the abstract idea of marriage, but he doesn't want the aggravation of having a real live wife. He wants the convenience of a home and hearth without wanting the emotional responsibility of its upkeep. It's like wanting to eat a great meal without cooking or cleaning up, or wanting to be a great musician without practicing. Sure, as a fantasy it's terrific. As a plan for life, it's a disaster.

In *Beyond the Male Myth*, Pietropinto and Simenauer quote a young man who describes his ideal relationship in the following terms: "Prefer steady girl with different address from mine. Would enjoy different girl every now and then just for sex. Can't stand the thought of getting married and losing identity and goals in life." Some men equate commitment with the loss of identity, underscoring the masculine fear that marriage involves an inevitable eradication of the self.

"WHY DID YOU MARRY?"

A permanent address, regular sex, and home-cooked meals seemed to be enough for a number of men who were raised to hold on to traditional expectations (in fact, a number of them would have settled for home-cooked sex, permanent meals, and a regular address). These men were often the most keenly disappointed after marriage. They thought they understood what they were getting into, only to find that much more was demanded of them than they expected. They felt that marriage was a bargain they didn't bargain for, "like signing up for two free books and then having to buy a hundred books a year for the next forty years," as one older insurance salesman put it. "I thought I'd hand her my paycheck—well, most of it anyway—and she'd hand me a couple of children, a clean house, and a couple of cozy bedtimes. Instead she wanted me to talk all night. It wasn't what I figured on, I'll tell you that." This man is well over sixty, but the young men with whom I've spoken sound as if these last forty years haven't made much of an impact on their expectations, hopes, and fears for themselves as husbands.

ONE WORD ABOUT HUSBANDS . . .

In an upper-division literature course titled "Sex, Politics, and Marriage" I recently taught, we started the semester by reading a few eighteenth-century novels, among them *Pamela, or Virtue Rewarded* by Samuel Richardson. *Pamela* includes a long and detailed prescription for exactly what is expected of a good wife in 1740. There are, however, only the most vague references to the qualities attributable to a good husband.

In Richardson's novel, Squire B (he is known only by his initial), the man Pamela ultimately marries, begins his "courtship" of servant Pamela first with seduction and then by attempted rape. When these don't work, he tries to buy her from her parents. Only after all endeavors to take her virginity fail does he propose marriage, an opportunity Pamela embraces despite her anger and terror at his earlier behavior. She puts all her resentment and fear behind her the moment he wants to legitimize the relationship, and falls in love with a man she had previously considered a brutish monster. After their wedding, Pamela discovers that he has an illegitimate child by a former lover, and Pamela—being the perfect lady, despite her lower-class origins—accepts all of this with good cheer because she is A Good Wife as designed by the author. Squire B can have children scattered around the country for all Pamela cares. As long as *she* was a virgin when they married, the union is solid. Pamela meets the requirements Squire B—and Richardson—lovingly set out. But what about Squire B as a husband? Does the fact that he finally breaks down and marries the object of his sexual desire because there is no other way to possess her, make him a good husband? Does the fact that he is rich make him a good husband?

I asked my present-day students what they thought of the role of the husband. Henry Felding, after all, a rival of Richardson's and author of *Tom Jones,* was so outraged by the presentation of the sickly-sweet Good Wife that he wrote a parody called *Shamela. Shamela*—clearly a play on both the words *shame* and *sham*—portrays a whore from London who disguises herself as a simple country girl in order to force the rich, naive, and weak Squire "Booby" to propose marriage. She flirts with him, arguing (like her counterpart in Richardson's book) that her body is sacred. But Shamela is, of course, bartering counterfeit goods. Her virginity was "given away" long ago, and by pretending to be "unused," she is viewed by Fielding as not only a dissembler but as a swindler as well. Squire Booby becomes the prototype of the husband-as-victim, the defrauded dupe of a matrimonial sleight of hand conjured up by a hypocritical seductress. The theme did not begin with Fielding, and it continues to be translated into contemporary mythology—despite revised expectations concerning a bride's virginity.

Consider the joke that concerns a young man who attempts to seduce a girl by promising to marry her after they sleep together. She refuses to become sexually involved until their wedding night. When the wedding has taken place and they are safely married for a while, the husband sheepishly admits to his wife that she "was right to say 'no' until the wedding. I never would have married you if you'd slept with me before we were married." "Tell me about it!" says the bride. "That's how the last five guys fooled me!"

"BUYING A GEO INSTEAD OF A LAMBORGHINI"

I asked my class for their most candid responses to the role of married men in the texts we were discussing. I decided to ask them to write, without censoring their responses, the one word they associated most closely with the word *husband*. They knew they were safe from judgments or recrimination; many of them were students who had taken several of my classes in other subjects, and so knew that I was eager to hear their true responses as long as they could substantiate their arguments. In this case, I asked them *not* to write their names (and guaranteed them anonymity even if, as a few of them suspected, I could decipher their handwriting from even one word). I did ask them to indicate their age and sex before passing the folded piece of paper forward.

I read the answers out loud in front of the class and we were all surprised. The results were fascinating. The captain of the lacrosse team sat in his corner at the far side of the room, arms folded, with a smug expression, as if to say, "I told you it would be like this." David had indeed argued regularly that guys were embarrassed to admit out loud what they really thought: that they were getting the losing hand in the hand dealt by the institution of marriage. The game seemed to be rigged against them, David asserted, and as if that wasn't bad enough, the young men knew that they were supposed to feel better about the prospect of marriage than they actually did. He would often preface his remarks by warning that "you're not going to like what I have to say," but I was always interested in his perspective. David told me that among themselves there was pretty much an agreement that for guys getting married was a last resort, like, he said, "buying a Geo instead of a Lamborghini." "You do it because you know you're never going to be able to get what you really want. So you settle for what you've got," he shrugged. "It may not be exactly like settling for your father's Oldsmobile," he continued, and I found myself wondering where Freud was when you needed him, "but you rarely end up with the sort of models you see in *Road and Track*." After a short discussion concerning the way that photographs of vehicles in car magazines resemble photographs of women in skin magazines—the doors of the cars opened slightly and at provocative angles, the hood raised so you can just peek underneath, carefully lighted and lushly furnished back-drops—we returned to the role of the husband, and to the role of woman as consumer item in our culture.

This highly informal survey mapped an astonishing fissure between the reactions of the male students and their female counterparts to the word *husband*. Reading the little slips of paper that replicated one another as if in some perfect genetic experiment, I realized I was opening each one with a certain breathless apprehension. It was like the Academy Awards; I began to see just how seriously the division between young men and women played itself out in terms of their perceptions of their image of the "husband." Not every male student responded like David, but to be honest, few boys imagined any "positive" qualities, although there were versions of the terms *friend* and *lover*.

A large number of women wrote *companion*, *provider*, or *partner* as the word they most closely associated with husbands. They seemed most concerned with the idea they would find, as one young woman put it, "my other half." At first glance, the women wanted an equal— not a savior, not a prince—although there were exceptions. One or two women responded negatively (one wrote, for some reason, *damp*), but by and large the women responded in a positive, if vague, manner. One twenty-four-year-old woman was very specific, however; she wrote the words *diamond ring*. It seemed a fairly specific request, more like a wish than a statement. Perhaps this woman's reply is emblematic of what the boys fear: She seemed to be that woman who wants a generic giver of gifts, status, and security.

"SURE, I WANT TO BE A HUSBAND—NOT!"

Their male counterparts, in contrast, most often responded with the words *trapped, caught, p—— whipped*—leaving out the first word of the usual street slang for an emasculated and powerless man, just in case the anonymity didn't take. A prevalent response from the male students was the word *NOT*, printed in block letters in order to indicate the inaccuracy of the original concept, as in "I'll be home early tonight—NOT."

By responding to the word *husband* by writing "NOT," these young men clearly indicated their lack of desire for the role, and were implicitly identifying with the adolescent basement-dwelling Wayne of the hit movie *Wayne's World*. Put another way, they saw the role of the husband as everything they were working hard to avoid. As much as they were looking forward to being certain things in a few years—to being employed, to having their own places to live—they were not looking forward to becoming husbands. Is it surprising that they would like love without commitment?

COMMITMENT TO AN INSTITUTION

Think of what the words themselves imply. Around the words *commitment* and *institution* hang the clouds of rules, straitjacketed conformity, restricted and uniform behavior. The real question is why don't we *all*—men and women alike—fear the confinement of a relationship, the restrictions of commitment, and the legislated nature of institutions? To be committed to an institution sounds more like what happens to you if you lose your mind rather than lose your heart, but these are the very words we use to describe marriage. According to stand-up comic Rita Rudner, "If you never want to see a man again, say, 'I love you, I want to marry you. I want to have children . . .'—they leave skid marks."

"What kind of word is 'commitment,' anyway?" ask authors Dan Greenburg and Susan O'Malley in *How to Avoid Love and Marriage*. " 'He was committed to an institution for the criminally insane.' 'She was committed to the federal penitentiary because she had committed manslaughter.' Right away you know that 'commitment' is not a fun word." They ask the reader to choose "the fun word from each of the following pairs of words: Petting/Commitment; French Kissing/Commitment; One-night-stand/Commitment; Cheap Thrills/Commitment." This is one quiz that we can all pass, as our fourth-grade teacher would say, without copying answers off our neighbors.

WALK LIKE A MAN, TALK LIKE A MAN . . .

Since popular wisdom (which might just be another oxymoron, like the "romantic marriage" we heard about earlier) has it that women are the ones who want to marry, it would appear that women are the ones arguing for the glory of commitments and institutions. Men appear to believe, in the style of George Bernard Shaw's mouthpiece Jack Tanner in *Man and Superman*, that if married, "I shall decay like a thing that has served its purpose and is done with; I shall change from a man with a future to a man with a past; I shall see in the greasy eyes of all the other husbands their relief at the arrival of a new prisoner to share their ignomy. The young men will scorn me as one who has sold out; to the women I, who have always been an enigma and a possibility, shall be merely somebody else's property—and damaged goods at that: a secondhand man at best." Shaw's hero nearly weeps at the thought of his own marriage the way you might shudder at the thought of your own funeral. Even at the end of the play, when indeed the hero and heroine marry, a servant offers the following caveat: "There are two tragedies in life, Mr. Tanner. One is to lose your heart's desire. The other is to gain it." The possibility for happiness seems to be out of the question, since even this traditionally "happy ending" can't guarantee it. Shaw's hero gives in to marriage, and his new bride gets the last word of the play. The thought that a man's life ends with marriage is, of course, in contrast to the idea that a woman's life will be validated by it.

"Marriage is a custom brought about by women who then proceed to live off men and destroy them, completely enveloping the man in a destructive cocoon or eating him away like a poisonous fungus on a tree," declares British actor Richard Harris. While many men might balk at his harsh terms, a shocking number of them seem to agree with his general sentiments. It's undeniable that many men feel enormous and often unarticulated anger toward their wives—regarding them as parasites and marriage itself as a form of "social disease"—especially those who believe that they married against their better judgment, instincts, and beliefs. Such men act as if any means of escape is not only allowed, but a right, a duty. Like the Allied prisoners in *The Great Escape,* they go from planning one run for freedom to another.

ACCEPTABLE, NOT EXCEPTIONAL

The twinning of the domestic with the generic is both a cause of and an emblem for the unexamined nature of the role of the husband. In the way that a domestic wine will be considered acceptable for everyday use and virtually indistinguishable from other domestic wines, so too—in conventional cultural terms—a husband becomes indistinguishable from other husbands. He becomes merely the man in the gray flannel suit; he goes from being a man with a future to a man with a past. He becomes a provider and protector, an instrument of family life instead of a heroic individual. When he acts courageously on behalf of others, sacrifices his time and his youth, he will be seen not as exceptional, but as acceptable. The man's response to the stresses pressuring him to conform to the publicly sanctioned script for a husband is often exhibited by his refusal to provide or accept the requirements of a private intimacy. He trades in his private life for his public life and becomes the image of a "good husband" without feeling as if he is truly emotionally invested in the role.

In order to maintain their self-esteem, such husbands construct walls between themselves and their spouses. "You've got a piece of everything I own and you think you know everything I do, but you don't have access to the *real* me," many men seem to be saying. "That's a part of me no one has ever seen. That's a card I won't play, so even when you think you've won everything over to you, there's still my ace in the hole." The ace in the hole, for many men, is what they regard as their soul, their inner self, and upon the integrity of this private, hidden self rests their masculinity.

PLAYING BY THE RULES

Husbands often feel that if marriage were cast as a game, then it would be cast as a game where the stakes are both very vague and tremendously high. As Ernest Hemingway's hero describes it in *A Farewell to Arms*, getting seriously involved with a woman may not necessarily begin with something that can be identified as love, but the method—playing the game—is the one element that is easily identified: "I know I did not love Catherine Barkley nor had any idea of loving her. This was a game, like bridge, in which you said things instead of playing cards. Like bridge you had to pretend you were playing for money or playing for some stakes," declares Hemingway. "Nobody had mentioned what the stakes were. It was all right with me." That a relationship is like a game where words are traded instead of cards or playing chips, suggests that words are a form of currency, emblems of value and invested with significance. The trading of words, then, assumes importance relative to the gravity of the emotional experience. The possibility of love gives weight to sexy small talk, the possibility of marriage gives weight to talk of love.

My gambling expert says there are such things as "money players," those who will rise to the occasion only if there is something on the line. Marriage puts money on the line in the game of love, otherwise it would remain, quite simply, a pickup game. To put it another way, when men decide to play house, they play for keeps. Men, like women, go into marriage believing that it will last forever. They want to get it right. Often a man brings his focused drive for success to bear on his marriage and wants his relationship to be the best, the most perfect, the most obviously flawless one around. In short, he wants to win—and casts the marriage in terms of competition and accomplishment. "I figure that in marriage you get only one time around, one role of the dice," observes Simon, a graduate student who is planning to marry once he gets his degree. "I want to make sure I walk away a winner. I consider my fiancée a real prize, and I don't expect that to change. I really won big when I won her."

But that does not mean that men always consider themselves lucky, even when they win. In his best-seller *Presumed Innocent* Scott Turow ponders the idea that even the avoidance of disaster doesn't constitute winning: "Even if luck, and luck alone, spares us the worst, life nonetheless wears so many of us down. Young men of talent dull it and drink it all away. Young women of spirit bear children, broaden in the hips, and shrink in hope as middle years close in upon them." Turow suggests that, no matter how well we play, there are forces beyond our control. To believe that you're not subject to the usual force is to invite disaster. "Every life, like every snowflake, seemed to me then unique in the shape of its miseries, and in the rarity and mildness of its pleasures." Life itself stacks the deck in a way that remains unfathomable to even the most expert of players.

WHY THE "NICE GUY" MARRIES

What are some of the reasons men marry? In the best-selling and influential 1922 novel *Babbitt* by Sinclair Lewis, we are offered a subtly nightmarish portrait of how a man might feel trapped into marriage not by the promise of sex but by an inability to figure out how to leave a relationship with his self-respect intact. Lewis tells us how George Babbitt was "hooked" by a woman, not through sex, but through tears: "One evening when he was weary and soft-minded, he saw that she had been weeping. She had been left out of a party given by [a friend]. Somehow her head was on his shoulder and he was kissing away the tears—and she raised her head to say trustingly, 'Now that we're engaged, shall we be married soon or shall we wait?'. . . but it was pleasant to have a girl in his ares, and less and less could he insult her by blurting that he didn't love her. He himself had no doubt. The evening before his marriage was an agony, and the morning wild with the desire to flee." Obviously, the "nice guy" of 1922 marries the girl who weeps in his arms.

In the 1950s, as we've already heard from Alvarez, men felt pressured to grow up, and so becoming a husband became like growing a beard: It was a mild annoyance but at least it proved that you were a man. In his novel *My Life as a Man*, Philip Roth explains that for young men "who reached their maturity in the fifties, and who aspired to be grown-up during that decade . . . there was considerable moral prestige in taking a wife . . . It was only within marriage that an ordinary woman could hope to find equality and dignity. Indeed, we were led to believe by the defenders of womankind of our era that we were exploiting and degrading the women we didn't marry, rather than the ones we did." This last point is a particularly interesting one: Marriage was considered the best gift a woman could be offered, so a man saved a marriage proposal the way a girl "saved" her virginity.

Many men were encouraged to see themselves as rescuers of the female race, since "unattached and on her own, a woman was supposedly not even able to go to the movies or out to a restaurant by herself, let alone perform an appendectomy or drive a truck," according to Roth. Young men were told that "it was up to us then to give them the value and the purpose that society at large withheld—by marrying them. If we didn't marry women, who would? Ours, alas, was the only sex available for the job: the draft was on." Some men viewed women in the same light as enforced conscription; if their number was up, it was up. It was an age when a woman married the man she wanted to be, since she could only define herself through her husband. ("We used to have to marry the men we wanted to be. Now we can be who we want to be, and marry the men we want to marry," says Betty Friedan.)

And so the "nice guy" of 1962, or 1972, or even 1982, was told that he should marry the girl who sleeps in his arms in order to provide her life with meaning and give dignity to her role. In a vein similar to the one opened by Farrell, Goldberg gives an overview of the "traditional" compromise for men when he argues that "until recently, most men made lifetime marriage commitments . . . while they were still unable to see the woman as a person beyond her vagina. Then, it was too late. After the wedding he often found himself again in the pathetic position of having to beg for the very thing he had paid so dearly for."

One forty-three-year-old novelist told me that "you couldn't get laid on a regular basis in 1963 unless you got married. Nobody believes that anymore but it's true. How were we to know that if we waited five years everybody would be taking their clothes off for the joy of it? In any relationship you get to the point where you either get married or break up. You either stayed in the game or you pulled out altogether— so to speak."

DO THE OLD REASONS
FOR MARRIAGE STILL APPLY?

Why do men marry in the 1990s? Surprisingly, many of the old reasons still apply. Now the line "We got married because she was pregnant" might be said by a successful stockbroker who's lived with his partner for ten years. It is no longer a phrase used exclusively by high school boys to explain why they have to drop out and get a job. But one of the interesting things about this particular rationale is that many of the misgivings felt by the high school boy might well be felt by his forty-year-old counterpart.

The boy and the man might still ask themselves, "Would we have gotten married if she wasn't pregnant? How do I know she didn't do this on purpose? Is she just using me to have a baby?" While women have gained some control over their reproductive rights, men often feel left out of the decision making when it comes to pregnancy— especially unplanned pregnancies. "She said I should tell her how I really felt and I told her that I thought we should wait. She decided not to wait, and we're married and I love our daughter, but my wife has never really forgiven me for telling her the truth ten years ago," said one financial manager. "I'm terrified that one day, in a fit of anger, she'll tell my daughter that I didn't want her. My wife has always had control of the situation even though she wouldn't see it that way."

ONE MAN'S ROLL

Some men feel like they were forced into marriage because they were never trained to make a home for themselves. Before they married they believed that it would be impossible for them to live on their own without ending up like Ray Milland in *The Lost Weekend*, Jack Nicholson in *Carnal Knowledge*, or Robert De Niro in *Cape Fear*. "I was afraid to live alone," affirms Billy, a mechanic in his mid-thirties. "I went from my parents' house directly to my marriage home without a break. It wasn't until my wife and I split up briefly three years ago that I lived by myself. I actually had to buy toilet paper. I ran out about eleven o'clock one evening and I was hit by the fact that there wasn't a roll tucked away somewhere because no one—meaning me—would think to do that. I started to see how much I was used to having somebody take care of me."

This didn't make him return, but instead made him resolve to learn to live alone before living with anyone else again. "In the end, my wife and I got back together only after I learned about how to take care of myself. It was important to both of us. Now we can have a relationship where she isn't my mother or my housekeeper. I didn't want to be a son or a tenant anymore, I wanted to be a partner in a real relationship. I came back home—and she took me back—not because it was just easier but instead because we both wanted it even if it meant putting ourselves out for each other."

There are men who celebrate married life. We should keep in mind that statistics record that men consider themselves happier in their marriages than women. Most married men believe, in fact, that being a husband has been good for them. In a 1990 issue of *Men's Life* an article titled "A Generation of Men Grows Up" by Carl Arrington describes a survey of 815 American men. It reports that "90 percent say their wives are their best friends. A staggering 88 percent said they'd remarry their spouse. Only 2 percent said they'd marry someone else; only 9 percent would elect to stay single."

The idea of having a partner appeals to most men, and seems to be the beginning, as they say, of a beautiful friendship. "She made me an offer I couldn't refuse," states Tim, a happily married high school teacher whose wife of twelve years is a social worker. "Nancy promised that we would be in this together and that I would never be left carrying the load." The fear of being left "carrying the load" should not be underestimated as a great force in the lives of many men. "She promised to work as hard as I worked, to spend as much time with the kids as I did, to work as much around the house as I worked, and to love me as much as I loved her. I have to live up to her expectations and she lives up to mine, and they're both pretty high. To use your gambling metaphor," he grinned, "we both always ante up. We not only see but raise each other's bets. When one of us wins, we both win. We both put so much into this marriage the 'pot' is always full." He adds, "I'm one of the few husbands I know who looks forward to going home at night because it really feels like home."

CHAPTER SIX

YOU BET YOUR LIFE

*Why Women Think Men
Make All the Deals*

WHAT DOES A HUSBAND DO?

I WAS TOLD as a child that if a man didn't drink, gamble, hit you, or run around with other women, then that man was a good husband. A good husband was defined not by what he did, but what he didn't do. It seemed pretty basic—not being hit, not being with someone who was controlled by compulsions—and it also seemed curiously negative. Couldn't you live alone and avoid all the problems?

Part of the challenge in approaching the topic of marriage is that it is not a static state, but a continuous process. At any point a wonderful spouse can stop being one; adultery usually eclipses years of fidelity, for example, or a broken rib eclipses years of nonviolence. Words, too, can be indelible; once said, they can alter the atmosphere in a room as profoundly as tear gas—and often with the same result. One destructive act has the potential to change the very definition of the relationship. A person can go from being a good husband—or wife—to a bad one in the space of five minutes. The nineteenth-century philosopher Kierkegaard pointed out that "romantic love can very well be represented in the moment, but conjugal love cannot, because an ideal husband is not one who is such once in his life, but one who every day is such." It's a tough assignment, being a good spouse every day. Men might be especially prone to the belief that, having been a good husband for an extended period of time (anywhere from six months to ten years), they are entitled to overtime. Bringing a workplace ideology into the home, a husband might feel as if he needs a "vacation" from the demands made upon him and so will stop making any particular effort at home. Or he might feel that as long as he fulfills the basic job requirements of a husband (paying the bills, making love three times a week, and being home for supper), he can do whatever he chooses on "his own time" (having an affair during lunch hours, for example, or drinking at a local bar every night on the way home) without jeopardizing his marriage. He might well balk at the idea that he doesn't get "time off for good behavior."

Instead, a good husband must reinvent and prove himself every day. Clearly the pressure to perform well on a daily basis can be a burden, even if "performing well" means simply being consistently there for someone, being honest and appreciative. Honore de Balzac wrote in a letter to a friend that "it is easier to be a lover than a husband, for the same reason that it is more difficult to show a ready wit all day long than to produce an occasional *bon mot.*" Surely, with the arduous task of being a husband ahead of them, boys are prepared by our culture to accept the mantle of such responsibility? Surely they plan their futures with as much attention as their female peers? Surely they are groomed to be grooms?

WHY THERE IS NO "GROOMS" MAGAZINE

Well, not exactly. As a number of people have pointed out, from stand-up comics to sociologists, there is no masculine equivalent of *Brides* magazine; it will be a long time before *Grooms* magazine hits the newsstand. College men do not usually discuss the potential members of their wedding party or possible colors for their cummerbund. When asked, most young women can describe their ideal wedding in detail, although they might hesitate to admit it for fear of seeming too eager to marry or for fear of seeming anachronistic in their wishes. When I ask, "What will your wedding be like?" young women will often describe weddings that would take more preparation than the coronation of the emperor of Japan. It is telling that they can do this in spite of the fact that they might not even have a boyfriend, let alone a fiancé, at the time. Not that there aren't slipups in the fantasy: One student of mine kept referring to her fiancé as her "finance" by mistake—not a good beginning.

The ideas of the dream wedding cherished by these young women were far more focused than their ideas of the dream husband, and their plans did not appear to depend in any way on the individual man they would happen to marry at the time. In contrast, the typical young man, when asked, "What will your wedding be like?" responds that he has not considered the event. He will then instinctively resort to the "passive voice" in constructing a sentence and say something along the lines of, "When it happens, it happens."

Of course, as one female student of mine muttered with a certain amount of bitterness, "All the guys have to do is rent a tuxedo. Why can't women rent wedding dresses?" Why indeed? A man might, presumably, have more than one occasion to wear a tuxedo in his lifetime, where a woman is meant to wear her wedding dress once. Yet she purchases the garment for what can be an astronomical sum while he rents the dark suit for what is comparatively a small amount of money, with no cash down. It's like the old children's game of finding "What's wrong with this picture?" Shouldn't it be the other way around? "A wedding dress is supposed to represent a woman's purity and emphasize the importance and uniqueness of the day," tutored a wedding consultant at an all-day seminar for prospective brides as she convinced eighteen-year-olds to purchase one of the more modest numbers—one of the mere thousand-dollar dresses.

What's the rented tuxedo on the groom supposed to represent, I wondered, the fact that the groom has been around the block a few times and is uncertain whether to commit himself to the relationship?

Or, perhaps more important, does the rented tux indicate that he is a sort of "generic" man, a figure who will not be the center of attention on this day? "The young men who come in to rent formal wear do not often have any say in the matter," says Paulette, a manager of a major rental outlet. "They are told what to order by their fiancées, and they don't feel like it's any business of their's to argue, even if they are uncomfortable with the choice. But the boys mostly seem to think along the lines of 'Well, she gets to do what she wants for a couple of months. Then I get to call the shots.' " There is obviously a fundamental inequality at work which can't help either member of the bridal couple survive life after the wedding.

Often the prospective husband believes he has "given" his fiancée the power to make decisions before they are married so that he will more firmly secure the right to make decisions after; the prospective bride, in contrast, believes he will always allow her the free hand she has had during courtship. Such patterns have little to do with love, and everything to do with power. Once the marriage is fully under way, the struggle for the right to make decisions and the right to steer the relationship in the "best" direction can become a source of conflict.

Psychologist Alfred Alder comments that "most married couples conduct themselves as if each party were afraid that one could see that *it* was the weaker." In other words, we often circle around one another, each unwilling to appear vulnerable or to show our worries. We sometimes are tempted to overcompensate for feelings of powerlessness by showy displays of superficial control. He might yell at her for not keeping the house clean enough because it makes him feel like she's not happy at home; if she doesn't like to cook, it might make him feel like she resents doing anything for them as a couple. She, in turn, might berate him for not knowing how to program the VCR because it makes her feel as if he isn't making any effort to help out at home, or as if he ignores her request for help. They bully one another because each fears that the other isn't doing enough to make the relationship work, and each partner feels as if the other is more powerful because he or she is less invested in the relationship.

Traditionally women worried more about their marriages because they often defined themselves exclusively through their relationships.

The cliché of the woman as petty domestic tyrant derives, paradoxically, from such a woman's feeling of powerlessness. She rules over dusting and dishwashing, yelling at anyone who touches a table or who leaves fingerprints on a glass, not because she was born a shrew, but because she needs to reassure herself of the extreme value of her role. She might well feel as if she was persuaded into a position that promised respect, affection, and esteem, only to find that she rarely sees evidence of any of these.

PRESSURES ON WOMEN TO MARRY

While many men feel conned by marriage, it's clear that many women share this same feeling. Although the same methods of coercion cannot apply, the sense of being pressured into marriage holds as true for women as it does for men. Women, as we've seen, are generally encouraged by our society to consider marriage as the validation of their desirability and femininity. But many women also resent the pressure to marry, the questions that follow them during their single days, the implicit assumption that they would be married if only they could find a willing mate. It's also true that many women feel pressured to marry not only by society in general but by the specific man they're dating. Obviously the dynamics of male pressure are going to be different from those of women. Doing a takeoff on the old male line, for example, Elayne Boosler does a routine saying, "My husband tricked me into marrying him: He told me I was pregnant."

Despite many men's views on the subject, most women do not feel like they are in control within the relationship. They are more likely to claim that they are trapped, that someone else is in charge. In striking contrast to the assumptions made by many men concerning the reign that women are seen to hold over the government of marriage, many women feel that men are the bosses—everywhere.

Women often see that at home: A husband will usually have final say on matters such as the purchase of a home or a car. When a woman divorces, her income usually drops while the income of her ex-husband usually rises. "Put it this way," dictates Gloria, a friend who returned to college after working as a nurse for twenty years to earn a Ph.D. in women's studies, "the systems of patriarchy have institutionalized marriage in order to validate the ritual debasement of the female of the species." Obviously Gloria doesn't believe, as Philip Roth was told, that marriage elevates a woman in the world. She sees it as an excuse to keep women out of the work force, and out of the running. "If marriage could remain a personal rather than an economic issue, then I'd applaud."

Erma Bombeck puts it in less abstract terms when she writes in *Motherhood: The Second Oldest Profession,* "Married. It was like a dream come true . . . Just think, soon her little girl would have unpaid bills, unplanned babies, calls from the bank and substandard housing. All the things a mother dreams of for her child."

WHY WOMEN ARE TYPICALLY MORE POSSESSIVE THAN MEN

Women are often more emotionally insecure and sexually possessive than their husbands since they literally cannot afford to be otherwise, according to researchers Blumstein and Schwartz: "We think heterosexual women are more possessive than men because they are more vulnerable and financially dependent . . . We find possessiveness especially among heterosexual women who are frightened of making a new life for themselves if their partners should leave them." As *American Couples* sums it up, "Men are less possessive than women because they are more powerful." It does not seem as if women are holding too many winning hands.

Although it will be discussed in more detail in a later chapter, it is worth mentioning the ways in which the impact of imbalances in the workplace affect our most personal relationships. Even in fields such as elementary education, publishing, or social work, which are staffed predominantly by women, the top executives are, in most cases, men. The most highly paid and most powerful positions—principal, publisher, or agency head—will usually be awarded to a male candidate. Women earn about 25 percent less than men who occupy similar positions. More women than men work part-time, a pattern which assures that they receive fewer benefits, and women are often far less prepared for injury or retirement than their male counterparts. In addition to all other concerns about the workplace, *Time* magazine recently reported that the leading cause of death on the job for women is homicide—42 percent of women who died on the job were murdered, 64 percent by gun. "Among men," declares *Time*, "homicides account for just 12 percent." The workplace doesn't seem as user-friendly for women as for men. In the minds of most women, men oversee both the home and the workplace, and women see men as running the system in both.

THE HOUSE—AND THE SENATE

In one obvious sense men have undoubtedly controlled women's lives because they have controlled both the House and the Senate. Certainly men have retained the right to make both governmental and church law, thereby legislating both official and unofficial systems of morality. "Wives, submit yourselves to your husbands," women are told by the Bible. Back when women were denied the vote they were patiently told that their husbands voted as the "head" of the household. The woman might be the hands and back and womb of the household, even the heart of it, but she certainly wasn't perceived as the head. She could have no direct say in the formation of her government but was, of course, still subject to all the rules and laws legislated "on her behalf."

In Benjamin Wadsworth's "Puritan marriage manual," *The Well-Ordered Family, or Relative Duties,* a woman in 1712 was advised that even if she was not "inferior" to her husband, she was nevertheless unquestionably to act as his subordinate. Wives heard from Wadsworth that

> though possibly thou hast greater abilities of mind than he has, wast of some high birth, and he of a more mean Extract, or didst bring more Estate at Marriage than he did; yet since he is thy Husband, God has made him thy Head, and set him above thee, and made it thy duty to love and reverence him. If therefore thou dost hate or despise him, revile or dishonour him, or disobey his lawful Commands; if thou dost usurp authority over him, much more if thou lift up thy hand to strike him (as

some shameless wretches will), then thou dost shamefully transgress the
plain Commands of the Great God: thou dost trample his Authority
under thy feet.

To go against your husband was, in effect, to take up arms against God
himself. Lucifer, we remember, got into trouble for doing no more
than this.

The Catholic Church positions women as subordinate to men,
since "the man is the ruler of the family, and the head of the woman." In an encyclical, or official papal letter, on marriage and the
family, Pope Pius XI gave the following instruction to his flock: "Because she is flesh of his flesh and bone of his bone, let her be
subject and obedient to the man, not as a servant but as a companion, so that nothing be lacking of honor or of dignity in the obedience which she pays." This should not be confused with equality,
however, since it is "the same false teachers who try to dim the luster
of conjugal faith and purity" that wish to "do away with the honorable and trusting obedience which the woman owes to the man.
Many of them even go further and assert that such a subjection of
one party to the other is unworthy of human dignity, that the
rights of husband and wife are equal; wherefore, they boldly pro-
claim, the emancipation of women has been or ought to be effected."
This is not an aim that can be endorsed, since basically the position
of women remains what Milton had declared it to be in *Paradise
Lost*.

Writing of Adam and Eve, Milton saw the chain of command as
follows: "He for God, She for God in Him." Eve should worship the
figure of God as he appears in the person of her husband. She needs a
translator, a go-between, a man who will be able to understand the
needs, rules, and regulations of a god. Her husband should serve the
Lord, and she should serve her husband. Heaven was presented as a
sort of men's club that admitted women only when they had an escort.
Certain faiths and congregations have allowed women equal access in
spiritual terms, and in these houses of worship female leadership is not
outlawed, and female lives are given a free range of expression. Often,
however, conservative religious groups regard women as naturally and
correctly subservient to men.

Published in 1973, *The Total Woman* gave advice similar to that of Wadsworth, Milton, and the Catholic Church by suggesting that a woman who wants to be happy in a marriage should become the wife her husband wants her to be. Marabel Morgan's book is only one of a flock of such texts marketed to women. These tracts, distinguished by their reliance on "scripture" and their emphasis on making sure that women are full-time homemakers, are full of practical advice on keeping a marriage alive—such as meeting your husband at the door swathed only in Saran Wrap. ("If I waited around the kitchen wrapped up like that," grumbles my friend Kim, "my husband would put me in the microwave without even thinking. He would figure I was just a big leftover.") A woman is encouraged to put aside her wants, needs, and dreams in order to be more accepting of her husband's desires. Marabel Morgan urges her readers to "adapt to his way of life. Accept his friends, food, and life-style as your own. Ask him to write down the six most important changes he'd like to see take place at your house. Read the list in private, react in private, and then set out to accomplish these changes with a smile. Be a 'Yes, let's!' woman some time of every day." Marabel Morgan also grounds her argument in the Bible's assertion that man should rule over woman. The rhetoric is different, but the message is the same: She should be for God in him.

Luckily, Cynthia Heimel offers a contrasting vision for those of us who have trouble believing that God wants us to dress as French maids in order to prove our devotion. Heimel suggests in *But Enough About You* that we should not look for God in heaven, but in less intimidating places. "For God is always to be found at the back of the refrigerator behind the moldy tuna fish casserole," she writes, "or sometimes He is found in the way the tailor at your corner lovingly stitches up the hem of your party dress, other times in the way a child sings along with a toothpaste commercial. Do not look for Him in the heavens; He only keeps a small locker there, only goes there to change." More recently and radically, attorney Sarah Weddington, who argued the victorious pro-choice position in the original *Roe* v. *Wade* case, was on a television talk show with an evangelical minister who offered to show her the path to the Lord. She turned to him and said, "I talked to God, and She doesn't remember you."

WOMAN AS CIVILIZING INFLUENCE

Men made the rules, but women had to police them within the domestic realm and on the community level. It was often left to women to maintain systems of religion and government on an every-day basis. This is, in part, the origin of the myth of woman as "civilizing" influence. We hear in 1 Corinthians that "the unbelieving husband is sanctified by the wife," despite the fact that we hear in 1 Timothy that the woman should herself "learn in silence with all subjection." A woman was the transmitter of godliness into her home, but she was barred from assuming any larger congregation since the same passage in Timothy declares, "But I suffer not a woman to teach, nor to usurp authority over the man but to be in silence." Women have always been permitted to speak with authority about domestic issues, but when the subject matter became more theoretical, they were silenced or dismissed.

In their reduced roles women were supposed to join godliness to cleanliness, and their spiritual chores were to be defined by the four walls of their homes. They were regarded as catalysts for men's good-ness, and were charged with the task of keeping men in line, while being tolerant of most transgressions. Women were considered the stabilizing influence, the ones who wanted to set up homesteads instead of wandering the plains. It was a woman who made you stop drinking and killing people (consider the role of Clint Eastwood's dead wife in the recent film *Unforgiven*—even her memory civilizes his behavior to a certain extent). In the home, a less savage environment, a woman forced you to wash your hands before you ate and it was a woman who made you go to church instead of wax the car on Sunday morning.

The wife was charged with being the conscience of the family, the holder of the family's super-ego (although Freud argued that women's super-egos were less developed than men's). "No woman ever in-vented a new religion," writes Hugh Walpole, "yet no new religion would ever have spread but for women. Cool heads invent systems, warm heads embrace them." But if women maintained the system, it was men who defined it, initiated it, and retained ultimate control over it. Husbands controlled the household, delegating the details to their wives, but never disowning the right to make any important decisions or even to reverse her decisions if they were deemed unacceptable.

1776 AND ALL THAT

Such a pattern of control becomes clear when we examine documents from as far back as 1776 and see that the same conversations that went on between Abigail and John Adams take place—in less formal language—in living rooms and bedrooms today. Consider the letter from Abigail to John written on March 31, 1776, in which she makes explicit her

> desire [that] you would Remember the Ladies, and be more generous and favorable to them than your ancestors. Do not put such unlimited power into the hands of the Husbands. Remember all Men would be tyrants if they could. If particular care and attention is not paid to the Ladies we are determined to foment a Rebellion, and will not hold ourselves bound by any Laws in which we have no voice, or Representation . . . [that] your Sex are Naturally Tyrannical is a Truth so thoroughly established as to admit of no dispute, but such of you as wish to be happy willingly give up the harsh title of Master for the more tender and endearing one of Friend.

Abigail Adams's plea is one that echoes through more than two hundred years of American history, but, for the most part, it has called forth only the most perfunctory responses.

Her husband's reply, in a letter dated April 14, 1776, complains that her "letter was the first Intimation that another Tribe more numerous and powerful than all the rest were grown discontented.— this is rather too coarse a Compliment but you are so saucy, I won't blot it out." In effect, his reply reduced her argument to a tantalizing bit of feminine nagging. He then proceeds to fob her off with excuses about the impossibility of equality. "Depend upon it, We know better than to repeal our Masculine systems . . . I begin to think the Ministry as deep as they are wicked. After stirring up Tories, Landjobbers, Trimmers, Bigots, Canadians, Indians, Negroes, Hanoverians, Hessians, Russians, Irish Roman Catholicks, Scotch Renegadoes, at last they have stimulated the [women] to demand new Privileges and threaten to rebel."

Even allowing for a measure of irony in this response, the message remains clear. The husband's indignation at his wife's wishes for a woman's right to make her own choice is a battle still being fought today. From the Supreme Court to the trailer home of a woman who wants to return to school to get her Graduate Equivalency Diploma, women of all classes and colors are still arguing for their rights to be heard, accepted, and respected. The husband, however, decides whether or not to listen to such requests.

THE STATUE IN THE PUBLIC GARDEN

It is undeniable that both men and women appear increasingly concerned about the discrepancy between the confused reality of their married lives and the idealized images created by the media or the expectations handed to them as a legacy of the culture. However, the issues raised by these discrepancies focuses almost without exception on the woman's place in the relationship.

But what does being a husband entail in the 1990s? The figure of the husband remains elusive and shadowy, virtually eclipsed in historical, social, and cultural studies by the attention given to the changing role of the wife. This imbalance of attention creates an illusion, however. All the chronicles charting the competing roles of the wife are in fascinating contrast to the lack of documentation focused exclusively on husbands. The demands on the husband seem unchanging in comparison with the shifting, evolving, and expanding expectations of the wife. The husband comes to resemble a stationary figure, like a statue in a public garden, which seems to disappear in the midst of the relentless, peripatetic motion of women. The nearly invisible and apparently static image of the husband as provider, protector, and patriarch is, like the statue, a representation of the demand for respect and public evidence of power. The role of the husband remains a manifestation of respect and power even when it is overlooked.

The idea that women can change their role as wives and thereby redefine marriage in contemporary culture without simultaneously altering the role of husbands creates a mirage, an inaccurate representation of the landscape we inhabit, and offers a false sense of hope. It's like being told to run with one foot nailed to the floor, or like entering a race with someone who doesn't realize he will be handed the baton and told to run. Either way you can't win and, because of lack of communication, no one will be to blame. Women still think they can make everything better all by themselves the way you might make a meal all by yourself in order to nurture others. The implications of this are emblematic of the way gender roles function.

The woman who takes the reins and gets the job done perhaps receives the benefit of the attention paid to her by men in their demonstrations of thanks and flattery—this rarely happens—or her efforts are taken for granted and ignored. A woman is left to decide whether it's better to end up with flowers and candy instead of respect and a renewed sense of her abilities or with nothing at all.

The woman in such an arrangement will remain, therefore, the *recipient*, rather than the *possessor*, of the power to evaluate and reward. She must wait for someone else to provide everything for her, including a definition of herself. The ways that women permit men to define their lives range all the way from allowing the government to rule on issues of a woman's right to choose whether to bear a child, to the simple way women have learned not to rely on their own judgment in small matters. Women are so often told that we don't know what's best for us, we learn to distrust our own instincts and wishes.

I am reminded of a twenty-four-year-old friend, Heidi, who said that she never knew what kind of music she actually liked until she split up with her husband. "The day I knew the relationship was really over," she told me, "was the day I changed all the preprogrammed buttons on the car radio. There wasn't somebody telling me what I really wanted to hear as if I couldn't figure that out by myself." It is a small matter, perhaps, but not trivial; it is emblematic of larger issues.

THE ORIGINS AND RETENTION
OF THE HUSBAND'S POWER

This brings to light a whole series of issues relating to the origins and retention of power in our culture. One reason the image of the husband is particularly strong is precisely because it has remained largely unexamined. This means that the powers associated with that role remain naturalized, viewed as somehow normal, valid and right since they appear stable and unmovable even in the midst of sexual and social upheavals.

Joanna Russ, in an article titled "Dear Colleague: I Am Not an Honorary Male," writes about the way most women back down from challenging men's authority because they have learned that they simply will not win in such a confrontation. "Your friend (or wife) knows better than to argue with a man, particularly about abstract matters," she counsels her male reader, because "from the age of three she has learned how to please Daddy: by finding out what he thinks and by admiring him (which includes agreeing with his opinions)." Russ explores this further by explaining that "your secretaries at work do not smile at you because they like you but because it is part of their job to be pleasant . . . Your wife doesn't cook dinner and mend your socks because she loves you but because it's part of her job. How can someone who depends on you for money, for social position, for status, even for her own self-esteem, even keep it clear in her own head whether she loves you or not?"

In response to Roth's anguished cry that the "slaves" in a relationship are actually the masters, Russ would argue that

> once you are in a position of controlling other people, they instantly become mysterious to you. Blacks know what whites want, children know what parents want, and women know what men want—power. The subordinate wants what the superior has. In fact, the subordinate wants what keeps the superior up there—power. But the superior cannot credit this . . . Their superiority is based on the assumption that it . . . is natural. Hence the bewildered cry, 'But what do they want? We've given them everything?' Everything but the power to dissolve the situation of superiority/subordinance.

The naturalized nature of men's authority in part derives from the way women hand over authority to them. "Nobody can make you feel inferior without your consent," advised Eleanor Roosevelt. We all do duets, and if, as women, we dance backward all our lives, then it is because we do not assume the lead.

CHANGES IN THE WOMAN'S ROLE VS. STASIS IN THE HUSBAND'S ROLE

Yet there have been significant, important, and sometimes startling changes in what can be considered the "woman's role" in the family. The role of the wife has undergone radical revision in the last thirty years or so, often moving her from housekeeper and childbearer to wage-earner and intellectual peer. The prescribed and conventional role of the husband in the 1990s, however, is strikingly similar to the role of the husband as defined in a marriage manual dated 1891: "The Husband must at all times guard against losing his Rights as Protector, Provider, and Mouthpiece for Providence in his Home." Men seem to have made a bargain with Providence in order to be permitted to invoke higher principles than their own sensibilities.

But there is a larger issue at stake here. Even if the modern man does not consider himself the mouthpiece of Providence, he probably still aligns himself with what he will call logic, objectivity, or reason, as opposed to what he regards as the more feminine traits of personal insight, subjectivity, and sensitivity. In his 1989 book, *Rediscovering Masculinity: Reason, Language and Sexuality*, Victor J. Seidler examines the alignment of masculinity with logic and femininity with inconsistency from seventeenth-century philosophy onward. Seidler argues that a "rationalist philosophy saw itself as essentially masculine, and was an integral part of establishing a new pattern of sexual relationships of power . . . This helped produce a fear of the personal as an integral part of our inherited moral traditions which has characterized our inherited masculinity ever since."

To put it another way, men see themselves as speaking The Truth, whereas women are relegated to speaking from a purely personal and subjective point of view. "This is a terrible movie," a man might announce. "Oh, but I'm enjoying it," a woman will counter, "I think it's funny." "Well, it isn't," he'll answer, defending himself by declaring, "It's sentimental and melodramatic." The difference between these statements reveals the difference between seeing yourself as speaking from an absolute and indisputable position of good taste and fair judgment, and seeing yourself as speaking from a subjective point of view that relies on personal response and reaction. This same authoritative sensibility, by the way, enables a man to declare, "It's hot in this room" instead of wondering, as a woman might, "Is it hot in here or is it me? I'm really feeling warm."

THE SUBJECTIVE VS. THE OBJECTIVE

Of course, a man is only speaking for himself—we can all only speak for ourselves, in the end—but he seems to have a chorus of voices behind him. These voices reassure him that he brings to bear on the issue the best that is thought and felt in the world, and his inflexibility is justified as integrity. Often men fear the lack of self-control that comes from having desires, feelings, and intuition.

In contrast, "women's talk" has been assessed as simply not up to par, not serious enough to interest men. As Virginia Woolf observes, it has always been "obvious that the values of women differ very often from the values which have been made by the other sex; naturally, this is so. Yet it is the masculine values that prevail. Speaking crudely, football and sport are 'important'; the worship of fashion, the buying of clothes 'trivial.' " It is a rare woman who has not heard, at some point in her life, that what concerns her is not really important. "Girl talk" is synonymous with triviality in the minds of men and women. Our culture aligns the feminine with frivolity and a lack of substance, and the masculine with gravity. And gravity, as we know, is a law we can't escape.

Girls used to be told that a good education was not important because they would only "go off and get married anyway," as if a woman had to choose between having ideas and having a husband. Women's books, plays, and works of art were denied critical attention because they dealt with "unimportant" issues such as birth, death, marriage, sex, and friendship as opposed to "important" issues such as hunting, travel, finance, or sports. Woolf emphasizes this point when she writes that "these values are inevitably transferred from life to fiction. This is an important book, the critic assumes, because it deals with war. This is an insignificant book because it deals with the feelings of women in a drawing-room. A scene in a battlefield is more important than a scene in a shop—everywhere and much more subtly the difference of value persists."

THE TRIVIALIZATION OF THE FEMININE

The belief in the male community that women's interests and women's language are somehow "soft," somehow "too personal" or "too trivial" to be of any significance, has gone a long way in institutionalizing the assumption that women are not to be trusted with authority and power. It's interesting, however, to note a potentially damaging side effect: The belief among men that they are inevitably interested only in the public, the profound, and the impersonal has gone a long way in preventing men from accepting their own seemingly illogical, emotional, and subjective responses. Therefore, men often translated the personal into the public, so that it really did become a matter of transforming "I'm warm" to "It's hot in here." This is one way that men's authority within marriage becomes codified. The voice of authority is passed down from father to son.

Studies done by such researchers as Robin Lakoff, Dale Spender, Carol Gilligan, and Deborah Tannen have documented that men and women use language differently to make their points, signify authority, and establish intimacy. In a piece titled "Friendship Among Men," Marc Feigen Festeau elaborates on how men address issues differently from women:

> In conversations with each other, we hardly ever use ourselves as reference points. We talk about almost everything except how we ourselves are affected by people and events. Everything is discussed as though it were taking place out there somewhere, as though we had no more felt response to it than to the weather. Topics that can be treated in this detached objective way become conversational mainstays . . . We plunge in for another round, trying to come up with a new angle as much to impress the others with what we know as to keep from being bored stiff.

My friend Chris complains quietly that she can predict exactly the topics of conversation her husband will raise in any social situation since "he seems to carry around a sort of memo in his head of which topics are on this week's agenda. They don't change depending on the situation, either. He'll start talking about a cold front coming in from the west to the seven-year-old boy from next door and not really 'get' that the kid isn't too thrilled to be talking about the weather. Or he'll talk local politics with his mother, who really only wants to talk about her hip operation. Those are this week's topics and he's flabbergasted by the thought that he might invent a whole new set of topics for each individual he sees."

So how do men get out of these conversational sand traps? How do they stop talking about the weather, mileage, sports, routes taken to and from the event, and taxes? By "allowing" women to join in. Festeau documents the fact that women in a mixed group are usually the ones to make "the first personal reference, about themselves or others present. The men can then join in without having the onus for initiating a discussion of 'personalities.' Collectively, the men can 'blame' the conversation on the women." But the blame being assigned here is more genuinely identified as a sign of relief, a welcome lifting of a self-imposed burden assumed by men who fear the revelation of the truly personal.

This seems to fit well with the argument we heard from Seidler, who maintains that

> since it has been masculinity which has been so exclusively identified with reason, it can hardly be surprising that men find it harder to build contact with our dream and fantasy life. Our lives can seem one-dimensional, lacking in depth. As men, we can discover ourselves to be more focused upon our activities than our relationships, finding it easier to apply universal rules and principles in our behavior than to respond in an individually caring way to the needs of others. It is as if we have been made to pay for the power we have in the social world, by a blindness and insensitivity in our personal relationships.

Men were encouraged to see the "larger picture," to give "overviews" of the situation rather than get bogged down in details.

That this can be problematic is an understatement. Cynthia

Heimel's injunction that we all steer clear of overviews is wise. "Someone who understands the situation in Lebanon but who forgets to call his best friend who just had a root canal is lost to the right priorities. He will also snap at his off-spring when they have innocent homework problems; he will not notice when his lover has a deadline." To have a great overview of everyone else's situation and be blind to your own is obviously problematic. The man who donates money to charity for orphans abroad but refuses to give a worker time off to care for a desperately sick child does not have an adequate perspective on the situation. Equally, a husband who demeans his wife in private and embarrasses her in public can hardly be considered a feminist, no matter how "politically correct" he would like to think of himself.

Men were not prepared to be anything at home besides head of the household. They were not meant to be the heart and soul of a family; that was considered the woman's job.

COSTS OF MASCULINITY

Cooper Thompson argues that "the costs associated with a traditional view of masculinity are enormous . . . The belief that a boy should be tough (aggressive, competitive, and daring) can create emotional pain for him. While a few boys experience short-term success for their toughness, there is little security in the long run. Instead, it leads to a series of challenges which few, if any, boys ultimately win. There is no security in being at the top when so many other boys are competing for the same status." Such information can help us to understand why we are the way we are. But this information cannot be useful if it goes nowhere. We need to translate it into changes we make in our everyday lives and in our daily conversations. For instance, Deborah Tannen presents a case for a radically revamped pattern of communication that takes into account these differences between male and female conventions: "The communication problems that endanger marriage can't be fixed by mechanical engineering. They require a new conceptual framework about the role of talk in human relationships." As she suggests, we must see male-female conversation as a form of "cross-cultural communication" which would allow both men and women to "understand the problem and forge solutions without blaming either party." Tannen, along with many of her colleagues who study patterns of language, believes that one key in establishing more successful male-female relationships is the honest exchange of emotional information without blame, guilt, or shame.

SURRENDER AS SUBVERSION

Too often we appear to give in even as we secretly hold out. We pretend everything is all right when it isn't so that we can sort of "jump-start" our lives into a better situation by acting as if our lives are the way we want them to be. This solution can be dangerous when misapplied or applied in the wrong dosage like the misuse of a pre-scribed drug.

Since girlhood, most women have been schooled in the arts of flattery, of disingenuousness and deceit, and told that these are femi-nine traits. "Laugh at his jokes even when you don't find them funny," we were advised as teenagers, and then as more mature women we decided it was okay to fake an orgasm every once in a while in order to make our partners feel more comfortable. We were counseled that we would be promoted at work if we made our bosses look good, even at the expense of our own recognition. Paradoxically, we were also told that we would get ahead by not being aggressive or assertive and by not exhibiting our own ambitions or flaunting our talents. That would put people off and ultimately hurt us. We were told that the best way to "get" a man was to pretend not to want one and that the fastest road to getting married was never to mention marriage. We were told that we can best get our way by seeming to let men get theirs, even if the message was never made explicit. No wonder men think they're Mister Right all the time—too often women have learned to say, "You're right, dear" just to avoid arguments. "Shouldn't we stop and ask for directions?" suggests the wife. "I know exactly where I am," the husband replies, "and we turn left here." There is a long pause as they enter a military testing site, but she still surrenders by saying, "I guess you're right, sweetie—I think I remember that 'Do Not Enter Under

Penalty of Law' sign over there." It's easier to surrender than it is to insist on the rightness of her position.

This idea plugs us right back into sitcom land. In "I Love Lucy" when Lucy Ricardo let Ricky believe every good idea was his, he was happy and things went well; when she insisted on doing something on her own without his support, it was inevitably a disaster and she had to learn to accept his wisdom for the future. We were brought up on the image of the scheming, manipulative woman who bats her eyelashes and appears vulnerable to her husband in order to get what she wants out of him. In a doubly distructive manner, she was often portrayed as the beroine of the tale: "A smart woman lets the man win." It was the epilogue of countless stories.

We were told not to beat him at tennis, not to sound too smart, not to be too witty. "If he wants everything his own way, let him believe that's exactly what he's getting," advised the mother of the kids I used to babysit for as a teenager. I had asked about how to deal with a boyfriend who, at fifteen, insisted that his way of dealing with the world was the only sensible one. "But if I let him pretend he's always having his own way, then he really is always having his own way," I whined. "Not really," said the young matron, balancing a baby on her hip while she unpacked the groceries and I cleaned up the five-year-old, who'd just mistaken dog food for Play-Doh. "You'll know deep down inside that you're the one in control because you're letting him have his way. That's how women really rule the world," she explained, "by letting men think they do." I nodded although I wasn't sure I understood. When I hear the argument repeated today, I think it's pretty dangerous.

In *Beyond the Male Myth*, the researchers quote numerous men who have enshrined the concept of feminine surrender. When asked how relationships should work, the men interviewed felt that they were "a little superior" to women and had a right to be. Furthermore, they wanted women to protect them from any possible feelings of inferiority or failure. "Women should let a man win a little more." But is this really a good idea? Does lying about or masking one's own abilities make for a healthy relationship? Even when "giving in" or "letting him win" might seem like a good idea, is it? We were told that it was in our interests not to provoke an argument because the only result is that he'll go for a three-hour walk, or turn the television up louder, or, worse yet, find someone else. It wasn't worth it. But I believe that the truth can be repressed for only so long, and when our hidden responses finally emerge, it's not with a whimper but with a bang.

THE THELMA AND LOUISE PARADIGM

That's why a movie like *Thelma and Louise* struck such a responsive chord: Susan Sarandon and Geena Davis embodied many women's contraband appetite for subversion and gave voice to all the unsaid, bitten-back words that women have lived with for years. Instead of offering us images of women needing rescue, the film offered us images of women setting out to implement their own form of justice. Most of the women I know loved that movie; many of the men I know were made uneasy by it. Women whooped and hollered when Thelma and Louise blew up the truck driven by the tongue-wagging, vicious, redneck harasser. Most men didn't like that particular part of the movie. (They thought it was okay for the girls to kill the rapist—after all, what's a Western for?—but they were uncomfortable with the destruction of personal property, especially vehicular personal property. That was going just too far.) But women loved the representation of a score settled, especially since the battle had always seemed a private one: When a woman walks down a street or drives by in a car and hears a man (or more often, a group of men) shout something obscene, she feels violated.

Even if it masquerades as a harmless compliment ("I was only saying you had great tits, what's wrong with that?"), the woman who is the object of such a remark knows that it's an invasion. She also knows that it would never happen if she were accompanied by a man—which, I am sure, is one reason why many men discount the experience as unimportant.

After watching *Thelma and Louise*, for example, a group of us went out for coffee. Chuck, usually a good soul, uncharacteristically sneered, "The bit with the truck driver was overdone, nobody really acts like that." He was speaking loudly and it seemed like every woman in the diner turned to glare at him. "Are you kidding?" cried Angie. "Yesterday some guy in a Camaro tailed me from New Haven to Hartford while sticking his tongue out and making, let's call them 'gestures,' in his lap area. It happens all the time." Chuck turned to his girlfriend and in one of the most perfect moments illustrating a certain kind of thought process said, "But how can you say that happens all the time? It's never happened while *I'm* around." We all laughed, and Chuck heard himself arguing, in essence, that if it never happened in front of him then it never happened. "The point is they would never say anything to a woman who was with a guy. But if you're unattached then you're up for grabs," Allison explained, driving the point home for us all.

But *Thelma and Louise* offered its viewers more than scenes of appropriate revenge. Despite its ending, the movie offered women a vision of the open road, and a chance to see what life could be like if one could cut loose from all "the ties that bind—and gag," as Erma Bombeck has called them. When Geena Davis, married to one of the world's worst movie husbands, calls home to hear her husband answer the phone with uncharacteristic politeness, she immediately slams down the receiver. "He knows!" she tells Sarandon, and they take off. All it took was her husband's one phrase—"How are you?"—to tip her off to the fact that the FBI was in her living room. Why else *wouldn't* her husband be screaming at her?

The two female characters in that film provoked the response that got them on the cover of *Time* magazine because they represented people who, once they stopped letting somebody else win all the time, turned out not to be the losers they thought they were. No matter that they were outlaws and that the ending was one few us would wish for ourselves—what Thelma and Louise offered was a vision of two individuals who refused to let other people speak for them, think for them, and act for them.

Letting somebody else win sets up all the participants as chumps because it turns a fair match into a farce. Boxers get thrown out of the ring if they take a dive; ballplayers get arrested if they throw a game. No one should be encouraged to say they'll lose when they know they have the chance to win. A man would never agree to do that. We should be encouraged instead to find someone who can match us talent for talent, ability for ability—not to be in the ring with us necessarily, but to wear the one we have earned the right to offer.

CHAPTER SEVEN

BREAKING THE GLASS SLIPPER

*The Trouble with Static Expectations
in a Changing World*

OKAY, YOU MIGHT say, so women should delight in the challenge of facing life head on, of finding a man who will be an equal partner, unencumbered by the fetters of dependence. But what if, like my friend Irene, you have been brought up with the idea that no woman should marry a man who is "only an equal"?

I was having lunch in New Haven with a former student of mine, a young woman for whom I have great respect and who is clearly nobody's fool. Finishing law school at the moment, she has worked her way through every degree, and intends to work in the family court system. Irene is ambitious, intelligent, attractive, and good-natured. Where is the problem? She wants to find a man who is decidedly *more* ambitious, intelligent, attractive, and good-natured than she is. She also wants someone more successful and established than she is, probably someone older, and, she says, it wouldn't hurt if he was taller and physically stronger. But she also wants a man who thinks of himself as her equal, who is sympathetic to feminist issues, and who will not look down on her. In short, she wants to look up to someone who will not look down on her. My sense of spatial relationships is not all that keen, but I have the feeling that this is asking for trouble.

CAN YOU LOOK UP TO A MAN WHO ISN'T LOOKING DOWN ON YOU?

Irene wants to be swept off her feet by someone who will nevertheless not dominate her. I should probably have prefaced all of this by saying this was a woman who actually liked the annoying, self-destructive, and wildly popular movie *Pretty Woman*. "There was a 'Hers' column in the *New York Times*," insists Irene, "which said that *Pretty Woman* was the first postfeminist fairy tale," as if that could put a stop to all further questions.

Even apart from the idea that "postfeminist" sounds like a woman's breakfast cereal or what women do when they write to each other (we can be postfeminists or telephone-feminists, whatever we choose), I find these ideas at best problematic. The high point of *Pretty Woman* occurs when the hooker character gets to buy clothes from a fancy store under the protection of her john: Is this a big moment because it is the first time anyone's heard of any man wanting to put *more* clothes on Julia Roberts? The central relationship in this movie is based on the idea that the male partner goes out into the big scary world and makes a living, thereby forfeiting his right to an emotional life; in contrast, the female partner cannot legitimately make a living except by selling her body, and so she is better off living an emotional life for two inside a relationship that protects her from the big scary world. This doesn't sound too modern to me. In response to the contingent that argues that *Pretty Woman* is a modern fairy tale, comedy writer Merrill Markoe says, "Excuse me, but where was I when they rewrote the fairy tale to start, 'Once upon a time, in a land far away, there was this hooker . . .'?"

I should mention that Irene also liked *An Officer and a Gentleman.* "I'm just an old-fashioned romantic," she insists. "What's wrong with that?" Well, for a woman who believes that women have the same rights and responsibilities as men, it's difficult to buy into the old-fashioned version of romance that depends heavily on having a great deal of time to spend waiting for a knight in shining armor ("Forget the knight in shining armor," joked my friend Meredith, "I'd settle for a night in the Plaza Hotel"). Irene will attract men who are looking for a woman who will be facing her own life in a straightforward way, and such a man might well be disconcerted to find that such a dynamic and independent woman *wants* to look up to him. He might not want to be viewed from that perspective; men, as well as women, can find pedestals uncomfortable. And those other types of men, the ones who want a sweet thing to look up to them, would not choose a woman like Irene in the first place.

Another woman I know has a similar problem. She attracts men who perceive her as a confident, self-assured woman. A graphic artist who has achieved a certain measure of professional fame, Sally is plagued by doubts about her ability to play the role of "girlfriend." Part of Sally's problem is that she approaches her relationships with a tentativeness that makes both herself and her partner nervous. "Jim and I started seeing each other sixteen months ago," Sally began, only to interrupt herself. "You know, I always describe the length of my relationships in terms of months, the way mothers say, 'Little Lulu is nineteen months on Tuesday.' " We laughed, but her next comment was quite serious. "Sixteen months is a year and a half, but since it sounds longer to say it in terms of years, I always use months so that Jim won't get nervous. I'm afraid that he'll see that we really are in a serious relationship, and that it'll spook him and he'll leave." Sally smiled nervously, and I can imagine that her nervousness could well spook Jim, who would like her to be as strong and secure in their relationship as she is in her professional life.

Sally is aware that her fears get in the way of her ability to sustain a viable relationship. "It's the same in all my relationships with men: I worry. I worry that I like him more than he likes me; I worry about being possessive; I worry about being jealous; I worry when I'm not jealous. Sometimes I worry about being stronger, or smarter, or more social, or more successful—even though it's hard for me to imagine that anyone could really see me in these ways." No one can reassure her enough to make her believe that she is acceptable since she can't cast herself as the "romantic heroine" of her culturally programmed dreams. "I'm not one of those women who flounce through life with an ankle bracelet and a feather boa. I admire women who believe that they have center stage. Me, I feel much of the time like I'm playing to an empty house." What would reassure Sally? "I've been waiting for Jim to come to the door with an armful of flowers, a diamond ring, get down on his knees, and ask me to be his wife. But I worry about that, too," she complained. "What if he does and I still don't feel the way I'm supposed to feel: safe, secure, and certain to be center stage forever? I know the whole business is an elaborate fantasy, but I feel stuck with it."

We do ourselves a disservice by associating our most personal and intimate feelings with generic fantasies. We should, each of us, reinvent romance for ourselves instead of accepting hand-me-downs from novelists, filmmakers, greeting-card writers, or our tradition-bound families. But we shouldn't ignore the fact that even the most romantic of us cannot live on love alone without becoming emotionally anemic. Living on love is like trying to live on after-dinner liqueurs; something that is best savored in small amounts becomes unhealthy— even unsavory—when offered as a steady diet. Dr. Sonya Friedman warns that "romance is a lovely diversion for a weekend, a honeymoon, a Thursday afternoon tryst, or as a momentary expression of affection on a special occasion, but it's not a way of life. If it were, humanity would have stopped functioning somewhere around the invention of the loincloth."

WHY ROMANCE IS SOMETIMES LIKE NUCLEAR WASTE

While nothing is wrong with being an old-fashioned romantic *per se,* the idea of the last-minute rescue from a disastrous situation by the knight in shining armor seeps into other aspects of our lives even when we think we can keep it self-contained. It's sort of like nuclear waste: We can bury it, but it doesn't ever go away and it can contaminate surrounding areas without our knowledge.

Here's a possible scenario, one that is familiar to many women. You start out by figuring that you and the man in your life can "rescue each other" even though you know that the world doesn't work that way, and that we are each responsible for our own lives. The relationship starts out pretty evenly. Then you figure that there's nothing wrong with being "taken care of" in various ways; what's a prince for? So you, someone who has always prided herself on paying her own bills, let him balance the checkbook and then you get a little careless about making sure that you pay for your share of activities or treats—he makes more money than you, so why shouldn't he kick in a little more? Then you start believing (as your parents might have taught you to believe) that the money the husband brings in should go to the support of the household and that your money—since there's less of it—should remain *your* money exclusively, used for those luxury items you are hesitant to count as important enough to be part of the household expenses.

Poof, you're back to the 1953 *Good Housekeeping* paradigm—you're being supported by a man who has the right to make the final decisions in the household because, after all, he's basically footing the bill. When the moment comes that he sees that he won't be promoted past his present position and applies for a job in a completely different (and to you, less appealing) part of the country, you uproot yourself and go with him without very much discussion since both of you can't afford to live on *your* salary because you've become slightly less ambitious over the years—there was a comfortable cushion to allow you a little breathing space, and you slacked off your professional pace. You suddenly find yourself underskilled, vague about your ambitions, slouching after your husband, and fully bound by his decisions—you have forfeited the desire to make decisions on your own. You are, in other words, in far more desperate need of being "rescued" now than you ever were while you were single.

Even if the roles are reversed, and a wife supports her husband, the same unbalanced patterns of financial and emotional dependence engrave themselves on the once healthy relationship. A woman who supports a man often ends up feeling exploited and valued only for her checkbook—even when that is not the case. If she attempts to "rescue" a partner who continues to show little interest in investing—

emotionally or economically—in the "partnership" then it is not worthy of the name. The supported spouse will almost inevitably come to consider him- or herself less than a partner and more like a dependent. Clearly, there are times in most relationships during which there will be imbalances. But when the economic imbalance reflects and becomes inescapably representative of an emotional imbalance, there are often grave problems. This is not, in anybody's book, a happy ending.

Of course, I'm not blaming all of this on Richard Gere movies, but I do have trouble accepting a general fondness for stories where women get swept off their feet. Women in today's world need both feet firmly on the ground in order to get anywhere. Even though the pull of the romantic ideal is strong, think of it this way: You wouldn't wait more than fifteen minutes in a shoe store if no one came to help you. Why wait a lifetime for some man to brandish a glass slipper?

WHY DO WOMEN SEE THEMSELVES AS DEPENDENT UPON MEN?

And yet many women continue to wait for their husbands to provide them with a structure for their lives. We need to have a better understanding of the function and iconography belonging to the husband so that the hidden causes of anger, frustration, and guilt so often attributed to the working through of individual emotions can be grounded in a larger cultural and historical context.

In the 1992 book *Men Are From Mars, Women Are From Venus*, John Gray argues that men and women are from different planets, meaning that men are somehow naturally aggressive, logical, and selfish, whereas women are born to be passive, sentimental, and selfless. So when faced with an unresponsive and self-centered partner, for example, women are counseled by Grey to accept that "by remembering that men are from Mars, a woman can . . . begin to cooperate with him to get what she needs instead of resisting him." In perhaps the most telling line in the book, the author suggests to the female reader that after she has made her point to her husband, "if he gets upset and doesn't like this comment, then simply apologize for being critical." The argument put forth by Grey's book appears to consider these patterns unchangeable except in the most superficial of senses.

WOMEN ARE NOT FROM DIFFERENT PLANETS, JUST FROM POORER NEIGHBORHOODS

I don't think men and women are from different planets, but I do believe that most women come from a poorer neighborhood. They make on the average 75 cents to a man's dollar (and that's a high estimation), and if they complain about this inequity, they have every right to be critical. Imagine men putting up with this. Many of the problems between men and women need to be understood not only within a psychological context, but within a social and economic one as well.

The Hearts of Men, written by Barbara Ehrenreich in 1983, ignores the rest of the solar system in order to intelligently explore the ways in which our gender roles on Earth have been scripted alongside our roles as earners and workers. Men and women are not from different planets, but they are raised differently and they are taught to behave differently in both their private and public lives. Ehrenreich argues convincingly, for example, that the "perpetuation of the family wage system has depended on two things, one a fact, the other an assumption. The fact is that men, on the average, earn more than women. The assumption is that men use their higher wages to support women, and hence that most women are at least partly supported by men." Ehrenreich establishes that the underlying assumptions of this economic pattern keep all of us—men and women both—in a loop that is difficult, if not impossible, to exit. Explaining that "if it is assumed that most women are already supported by men, then they can, in good conscience, be paid less than men," Ehrenreich makes the case that "if women cannot expect to earn a decent wage on their own, they will indeed seek the financial support of individual men. Which reinforces the assumption that men, as supporters of women, deserve higher wages than women, and so forth." She does not blame some version of "innate passivity" for women's difficulties in breaking through the glass ceilings at work, but instead shows the ways in which women's contributions in the workplace and in personal relationships are devalued or ignored.

Ehrenreich's book, which deals with the contemporary man's "flight from commitment," takes on many such fundamental gender constructs and vivisects them meticulously. She argues that "male culture seems to have abandoned the breadwinner role without overcoming the sexist attitudes the role has perpetuated: on the one hand, the expectation of female nurturance and submissive service as a matter of right; on the other hand, a misogynist contempt for women as 'parasites' and entrappers of men." She concludes that "in a 'world without a father,' that is, without the private system of paternalism built into the family wage system, we will have to learn to be brothers and sisters."

Changing the paradigm is in itself fascinating: Instead of women searching for a husband who will be a sort of "Big Daddy" or, to employ what now seems a slightly quaint term, a "Sugar Daddy," women should look for an equal, a brother who will be in the same league, who will work with them side by side. But looking for an equal might appear problematic to the woman hooked on romance.

LEARNING THE CURRENCY

Women often hand over control without thinking very much about it, especially in the small matters that loom large only in retrospect. At a party a few years ago, a group of us were exchanging travel stories about missed trains, great restaurants, and strangely intimidating museums. When the conversation came around to the trials of trying to exchange monies into various currencies, a friend told a story about trying to talk her way into a room in a hotel in Madrid after midnight by brandishing Irish pound notes. Turning to a woman who had spoken earlier about her trip to Europe, my friend asked whether she had trouble remembering what currency to use in what country. The woman answered condescendingly, "Oh, I never had to learn the currency; my husband took care of everything." A small shudder ran through the group. We were as terrified on this woman's behalf, and as frustrated, as if she'd just said she was going to get drunk and drive around all evening. What would happen to her if, as happens to many women in the course of a lifetime, she were left on her own without a man to "save" her from her own calculated ignorance? Not knowing how to look after yourself stops being appealing after a certain point—and the sooner we realize that, the better.

Whether in a distant country or in a corporation, women must know the currency; they must understand how things are valued and they must figure out the intricate workings of a system that occasionally seems foreign. Generally speaking, men make it their business to have control over their situation. Women, on the other hand, are often tempted to hand over the responsibilities of life to others. Traditionally, a husband "looked after" his wife by assuming she was childlike in her inability to take care of herself. But, in the long run, both men and women resent the process.

It's easy to simply say yes when someone offers to make everything easy for us as long as we're nice to them. Yet we should resist. We knew enough not to take candy from strangers because we knew we were making a bad bargain of some sort, even if we didn't know the details. The same sort of wariness should caution us when someone gives us a deal that looks too good to be true. We have to know the cost of whatever it is we're doing, of whatever choice we make. It's like going into a small, elegant store where there are no price tags on anything; it doesn't mean the merchandise is free—what it means is that it probably costs more than you can afford. Anything that looks like a free ride isn't. And, obviously, I'm talking about more than money.

NO FREE RIDES

I can speak to the idea of "free rides"—quite literally—because I didn't learn to drive until I was thirty-three. While there were plenty of excuses (I'd grown up in a city, I couldn't afford a car, and so on), they were not the real reasons that I never bothered to learn. No, the real reason was that there had always been a guy ready to get behind the wheel. I used to see my role as that of the entertainer: I'd keep the driver awake by making small talk, pointing out interesting land-marks, and finding the best music on the radio. I figured that as long as I rubbed the back of his neck then I was doing my job; I told myself that men *liked* to drive.

It worked for a while, even though I had to wait for a second opinion on whether I needed to go to the mall. I told myself that it didn't cramp my style too much; after all, I usually had what I really needed. That seemed fine to me until I recognized one day after the end of my first marriage that I was about to go buy a week's worth of food at a store that seemed to stock two items, Spam and orange soda, because it was the only store within walking distance. I realized that if I didn't get my license, I was destined to be taken only where someone else wanted to go, bumming rides to whatever store was on *their* list. Alternatively, I had to wheedle and cajole people into going where they *didn't* want to go.

Neither option was particularly healthy. I got my license and the picture is terrible but the smile is genuine—as bad a driver as I was when I first started, it was emotionally safer than playing the per-petual-passenger game. I found out that I wasn't the only one to participate in this game, even if many women did metaphorically what I did literally. As Terry McMillan puts it in *Waiting to Exhale*, "But you were his wife, and you had done what you'd been taught to do: let him take the wheel while you took the back seat." Handing over the wheel or taking the back seat isn't a bad thing if you've done your share of the work, but otherwise it's just an excuse to nap through what could be the most interesting part of the journey.

Historically, women have been offered passivity as an option, but it is far from a real option. It is the removal of options, the relinquishing of possibility, and the embrace of defeat. The horizon of power will then remain out of focus and out of reach for many women because the terrain is relatively unmapped. Taking control of our own lives—even and especially when we are married—has nothing to do with a lack of or a distrust of love. Quite the opposite, in loving ourselves enough to care for the independent person we were always meant to be, we are better able to love others.

Does the taking of a husband represent, for most women, the triumph of reason over confusion, or ease over hardship? Is it the basest form of capitulation to convention or the refuge of the weary and the frightened, who will make any creature walking upright into a husband for the sake of saying that she is not alone? Or are women, once they are able to examine, explore, and sort through all their inherited and invented notions about marriage, capable of deciding to choose a man they respect, enjoy, and love?

Women should not look at the "marriage market" the way that a shopper at Kmart looks for the flashing blue-light special. There's more to choosing a mate than finding someone with a Y chromosome. A number of us are recovering from the wave of "told-you-so" fear that swept the country when the infamous *Newsweek* headline of June 2, 1986, proclaimed that we were now issuing in the era of "The Marriage Crunch."

I actually know some women who heard about that headline and remember it the way people remember where they were when Kennedy was shot. "Oh, I was on the floor of the Stock Exchange when I heard the news," or "There I was, taking the MCATS as the news was breaking." What was the news? Susan Faludi, author of *Backlash*, a 1991 book that debunks the "marriage crunch" myth, sums the initial study up as follows:

> Bennett and his colleagues, Harvard economist David Bloom and Yale graduate student Patricia Craig, predicted a "marriage crunch" for baby-boom college-educated women for primarily one reason: Women marry men who are an average of two to three years older. So, they reasoned, women born in the first half of the baby boom, between 1945 and 1957, when the birthrate was increasing each year, would have to scrounge for men in the less-populated older-age brackets. And those education-minded women who decided to get their diplomas before their marriage licenses would wind up worst off, on the theory that the early bird gets the worm.

The point was driven home to American women in an especially horrifying way when they were told that an unmarried woman of forty supposedly had a better chance of being shot by a terrorist than she had of marrying.

This became translated into the idea that if you weren't married by the time you were forty, you would *automatically* be shot by a terrorist. Women with briefcases started looking over their shoulders. The theory grabbed hold of our innards because it confirmed our fears. It was compelling at the time because it had a McCarthyish tinge to it that rendered even the most self-confident woman slightly paranoid. Reading the report or listening to the endless talk shows it sparked was a little like looking at road kill, or watching a house burn down in the middle of the night. It validated the warnings we had heard all our lives and had ignored: Put your work/life/feelings/mind before your job of finding a husband and you'll never marry.

But now Faludi has proven that the scare was just that: a case of media-induced panic. The figures were never accurate; a woman who wishes to marry does not have to fight her way out of a terrorist organization unless she is Patty Hearst. (Remember Patty Hearst? My students think that Patty Hearst is Ronald Reagan's novel-writing daughter.) Faludi exposes the mechanism behind the numbers to show that they were part of a "backlash" against feminist values in much the same way that Simone de Beauvior and Betty Freidan charted the backlash against the gains made by women in the earlier part of the century.

This is not an idle conspiracy theory on Faludi's part, but rather a search for the truth behind the fear. Think of Dorothy in *The Wizard of Oz*, who trembles when she enters the temple and sees the fierce image of the Wizard. Dorothy then finds a little old man manipulating the machinery, who cries out, "Pay no attention to the man behind the curtain!" Dorothy is expected not to expose the real origin of all that fake authority. Faludi shows us the men—and women—behind the curtain who made women feel that they were supposed to marry any man with a pulse.

Indeed, Faludi examined studies of women's attitudes compiled from fifteen years of national surveys of ten thousand women and "found that marriage was no longer the centerpiece of women's lives and that women in their thirties were not only delaying but actually dodging the wedding bands." She reports that a 1985 Virginia Slims poll declared that "70 percent of women believed they could have a 'happy and complete' life without a wedding ring," and that a 1989 "New Diversity" poll found that the "proportion had jumped to 90 percent."

So if indeed there is no "marriage crunch," no appalling male shortage, no need for women over thirty or women holding advanced degrees to start hanging around car showrooms, walking large dogs, or volunteering at federal prisons in order to meet eligible men, what are the issues? Despite the fact that women are usually identified as the ones who want to get married, and men are identified as the ones trying to "get away" before they get hooked, it is interesting to note, as Caroline Bird does in an essay titled "Why Women Should Stay Single," that

> single women over thirty are brighter, better educated, healthier, and happier than single men over thirty. Bachelors are worse off than spinsters in every way except salary. Age for age, single men are more apt to be mentally ill, three times as apt to say they are unhappy, four times as apt to say they don't like their work. They are more apt to get sick. They die younger—by their own hand as well as from other causes. And so far as happiness can be measured, they lose out this way. On the Happiness Scale devised by Norman Bradburn of the National Opinion Research Corporation in Chicago, single men score less happy than single women.

Jessie Bernard makes a similar point in her book *The Future of Marriage* when she demonstrates that there is "research literature reaching back over a generation which shows that: more wives than husbands report marital frustration and dissatisfaction; more report negative feelings; more wives than husbands report marital problems; more wives than husbands consider their marriages unhappy, have considered separation or divorce, have regretted their marriages; and fewer report positive companionship." So if single women are happier than married women, and if married men are the happiest of all the groups listed, we must ask ourselves: Why are the images presented to us from childhood onward those of unhappily married men and unhappy single women?

In part, women who focus almost exclusively on relationships are bound to be disappointed by any actual relationship with their husbands. If a woman looks to a man to change her life, she's looking in the wrong direction. Instead of mapping out a course for herself, she's swept up by the current of her husband's life, and then wonders why she's out to sea without a compass or chart of her own. When she signals for help, drowning in another person's life, it simply looks like she's waving at the shore and yet she wonders why no one comes to the rescue. If you're promised a life jacket, you're unlikely to learn to swim.

HAPPY EVER AFTER?

A wife whose life is fraught with anxiety about her own identity and role, for example, might well believe that her husband has translated her story into his own. In despair and with anger she comes to see herself as relegated to the footnotes and marginalia of the text—*his* text. She is night to his day, shadow to his substance. He is "the One" and she is "the Other," defined only in terms of her similarity to and difference from him.

A wife, feeling confined by her role, might believe, like Nora in Henrik Ibsen's play *A Doll's House,* that she was coerced into participating in a system that forced her to remain a child. Nora tells her husband, "Our home has only ever been a playroom. I have been your doll-wife, as I was my father's doll-child, and as I have made the children my dolls. I thought it was great fun when you played with me, just as they think it's great fun when I play with them." But Nora is no longer content to be part of someone else's game, and she rejects her role of the "good little girl" who does what she is expected to do without a murmur. She believes that she must leave her husband's home in order to develop a sense of herself as an adult. One of the first portraits of a woman who decides to leave home rather than play house, Ibsen's heroine still speaks to the struggles of many women today.

The catalog of contemporary novels, films, and made-for-television movies that have as their central theme a wife's refusal to stay in a confining marriage is too long to list in detail. Thinking of just a few representative titles, however, we can see that from *Fear of Flying* to *The Women's Room,* from *The Burning Bed* to *Thelma and Louise,* from *The Color Purple* to *Heartburn,* the woman who walks out on a bad marriage is shown as possessing heroic qualities. She is breaking free of the bonds that prevent her from attaining knowledge and expressing her true self.

"When a woman walks out on her marriage she's strong and sure of herself," complains Mike, a twenty-four-year-old electrician, "but when a man walks out on his marriage he's a schmuck. How come?" In part, a woman who leaves a marriage is usually seen as weaker financially, more marginal socially, and more vulnerable emotionally than her husband. We also assume, sometimes very wrongly, that a woman will only leave a marriage when it has become truly intolerable, where the assumption is that a man will leave a marriage when he is merely bored or uncomfortable.

In reality women's reasons for getting married are remarkably similar to men's, although few might imagine that this is the case. "I got married because my family thought I should," explains a divorced journalist in her late forties. "I was finished with school and I wasn't sure what to do next. Getting married seemed to be a step in the right direction. It made me feel grown-up and ready to face the world. I didn't know that just getting up in the morning to go to a good job at twenty-two would have made me feel the same way. I wish I could go back and give my younger self some advice: Don't be so terrified of life that you hide out in a marriage to escape it." Like her male counterparts, this woman saw marriage as a refuge from the scary world of adult life, even though she was not particularly well prepared to make the marriage work.

Is she unusual in feeling pushed into marriage? Not at all. "He definitely wanted to get married before I did," explains Karen, who is returning to college after dropping out in 1978 to have the first of four children. "He made a lot of comments about how I would never do any better than him. Finally he convinced me, but now I wonder why he kept saying that. He told me that if I didn't marry him I'd probably never marry. It wasn't very flattering but it was persuasive, although I now have my doubts about whether he was right. I feel like I got talked into marrying too young." ("We're all too young to marry," said one rather cynical friend when I read her this comment. "Hell, I got married at thirty-eight and I was too young.")

When I asked women, "Why did you marry?" they often said, as did the men, that they were worried about living alone. "He said he'd take care of me," explained Sophie, an actress in her early thirties who has been married for twelve years. "I came from an abusive family and he offered stability and comfort and that's all I wanted," Sophie said, adding after a moment, "At least that's what I thought at the time."

Other women had more active reasons for wanting to marry. "I got married because we were living together for so many years—four in all—that it became increasingly annoying and intrusive to have to explain why we weren't married," declared Jennifer, an accountant in her late twenties. "When I called his office, for example, and the switchboard operator answered, I had to go through this long routine in order to leave a message. 'Yes, he knows where to reach me. No, you don't have to spell out my last name. Yes, he can call when he gets out of the meeting.' I wanted to be able to call and leave a message asking him to get in touch with his wife."

Forty-six-year-old Faith considered my question for weeks before answering. She, too, had lived with her lover for quite a while before deciding to marry. "I'd loved him for years and I wanted the world to know we weren't just a couple for the sake of convenience, although no doubt many marriages are just that. But I wanted to be able to shout from the rooftops that not only was this for good—it was for better and for worse. I wanted to make a new family out of the combination of our lives. I wanted our relatives to be related to one another. I wanted to be able to use all the usual terms: sister-in-law, niece, stepchild, whatever. Names and naming are important and should not be underestimated. The first time I heard his adult daughter describe me as her stepmother, we both laughed at the connotations but it was still a relief to have a name for what we were to each other. Suddenly we were also legitimate and official." She paused, and in the way that many women have, ended her statement with a question: "Does that make any sense the way I've said it?" I thought it made enormous sense and told her so.

But of course that doesn't tell the whole story. Nancy Cobb's book How They Met chronicles the beginnings of long-term marriages between notable couples, and one of the most striking aspects of the volume is the descriptions of initial meetings given by men. Husbands are at least as invested in their relationships as their wives, seem to remember as many details, and appear to be as committed to preserving the best of those moments. Although a self-admitted "die-hard" romantic, Cobb is not coy about the perils of relationships; after all, she dedicates the book to her parents, "who couldn't live with or without each other." The tales are a testimony to the enduring nature of both men's and women's delight in finding someone who adds to an already full life.

Ranging from the lines that seem to be scripted by Preston Sturges (such as the one Cobb tells of Walter Matthau's proposal, sent by telegram. " 'I told the operator to write, 'Darling, will you marry me?' The operator paused and said, 'Is that all?' I said, 'Isn't that enough?' ") to ones that seem as if they could be scripted by anyone we know, Cobb supplies evidence for the "promise of possibility" between women and men. My favorite is the one told by writer Mavis Leno, who couldn't imagine ever marrying since she feared it meant ending up in a cold-water flat like Alice Kramden. The decision to marry came not only after she'd met Jay Leno but had lived with him for quite some time. "It was as if there was a party going on somewhere and I couldn't get to it. Then, one day, I woke up and I realized, I'm at the party . . . It's Jay; he's the party . . . and it was the goddamnedest feeling."

"The goddamnedest feeling" is the sense you have when you get into the car and your favorite song is just beginning the moment you turn the radio on; it's the feeling of getting an A on a test in a class you enjoy but didn't study for; it's the feeling of relief when you discover, having gathered all your courage together, that the noise in the other room is just the cat chasing a moth. "The goddamnedest feeling" is a combination of luck, timing, strength, and courage you might not have known you had. It's the kind of relief that ends in laughter, the grin that's so genuine you close your eyes and shake your head in disbelief.

By the way, there's nothing "politically incorrect" about falling in love. Propagandizing the idea that a feminist is a woman who doesn't fall in love is one of the tricks played on women by those people who are too frightened by the possibility of women's independence to admit that you can have control over your own life and still care deeply about someone else. As Mary Wollstonecraft wrote in her 1792 *A Vindication of the Rights of Woman*, "I do not wish [women] to have power over men; but over themselves." And securing the right for women to have power over their own lives does not mean that men are unmanned in the process. I often think of Ellen Currie's line from her novel *Available Light:* "I like men, God help me. Not that I'm a siren on a rock, I just like them, the way some women like cats and some others hate spiders." I applaud Currie's sentiment and I believe that women can love men and ourselves at the same time. After all, monogamy doesn't mean loving your husband instead of yourself.

CHAPTER EIGHT

THE EMOTIONAL
MENAGE A TROIS

*Can You Love Two Men
at the Same Time?*

By way of preface, and to address the needs of any reader who might
have turned directly to this section for clarification, the short answer
to the question "Can you love two men at the same time" is "Yes—sort
of." Usually what happens is that one man offers security and de-
pendability, and the other offers adventure and freedom. We all want
everything. Is that so difficult to understand? Examining the reasons
why we carve people up into these categories is the first step in
understanding why the emotional ménage à trois is desired by some
women, and lived by others.

THE EXOTIC AND THE EROTIC

Real men are not meant to be husbands, according to the folk wisdom
pervading our culture from the frontier days onward; Shane rides away
unmarried. Heroes move toward the far horizons of experience with-

out the shackles of marriage; all but Bruce Springsteen's most recent songs emphasize that only the man who travels alone can travel fast. Such mythologies fit neatly into the conventional patterns of masculine and feminine psychology and behavior. We understand that it isn't just the Garden State Parkway that makes Springsteen see himself moving swiftly through the night in order to avoid the ties that bind. To find the truly erotic lover, we are encouraged to look for the truly exotic lover.

THE CONVENTIONALLY MASCULINE VS. THE CONVENTIONALLY DOMESTIC

Women's apparently paradoxical reluctance to enter a calmly satisfying relationship when they seem to want one is a point made repeatedly by one of the best-selling self-help tracts of the eighties, *Smart Women, Foolish Choices.* The two men who wrote this book, both California psychologists, describe a pattern they see as creating havoc for many women. They argue that women sometimes "seek out states of tension, challenge, and excitement in relationships because as girls they were geared to see relationships as a primary goal in life. Boys, on the other hand, were taught to look for excitement in their jobs and in athletic competitions and so tend to view relationships as less primary. Most men don't look to relationships for excitement and thrills." Women seek out drama and adventure in their relationships since they are taught to see emotional territories as the only ones open for their exploration.

Invoking Ellen Moers's *Literary Women,* we can agree that in their emotional lives, women "could enjoy all the adventure and alarms that masculine heroes had long experienced, far from home." To put it another way, women are encouraged to regard relationships as the defining force of their lives. They fear that too tepid a relationship will not provide them with a sufficiently breathtaking plot or breathless pace. If their relationships are boring, their lives will be boring. If their relationships are stormy, then the days won't so easily blend into one another. Such a woman will create crises in her emotional life in order to feel "more alive" the way a physician whacks your knee with a hammer to see if your reflexes are working. The crises of such a woman's emotional life is indeed a sort of reflex response to her fear of boredom.

PASSION PLAYS

Dr. Alexandra Symonds records the case of one woman who "lived alone, worked hard, traveled, and had many friends" and yet "was always very cautious about becoming involved (romantically) because she knew that 'only a strong man could take me.' " It becomes clear that a "strong man" is synonymous with one who treats her badly. If he didn't treat her badly, she *acted* badly herself, often by becoming voracious in her needs. Symonds found that as soon as this woman met a man who was compatible, she seemed to change from being independent to being extremely needy. "She had no interest in going out or entertaining friends. She was interested only in her boyfriend, had tremendous sexual desires, and looked forward to getting married, cutting down on her work or giving it up completely. She clung to her boyfriend physically and emotionally, looked up to him in a little-girl manner and conducted herself in a submissive sycophantic way in his presence." She lost all sense of pride or satisfaction in her work or any area of her life apart from the romantic involvement. The independent woman declared, in effect, that in a relationship she could only behave as someone whose behavior needed a "strong man's" influence. Not only did she give up her independence, but she contrived a situation that was dramatic, tense, and laced with stress.

A woman like this might even be attracted to someone who will cause her emotional pain, since she has come to associate pain with her deepest feelings and most intimate relationships. In extreme cases, this can spill over into the toleration of physical as well as emotional pain. There is an arcane school of romance that assigns pain as proof of love.

"HANDSOME, RUTHLESS, AND STUPID"

Author Dorothy Parker was quoted as saying that "I require only three things of a man. He must be handsome ruthless and stupid." Parker's line is suffused with the sharp edge of irony that characterizes her fiction. This line, however, is from her biography. Just because a woman can vivisect an unhealthy relationship by describing two mismatched characters to perfection, it unfortunately does not guarantee that she will be able to see with such clarity the details of her own intimate relationships. Parker, who at one point married the same man twice ("There are several people at this wedding who haven't spoken to each other in years," she said at the occasion of her second marriage to Alan Campbell, "including the bride and the groom"), did not seem particularly insightful in choosing men who would treat her well. In fact, she seemed to seek out those who would most obviously devastate her. It is a cliché that a woman is more responsive to a man's forgetfulness than to his attentions, and men have noticed this as well as woman. Oscar Wilde wrote that "I am afraid that women appreciate cruelty, downright cruelty, more than anything else. They have wonderfully primitive instincts. We have emancipated them, but they remain slaves looking for their masters all the time." Wilde's flippant statement is no less poignant for its "bitchiness": He focused on the drive that some women have to find the man who will colonize their emotions, enslave their passions, and rule over their lives—and so in the name of finding love, they find a fascist.

Sylvia Plath, in one of her most moving poems, asserts that "every woman adores a Fascist," who has the "brute heart" of "a brute like you." Her poem goes on, in painful and careful verse, to describe the "Love of the rack and screw." The play on words is anything but playful; obviously *screw* is as much a word that connotes torture as it is a description of the sexual act. In a similar manner, one of Margaret Atwood's narrators suggests that she and her lover go together like a "hook and eye." Nice, the reader might think, a domestic poem, with metaphors that fit romantically in the world of needle and thread. The comfortable images from a sewing box soon dissolve and the reader discovers instead that the imagery is drawn from the hunter's arsenal, images of curved steel and pain: Atwood is describing "A fish hook. An open eye." The reader reflexively blinks, and the transition from believing something is a perfect fit to believing it will be the death of you is swift and shocking.

Finally, there are those who feel, as one French philosopher put it, that "if no one had learned to read, very few people would be in love." Novelist Margaret Drabble, for one, locates the responsibility for such misplaced desires in the way we are taught to envision "real romance" as tragic. "I blame Campion, I blame the poets," fumes Drabble in *The Waterfall*. "I blame Shakespeare for that farcical moment in *Romeo and Juliet* where he sees her at the dance, from far off, and says, I'll have her, because she is the one that will kill me." When I read that I thought of the high school gymnasium dance in *West Side Story*, where Tony and Maria look at each other as everything else blurs. You knew from that first glance that Tony and Maria were as good as in bed and as good as in the grave—sort of coming and going at the same time.

"A MAN WHO HAS TIME FOR ME ISN'T BUSY ENOUGH"

While many women will not actually look for a painful relationship, they might well look for a man who seems to be a little "too good" for them. Women will focus, for example, on the man who apparently likes but ignores them rather than devote their attention to the man who likes and is adoring of them. "A man who has all the time in the world for me," says my friend Anne, "just isn't busy enough." Thomas Hardy suggests that "women never tire of bewailing man's fickleness in love, but they only seem to snub his constancy." His words still ring true today. Women will often choose to pursue the man who retreats from them rather than accept the hand of the man who offers himself openly. Why?

There are, of course, many possible answers, but few of them are reassuring. "It's no news to anyone that nice guys finish last," cartoonist Lynda Barry tells us. "Almost every female I know has had the uncomfortable experience of going out with a 'nice man.' Spelled 'N-E-R-D.' How many times has your girlfriend said, "He's SO sweet and so cute so why don't I like him?' Let's face it, when an attractive but ALOOF ('cool') man comes along, there are some of us who offer to shine his shoes with our underpants. If he has a mean streak, somehow this is 'attractive'. There are thousands of scientific concepts as to why this is so, and yes, yes, it's very sick—but none of this helps." Barry makes us laugh, but many of us also wince in recognition of the pattern she describes.

PAIN AND LOVE

Just what are these scientific concepts Barry mentions? As Jules Masserman writes in *Individual and Familial Dynamics*, "Peaceful, noncontentious living" is often "unattractive and unbearable" to such a woman. There is no easy way out of the familiar pattern of refusing to believe that one can live both calmly and well in the presence of a man who is both loving and lovable. If a woman like this comes close to a man who might actually love her, she finds a reason to abandon him. He dresses badly; he is overweight; he is not ambitious enough; he is too ambitious; he can't parallel park—any reason will allow her to justify ending a relationship with a man who might treat her well. This woman will not be able to respect a man whom she regards as "weak" enough to have fallen under her spell. She loses her regard for him the moment he loses his heart to her.

For example, Scarlett O'Hara, as we remember from Margaret Mitchell's *Gone With the Wind,* spends most of her adult life pursuing the one man who refuses to succumb to her charms. Scarlett is driven by her love for Ashley Wilkes, despite the fact that he refuses to become her lover. Why?

Perhaps the answer lies in a minor transformation of the sentence: Scarlett loves Ashley not *despite* the fact that he refuses to become her lover, but *because* of that very fact. Scarlett wants the Impossible Man, the Unavailable Man, and makes sure that she focuses all her attention on the very man who keeps his distance. Toward the end of the novel, when Ashley is free to marry her, Scarlett herself understands clearly that she never really loved him: She merely loved the *idea* of having him.

Once he is available, he is no longer desirable, and Scarlett sees that "Ashley was only a childish fancy, no more important really than her spoiled desire for the aquamarine earbobs she had coaxed out of [her father]. For, once she owned the earbobs, they had lost their value as everything except money lost its value once it was hers.

And so he, too, would have become cheap if, in those first far-away days, she had ever had the satisfaction of refusing to marry him." If he had ever loved her, Scarlett never would have loved him. Scarlett is not the only one to come to this conclusion; Rhett Butler, her third husband, also understands that Scarlett wants only what she cannot have. Rhett tells her, "You are brutal to those who love you, Scarlett. You take their love and hold it over their heads like a whip," and so Rhett learned to assume a cynical air toward her in order not to reveal the depth of his emotion.

Finally, he is driven away by her inability to accept his love: "I loved you so, Scarlett. If you had only let me, I could have loved you as gently and as tenderly as a man has ever loved a woman. But I couldn't let you know, for I always knew you'd think me weak and try to use my love against me." Undercutting the confidence and self-esteem of anyone weak enough to fall under her spell, Scarlett is a character who represents the dilemma faced by many women: How can she love a man who submits to her, when what she is really looking for is a man to whom she can submit? How can she love a man whom she has "tamed," when she really wants a man who will tame her?

In her influential article "The Alienation of Desire: Women's Masochism and Ideal Love," psychologist Jessica Benjamin explains that women are not looking for a man who will hurt them *per se,* but are instead looking for a man who will "tame" them in some crucial way. They do not desire pain, but they do desire someone who will require their submission. "The idea of 'pleasure in pain' is misleading," Dr. Benjamin explains, "insofar as the crucial point in masochism is not the experience of pain, but of submission. Submission may involve eroticized pain, but more often pain is a symbol or metaphor for submission." They want to submit to a man in order to subdue their own fears and anxieties, and paradoxically, submitting to a man who they know will cause them some measure of distress allows them to have a feeling of control.

When such women are loved in return, they find reasons to undercut the man who dares to love them. Dr. Karen Horney explains that "when these women succeed in getting one man after another to fall in love with them, they are able to conjure up reasons for depreciating their success—reasons such as the following: There was no other woman about for the man to fall in love with; or, he does not amount to much; or, I forced him into the situation anyway; or, he loves me because I am intelligent, or because I can be useful to him in this or that way." There is no way to win in such a situation, and pain becomes inevitable.

"NEEDING" TWO MEN

In *Beyond the Male Myth: What Women Want to Know About Men's Sexuality*, Anthony Pietropinto and Jacqueline Simenauer assert that "since women do not need two distinct types of men in their life, the virtuous and the profane, they are more easily monogamous." My response to this assertion is: HA! Statistically women may be more monogamous than men, but that doesn't mean that it's been easy. Of course, women "need" two types of men in their lives—as much as any man has "needed" two types of women.

Perhaps one of the most revealing paradigms of the dangerous, exotic, eroticized lover in contrast to the safe, domestic, and neutered husband can be found in Emily Brontë's romantic novel *Wuthering Heights*. Generations of readers first came across it as students, and read it as if our lives as well as our grades depended on it. It was one of the few books by a female writer to be assigned in high schools and colleges, so Emily Brontë achieved a kind of cult status as the writer of the "woman's story." The love between Cathy and Heathcliff has become so familiar that it is the stuff of pop songs and Monty Python sketches. Indeed, *Wuthering Heights* is the template for thousands of other novels, including a recent novel based on the "untold" story of one of the main characters. If *Wuthering Heights* were an item on a menu, it might be described as "a surprisingly rich dish, flavored with strong sexual longing, a pinch of incest, a sprinkling of life and love after death, prepared in perfectly heartbreaking portions, of which many feel the first bites are the best. Served with a Gothic sauce. Goes well with aged wine, and the film version goes a little too well with cheese."

Catherine Earnshaw is a wild, hearty child who befriends the orphaned and inarticulate foundling Heathcliff. Cathy and Heathcliff roam the moors and play with the passionate attachment of a childhood romance. They are devoted to one another. In Cathy's company, Heathcliff becomes an able young man whose native intelligence nevertheless remains undervalued in his position as a servant to the household. The bond between Cathy and Heathcliff appears unbreakable, despite her family's deep-seated concern with the direction of her affections.

This childhood romance, which is convincingly presented by Brontë, lasts until Cathy meets Edgar Linton, the man who will become her husband. Cathy has never seriously considered marrying Heathcliff. After all, as she tells her maid and confidante Nelly, "Did it never strike you that, if Heathcliff and I were married, we should be beggars?" Even as she cried into the night wind one of the most famous declarations of love, "I *am* Heathcliff," Cathy was preparing for her wedding to Linton. Cathy was nothing if not practical.

In the early film version, Laurence Olivier plays Heathcliff to David Nivens's Linton, and they are impeccably matched. (Merle Oberon plays, unfortunately, a rather shrill Cathy.) Olivier is shown, in the first shot of Heathcliff as an adult, filling a door frame. He is enormous, dark, and brooding, and his shirt is stained and opened at the neck. Nivens is presented indoors, part of a magnificently decorated room, part of music and light and culture.

If Heathcliff represents nature, then Linton represents culture. If Heathcliff represents the physical, then Linton represents the intellectual. If Heathcliff represents the sexual, Linton represents the conventionally romantic—and that is a large part of the problem. While she is trying to decide between the two men, Cathy becomes increasingly impatient with Heathcliff's once beguiling silence.

In a line that could be straight out of Deborah Tannen's book on the problems of communication between the sexes, *You Just Don't Understand,* Cathy asks Heathcliff in great frustration, "What do you talk about? You might be dumb or a baby for anything you say to amuse me . . ." Complaining, sometimes peevishly, sometimes furiously, about Heathcliff's recalcitrance, Cathy echoes every woman who has demanded a verbal response to an emotional situation from a man who cannot or will not supply one. (Erica Jong will echo Emily

Brontë more than a hundred years later when she laments in *Fear of Flying* that although she was initially drawn to the stoic silence of her husband, "How was I to know that a few years later, I'd feel like I was fucking Helen Keller?")

In contrast to Heathcliff, Linton can speak and write to Cathy in the accepted and carefully embellished language of romance. He woos her with soft words and the promise of a good life. When asked whether she loves Linton, Cathy unhesitatingly replies, "Of course I do," and then rattles off the reasons why: "He is handsome and pleasant to be with . . . because he is young and cheerful . . . because he loves me . . . and he will be rich, and I shall like to be the greatest woman of the neighborhood, and I shall be proud of having such a husband." But, as Jane Austen cautioned her readers early in the 1800s, "a woman is not to marry a man merely because she is asked or because he is attached to her, and can write a tolerable letter." In effect, Austen is telling her readers that for the relationship to work, you must admire something in your potential spouse besides his good taste in choosing you.

Although Cathy, at twenty-two, can recite the proper catechism of romance in order to prove she should marry Linton, she is troubled by one thought: *not* that she will be *unhappy* in her marriage, but instead that she will be *too* happy. "I've no more business to marry Edgar Linton than to be in heaven." She associated having a good relationship with having a boring one, and for her the two become synonymous.

Cathy, we can see, fears that she will be bored by Linton's heaven since it will give her a constant sense of security and public worth. She associates intimacy with pain, and what Linton offers does not look like intimacy to her. She will no longer experience the roller-coaster ride of quickly shifting emotions she experienced with Heathcliff. In some way, then, Cathy would be more comfortable with unhappiness because at least it is familiar. Unhappiness is what she knows best. With a father who had "always been strict and grave with his children," with a drunk and abusive brother, living motherless in a desolate corner of Victorian England, Cathy was weaned on disappointment and fed on misery. With Heathcliff, whose soul is made from the same "stuff" as Cathy's, she knows she would be unhappy. There is something appealing in this guarantee of unhappiness, as odd as it might sound. Cathy longs for a high-tension relationship because it is the sort of relationship she best understands.

When she finally rejects the possibility of marrying Heathcliff, however, we should note that Cathy is not acting out of a desire for her own happiness but out of a sense of misguided pride. She rejects her childhood sweetheart simply because "it would degrade me to marry Heathcliff now." She is forced to choose between social standing and sexual longing. Cathy feels she must forfeit one desire for the other, and in terms of society's acceptance, indeed she must.

If Heathcliff represents the raw, to employ the terms presented by anthropologist Lévi-Strauss, then Linton represents the cooked. Heathcliff is destined by his very soul to be the lover; Linton, equally bound by his destiny, is the husband. In one telling scene, Brontë shows us a very young Cathy dividing her food and attention between a fierce guard dog that has attacked her but is now gently won over to her side, and a small indoor-pet dog that is equally affectionate. It is clear that the dogs represent the two men. This becomes especially clear when Cathy pinches the nose of the guard dog to hurt it slightly, but she still keeps it by her. So will Cathy and Heathcliff torment each other but be unable to separate.

"HAVING THEM BOTH"

Women's desire in *Wuthering Heights* is explicit and catalytic. Women speak their desire and act on it. Cathy can articulate quite clearly her attraction to Linton as well as to Heathcliff; some critics seem remarkably surprised by the very idea that she can desire two men simultaneously. Albert Guerard, in a preface to *Wuthering Heights*, suggests that "the oddity is that Cathy expects to 'have them both', finds this expectation entirely 'natural', and is enraged because neither Heathcliff nor Edgar [Linton] will consent to such a ménage à trois." It is, of course, not a ménage à trois that Cathy wants. In fact, women rarely fantasize about two men making love to them in the way that men are hooked on the fantasy of having two women in bed, a situation that appears in almost every issue of *Playboy* and *Penthouse*.

Instead, what she wants is *one* man who can be both lover and husband at the same time. She doesn't want two men; she wants one man who can meet all her needs. " 'I wish I were a girl again, half savage and hardy, and free . . . and laughing at injuries, not maddening under them!' " Cathy longs for the prelapsarian moment, the time before her fall into the world of romance, in order to escape from the decision of having to choose between the two men. She does believe, briefly, that she can have them both in her life.

When Linton protests that Heathcliff holds too important a position in his wife's affections, that he won't allow her to be "just friends" with him, Cathy asserts that "if I cannot keep Heathcliff for my friend, if Edgar will be mean and jealous, I'll try to break their hearts by breaking my own." This she does with alacrity. Cathy dies from her rage at being unable to find in one man characteristics of both the lover and the husband, but it is still essential to examine the fact that she did not hesitate to marry Linton when he proposed.

Brontë makes clear that Cathy was happy with Linton until Heathcliff returned in the role of a gentleman, having made money while he was abroad. Cathy was perfectly content with the "heaven" offered by her newly fashioned domestic sphere until Heathcliff appears at the door like a fallen angel in a good suit. He has made enough money to buy up several aristocratic drawing rooms, whether he cares to sit in them or not, but he still retains his "Otherness," his sexual and "outlaw" side. It is not so much that Heathcliff is diabolical himself, but rather that he brings out Cathy's wild side when she is with him.

Heathcliff always represented adventure and possibility for Cathy because she could seek them out in herself while in his company. He is a "carrier" of adventure the way someone might be a carrier of a certain gene. But it is these very things she has agreed to renounce in order to be a good wife.

REPLACING BUNGEE JUMPING WITH JUMP ROPE

So Cathy gives up Heathcliff for Linton as you might replace bungee jumping with jump rope. She marries for money, social position, and the promise of a cheerful spouse. It turns out, to everyone's surprise, that Heathcliff would indeed have made a good husband in at least two out of three of these fields (he will never be cheerful) since the intervening years provided enough polish to his rough exterior that he can now be permitted to eat inside the house.

Only after seeing Heathcliff as a potential husband does Cathy find her married life to Linton intolerable. When she believed Heathcliff was too far below her to marry, she was satisfied with her situation, but when Heathcliff appears as a potentially viable marriage partner (since he would no longer "degrade" his wife), Cathy dies from frustration and anger. Women were permitted to do that in tales of romance— perish from an inappropriate lack of love, waste away, or melt down in the referred heat of their rage at the loss of a romantic ideal.

Cynthia Heimel provides a useful summary of the romance heroine's plight in her 1983 collection of essays, *Sex Tips for Girls*. Heimel asserts that "back in say, 1807, heartbreak was treated with the respect it deserves. Women whose hearts were broken went into an immediate decline and spent months in bed having vinaigrette pressed to their noses and laudanum poured down their throats. Anxious relatives hovered about the heartbreak victim's bedside, hoping she wouldn't die. Sometimes she did." We can no longer throw ourselves after men. As Heimel puts it, "If you really want to be self-destructive, you can always become a heroin addict." One might say, too, that it is possible to become a "heroine" addict by mainlining too many romance novels.

WHY MR. RIGHT IS RARELY MR. RIGHT NOW

Brontë's heroine dies out of her fury at being unable to satisfy all her needs. It could be said that, like Mary Shelley's Dr. Frankenstein, Cathy wanted to make a perfect whole out of the parts of people. And it could be said that all forms of popular culture reinforce this sense of division, from soap operas to romance novels.

The queen mother of contemporary romance novels, Barbara Cartland, certainly subscribes to this division of men into classified groups. Cartland describes her heroes as "dark, handsome, and great sportsmen, but cynical and disillusioned. It is only the unique and perfect quality of the heroine which can wipe the mocking words from their lips and find that after all they have a heart." (Going back to Victor Seidler's explanation of the division between "reason-as-male" and "emotion-as-female," the awakening of the hero's stillborn emotional life means that he can discover the "feminine" part of himself and therefore risk making himself vulnerable, whereupon, no doubt, the Cartland heroine will no longer like him.) Cartland and many women prefer this image of the cool and distant lover to the image of the angelic, nice man. She makes her feelings clear when she writes that "most girls dream of falling in love with an angel but what would he be like? Weak, effeminate, eternally cluttered with a white nightgown." Barbara Cartland, like Cathy, seems to fear the boredom that heaven might provide.

And, ironically, there appears to be genuine risk in choosing the possibility of boredom in order to secure a placid existence if indeed a placid existence is what is simply prescribed instead of what is actually desired. Angels, like good intentions, might lead us in the wrong direction. In *The Waterfall*, contemporary British novelist Margaret Drabble offers chilling insight into the reasons why a smart, perceptive, and creative woman is conflicted over her decision to marry her "nice" suitor.

Drabble's words are unnerving because they cut so close to the heart of the matter for many women. Her first-person heroine writes:

> It is a curious business, marriage. Nobody seems to pay enough attention to its immense significance. Nobody seemed to think that in approaching the altar, garbed in white, I was walking toward unknown disaster of unforeseeable proportions: and so I tried to emulate—I emulated successfully—the world's fine, confident unconcern. Such an emulation had paid off so well on so many other alarming occasions (anesthesia, for instance, or diving off the top diving board, both events which, I was assured, despite a natural reluctant fear, would not harm me) that I was prepared to take the world's calm view of marriage too, distrusting and ignoring the forebodings that even then possessed me: in such a mood, assured that it is a normal event or a commonplace sacrifice, one might well lay one's head upon the block or jump from a high window.

Wanting to put as much distance as possible between her real passions, desires, intelligence, and creativity for fear of "overdoing" it, she chooses for a husband a man who is not her match—"because she had always believed that her passions, if revealed, would in some way scorch and blister and damage their object."

Yet she knows, more consciously than Cathy, that she needs passion and intensity, things she fears her husband will be unable to provide. Drabble's heroine dutifully attempts to gamble with, not against, the house even as she suspects that she might be placing a losing bet. "Did I marry because monogamy, cruel though it may be in its initial selection, seemed safer, more honorable, more innocent, than endless choice and endless realignment, in which the victims could merely lose more and more often, and the takers more often, more surely, take all . . . ?"

IN AVOIDING OUR FATE, WE RUSH TO MEET IT

Drabble's heroine marries, in short, because she looks for someone who will allow her to avoid her fate and provide a safe life for her: "I thought [while marrying], oddly enough, that I was denying myself tragedy, that I was choosing companionship and safety and dignity, and avoiding thus the bloody black denouement that I had been sure, as a girl, would be mine: the lyric note, I thought I had chosen . . . not those profound cries that I was later to hear issuing from my own throat in childbirth and abandon. Often, in jumping to avoid our fate, we rush to meet it: as Seneca said. It gets us in the end."

The central question remains: Should passion, an insecure emotion, be chosen over domesticity? Is the passionate heroine best linked to the quiet guy with whom she will settle down? It is no accident that generation after generation of readers and film audiences have been fascinated by the quandary of whether or not the heroine should love the nice guy. *His Girl Friday*, released in 1940 with Cary Grant, Rosalind Russell, and Ralph Bellamy, is widely regarded as one of the best movies ever made and it, too, posed the question. Ace reporter Hildy Johnson has to decide whether she should marry the insurance salesman from Albany (where she says she will settle down, "have babies and give them cod liver oil and watch their teeth grow") or stay with the ruthlessly charming and selfish newspaperman played by Cary

Grant. Audiences debate whether the heroine from *Broadcast News* should have gone with the sweet, vulnerable short guy or with the narcissistic, charming tall one. Does Cathy, finally, love her kind and generous husband, in addition to loving Heathcliff? Did she simply use Linton for her own purposes or was her relationship to him, in fact, a true portrait of affection's triumph over her simple obsession for Heathcliff?

OBSESSION VS. LOVE

The same questions asked about *Wuthering Heights* can and have been asked about the classic film *Casablanca*. The theme of *Casablanca* was even reframed in the seventies within a contemporary context in the Woody Allen film *Play It Again, Sam*: Can a woman love two men at the same time? Can she truly love both her husband and her lover? As we've seen, the thought that a man could love two women simultaneously appears more than slightly acceptable; a woman, in contrast, must "choose."

In *Casablanca*, a woman must choose between her outlaw former lover and her honorable, devoted husband. Ilsa (played by Ingrid Bergman) is drawn to the seeringly snide Rick (played by Humphrey Bogart) because she can see how deeply wounded he is and because he represents a raw, uncensored, and powerful sexuality despite—or perhaps because of—his pain. Her husband, Victor Lazlow (played by Paul Henreid), is a great leader of the underground movement against the Nazi party yet represents the sort of masculinity that appears in a completely different context from the one represented by Rick. Lazlow is a thoroughbred, an intellectual, a public hero. In contrast, Rick is unpredictable, smoothly cynical, and a street-smart loner.

I remember waiting on line to see that movie with a male friend once and saying that I couldn't understand how Ilsa could leave Rick and stay with a man she didn't love. I hadn't given my comment too much thought before making it, it was an offhand, standing-on-line remark, the kind of thing you say to fill up time. But I touched on a nerve I never knew my friend possessed. He was astonished. "You think she doesn't love Lazlow? Are you kidding? Look at her face when she watches him lead the singing of 'Le Marseilles' to drown out the Nazi bastards in the restaurant. She adores the man! She looks at him with complete passion. Of course she loves her husband. Maybe she wants to sleep with Rick, but she certainly loves Lazlow. You've got to see that!" I watched the scene carefully. My friend was right. Ingrid Bergman looks at Paul Henreid like a schoolgirl looking at a rock 'n' roll idol. She worships him. Maybe that is part of the problem. Maybe this husband, too, is slightly too good for the heroine's tastes.

Despite the fact that Ilsa reveals to Rick that she fell in love with her husband because he is a good man, because he was a father/teacher figure to her, there is more than intellectual passion at work in the relationship between Ilsa and Lazlow. Needless to say, it is easy to see that Ilsa loves Lazlow with her mind and her heart, and that her love for Rick is instinctive and electric, a current that suffuses her very skin. So why does Ilsa go off with her husband as he leaves Casablanca at the end of the film even though she has made the conscious decision to stay behind with her lover? Ilsa, remember, had decided that she wanted to stay with Rick. It was a painful choice, but she made her decision and so prepares to explain to her husband at the very last minute why it is impossible for them to resume their lives together.

Yet finally, and most significantly, it is not up to her at all. The men make the decision for her. They decide with whom she "belongs." Rick gives her to Lazlow at the airport like he was handing over a piece of American Tourister. Ilsa turns out to be portable property, emotional hand luggage, something to be given by one man to another man no matter what she wants for herself. It is Rick who decides that her place is by her husband's side, and leaves her no say in the matter. He gives her up for her own good, whether she wants to be given up or not.

In *The New Male*, psychologist Herb Goldberg presents the argument that when men make gestures such as Rick's, it is clear that they are doing it to meet their own needs, not the needs of the woman involved. Goldberg provides a useful illustration: "A former police chief of Los Angeles, noted for his 'macho' attitude, a man who liked to call himself the 'meanest man in town,' revealed in a recent interview: 'Men have the responsibility to protect women in the classical sense—to open the door of the car for ladies.' When the interviewer asked, 'You still think so today?' the former chief replied, 'I still do it. The heck with them if they don't want it.' "

BORING/SWEET VS. MEAN/ATTRACTIVE MEN

What are the implications? Men get the message that they are split into the boring/sweet guy or the attractive/mean guy, according to Warren Farrell in *Why Men Are the Way They Are*. Farrell declares that the great fear of many men is that "once a woman has her security needs met, she'll be off with someone else who is really exciting"— much as Linton might worry about Cathy's discarding him for Heathcliff, or Lazlow might worry about Ilsa leaving him for Rick.

Farrell contends that men get the message, "by the distance they feel when they are not exciting enough, or their rejection by women if they don't have their success act together—not rejection or distance from all women, but rather the women they are taught to want most—the women who have options."

For clarification, "the women who have options," as defined by Farrell, are conventionally beautiful women. He argues in his 1986 book that the sexual possession of a beautiful woman is the primary male fantasy, that a young woman with a beautiful face and body is the real thing that most men are brought up to desire. It is disappointing to hear this, but similar information comes from numerous sources. In a recent issue of *Glamour* magazine devoted to figuring out what men are up to in the 1990s, Eric Goodman had a short personal essay on "Men and Their Porn Pleasures." In it he admits that a "centerfold is sexual comfort food. In America, most males' first sexual experience involves pornography. Some men never get beyond it. Years later, we remember a Playmate's name. We recall, with a tightening in our throat, her airbrushed nipples. Until the average man moves in with a wife or lover, he's had more orgasms with a favored centerfold than with any single living woman."

Both Goodman and Farrell are, in their own ways, affirming what the "thirtysomething" men are saying, that women are objectified in terms of beauty. But Farrell's choice of words is fascinating. When I asked women what they think of when they hear the phrase "women who have options," they inevitably think of women who are successful at work, able to earn well, and those who are well-educated and able to move easily. They do not think of beautiful women as women with the most options. It seems to me an interesting difference in the gender-specific perception of the term.

Although she doesn't refer to them as "women with options," Cynthia Heimel does an excellent job of describing the type of woman Farrell frames as the object of desire. Heimel, in her 1991 collection of essays, *If You Can't Live Without Me, Why Aren't You Dead Yet?*, addresses these issues by confronting what she called "Professional Girls," who "exist solely in the mainstream of society. They've bought the whole cloth of traditional mores. In the deepest recesses of their souls, they firmly believe that men have been placed on this earth to take care of them. And they fully expect and want to be taken care of. Most of their actions are directly related to the goal of having someone else pay the bills."

In addition, Heimel makes an important distinction between "Amateur Girls" (what the women I talked to thought of as "women with options") and their "Professional" counterparts (what Farrell calls "women with options") by telling us that "Professional Girls are desperate for a boyfriend with a platinum Amex card. Amateur Girls are desperate for a boyfriend who can deliver a good punchline . . . Professional Girls want security. Amateur Girls want hot sex." And she acknowledges that "Other Amateur Girls and I have been saddened by the knowledge that most men what Professional Girls."

THE RELATIONSHIP OLYMPICS

In *The Men from the Boys: Rites of Passage in Male America*, cultural anthropologist Ray Raphael quotes a young man as saying what every Amateur Girl fears hearing. To prove his manhood, this individual competes in something like the Relationship Olympics whereby the number of women you sleep with and leave is in direct proportion to your masculinity. Here he discusses the arts of seduction:

It's an accomplishment I'm proud of, a track record, a hit-and-miss ratio, a statistic. It's a skill you get good at, like having a good batting average in baseball or like going to school and saying, "Yeah, I made straight A's." I take pride in that. I'm happy about it, but that's not really important. What's really important is that I haven't missed out on things, that I've had some really beautiful women. I don't have regrets like, "Gosh, I wish I had this one there." Some guys I know have never had a beautiful woman, but I've been through all types of women.

Despite the fact that by saying he has "been through" all types of women he makes himself sound like some kind of emotional Drano, this man is living the fantasy that men are handed as boys. He has decided to sleep with as many women, preferably beautiful women, as possible in order to make himself believe in his own worth.

Men also learn to distance themselves from their emotions, in part so that they can remain invulnerable to women. A really lovable male friend from my college days clued me in to what appears to be a significant trend when he said his latest girlfriend had broken off their relationship because she felt she wasn't being "challenged" by him. "She told me that everyone described me as 'sweet,' but that while sweet was something a man should be, it shouldn't be the primary thing he is. What I am supposed to do, spit a lot? Belch? Yell? Kill small unarmed animals during hunting season? How do I stop being sweet?" When he expressed his feelings, so to speak, he was judged as inadequate. You can be certain that, in his next relationship, he was as tight-lipped and reserved as he could be. "Men who cherish for women the highest respect are seldom popular," wrote Joseph Addison several hundred years ago. Is the same still true today? Women can, indeed, fear commitment and flee from the confinements of an intense relationship. Unhappily, they will often flee to the reluctant arms of a man less devoted and less intense, which will make everyone miserable.

This fear that an honest, straightforward, nice man will lose to his more evasive, sneaky, and selfish rival is grounded not only in personal experiences but in literature and popular culture as well. In endless soap operas, we have two male characters offered to the viewers as possible love objects. The cute, compact, nice guy is always around to marry the girl who gets into trouble and to offer a shoulder for female characters to cry on. He's the "best friend" type, and only the youngest viewers—those under thirteen—will write into the network for a signed photograph of this character. On the other hand, there is the inevitable thug with the eye-patch. Mr. Eye-Patch is played by the actor with broad shoulders, prominent thighs, and a bass voice. He's sexy, he's gutsy, he's dangerous, and he's disdainful of everyone around him. So what's the result of all these problems? Female characters, pre- and postmenopausal, fling themselves at this guy's feet like he's got money in this socks. He certainly isn't loved because he's successful—these guys are always on the run because they're being chased for some crime they didn't commit—but because he's an outlaw. He's not the man you want your daughter to run away with, but you might just want to run away with him yourself.

Is it only aloof, disdainful, and slightly evil men who attract women? Do women think of men as either wimps or tyrants, the way that men think of women as either madonnas or whores? Are women's categories for men as blind and unbending as we have always declared that men's categories for women have been? Are women's fantasies dangerous?

Women, of course, have not gone out to rape or commit other acts of violence against men after reading romantic novels or watching sexy movies and this is just one way in which fantasy for women differs from some hard-core fantasy literature and films for men. (When I say "fantasy," I'm not referring to Dungeons and Dragons but to *Debbie Does Dallas*.) Nevertheless, women as well as men must recognize that any fetishization of a trait—breasts, buttocks, height, or financial acumen—is unhealthy. Women are as responsible for these confining images of men as men are responsible for airbrushed and navel-stapled visions of women. Consider, again, the "wisdom" imparted to millions of devoted readers by Barbara Cartland when she says that "women have always been fascinated by abduction by a brutal, determined villain who, of course, eventually is reformed by love." This is the fear of every man who wants to express his vulnerability: He will not be sexually attractive because he is not a brute or a villain, or sufficiently "above" the object of his affections.

While relationships between men and women have indeed changed in the last fifty years or so, perhaps they have not yet changed as much as they will—or should. One thing is certain: We can still see the undercurrents of this dichotomy, this split, between the figure of the "husband" and the "real man" shaping plots in such recent films as *Moonstruck*, which was released in 1987.

The older brother in this movie is perfect "husband material"; he is stable, domestic, and predictable. His personality is in direct contrast with that of his younger brother, who is tormented, volatile, and sexual in nature. The character played by Cher becomes engaged to the older brother—for whom she already shops and cooks—because she figures she can do no better at her age and because generally she has had "bad luck with men." Cher's character feels it is best to settle for what British psychologist Donald Winnicott might have called a "good enough" marriage, or what I call the "perfectly good husband." When her mother asks whether she loves her fiancé, she replies, "No," to which her mother replies, "Good. When you love them they drive you crazy."

Our general preoccupation with the draw of the exotic, however, still cannot be fully eclipsed by the promises of the domestic. The lover is the exotic figure, the "real man" who is undiluted by the feminine in culture. The younger brother in the movie is, at first glance, not good husband material because he is wolfish in his appetites, his rage, and his desire for freedom. Yet these are the very elements that cause him to be desirable; these are the elements that, although they may well cause her pain, seem to force the main character to forgo security for romance. He will remain a man even within the context of the relationship, the narration implies, while the older brother will immediately become soft around the edges.

CHAPTER NINE

HAVING MORE
THAN YOU SHOW

The Trials and Rewards of Independence

To LIVE WITH a man to whom you are not truly vulnerable emotionally appears to offer a balance to the power the husband will exercise in all other aspects of married life. To be vulnerable emotionally to a man offers him your private life as well as your public one; it is best, according to some women's mythologies, to keep something to yourself.

Perhaps you know stories of women who, while financially dependent on their husbands, nevertheless squirreled away hundreds, even thousands of dollars, by skimming small amounts of money off their usual "allowance" for household costs. I had an aunt who could have bought a Ferrari on what she managed to "put away." She didn't see this as cheating her husband or family, but instead she regarded it as prudent. It made her feel safe; it made her feel like she was ready for an emergency or a "rainy day."

Sometimes this desire for private information can include the serious secrets of an affair or an undisclosed sexual history. But it can also encompass seemingly harmless everyday secrets, like not admitting exactly how much a purchase actually cost, saying it was on sale when it wasn't, explaining it was a gift when it wasn't, or saying a dress had been hanging in the closet for months rather than admitting it was bought that day. These "white lies" offer some women an emotional buffer zone from their husbands that enables them to feel more in control. She ciphers out of the relationship anything she feels will not be missed. She appears to be a "team player," while refusing to pool her resources. She comes to mistake her "withholding" for genuine independence. Such a pattern of even minor deceits offers, however, only a dangerous method of securing a sham form of independence.

SELF-STORAGE

Some women go through similar motions in terms of their emotional lives: keeping feelings of happiness or sadness, shame or guilt, pleasure or joy to themselves in order to keep something back from their husbands. They create a version of an emotional Independent Retirement Account; they believe that their husbands don't need to know everything about them. In fact, the less they know, the better off everyone will be. These women put their genuine wishes and dreams into a form of "self-storage" in order to keep them free from the contamination of the everyday.

Years ago, women were often counseled to avoid emotional dependence since financial dependence, for example, was assumed. If we could hold something back for ourselves, we could retain a small measure of autonomy—although nobody would have thought of it in those terms. It was a way women found to subvert the authority they felt they had to hand over to their husbands. It also permitted them a form of breathing room. And, perhaps most important, it provided insulation against the pain that someone you loved deeply would be capable of inflicting.

Such a pattern for behavior often derived from the experience of pain. In Zora Neale Hurston's novel *Their Eyes Were Watching God*, much of which is written in dialect, we hear a grandmother advise her granddaughter not to fall in love since "dat's de very prong all us black women gits hung on. Dis love! Dat's just whut's got us pullin' and uh haulin' and sweatin' and doin' from can't see in the morning 'till can't see at night." The heroine nevertheless marries a man she thinks she loves, only to be hurt by his bullying and contempt. In order to keep the relationship intact (until she can somehow escape it), she learns to insulate herself against the pain her husband causes her. Something "falls off the shelf" inside her after he humiliates her on one occasion too many, and so "gradually, she pressed her teeth together and learned to hush. The spirit of the marriage left the bedroom and took to living in the parlor. It was there to shake hands whenever company come to visit, but it never went back inside the bedroom again . . . The bed . . . was a place where she went and laid down when she was sleepy and tired." The idea that "the spirit of the marriage . . . took to living in the parlor" is a phrase that brilliantly sums up the way passion dissolves into mere politeness for some women who learn to distance themselves from their husbands in order to keep their self-respect. They might well go through the motions of lovemaking or dutiful wifeliness, but the sense of enthusiasm that once informed these gestures is gone and the experiences become hollow. Often the saddest aspect of this for many women is that their husbands seem not to notice any difference.

Hurston's story is the story of many women's marriages: The fear of being hurt cocoons women into an emotional ball of wool that prevents them from feeling deeply. They do not wish to risk being open to anyone, and so they shut down. They return to and learn to believe in the advice they heard from women like the grandmother in Hurston's book: Better for a woman not to be in love with her husband because she'll only be hurt.

FEAR OF DEPENDENCE

No wonder, too, that it seems wise to marry a man you don't love in order to preserve your dignity and self-esteem. This sort of caveat maintains that the less someone knows about your inner life, the fewer emotions you invest in a relationship, the better off you will be.

We saw some friends marry men who seemed odd, sometimes desperate choices, although we never referred to them that way. We'd say things like "Do you really think he's 'enough' for her?" or "How did *she* end up with someone like *him?*" and although we couldn't put our finger on it, we suspected and worried that these relationships wouldn't work.

THE "SECOND-CHOICE HUSBAND"

If a woman has been hurt, if she has experienced abandonment or loss, she might be driven to find a new man whom she believes will never leave her. Psychologists refer to the man in this arrangement as a "second-choice husband." The "second-choice husband" is a sort of consolation prize awarded to—or seized by—a woman who cannot win, or for one who walks away from, the man she truly or originally desired. The second-choice husband is a stand-in, a substitution for the "real thing."

"In this pattern," explain researchers, "the wife lived an adventurous, sexually free life while single. Then, for some reason, perhaps pregnancy or an unhappy love affair, she lowers her sights to select a sturdy, responsible, dependable husband, who is probably thought physically unattractive." She will therefore choose a man who is less than attractive or less than charming in order to feel as if he couldn't "do better" than her. This quiet, passive, and usually kind man is expected to stick around since everyone knows he doesn't really "deserve" his attractive, vibrant, and lively wife. The marriage is based on her acceptance of this man as a sort of talisman against pain. He will never leave her. He will always feel lucky to have such a woman by his side.

Scarlett O'Hara's first marriage to Charles Hamilton in *Gone With the Wind* is the paradigm of a woman's deciding to marry a "second-choice husband." Scarlett's behavior fits the pattern described above perfectly. Scarlett, the impetuous, impatient, and passionate young woman, has just declared her undying love to longtime family friend Ashley Wilkes. Wilkes, a gentleman of the old school, knows that he and Scarlett are mismatched, however attracted to each other they may be. Ashley gently explains to Scarlett that he is engaged to Melanie, and they must never speak of love again. Scarlett, infuriated, slaps Ashley, and smashes a piece of china against a wall. She runs out of the room and accepts Charles Hamilton's proposal of marriage.

Author Margaret Mitchell makes it clear that Scarlett is in no way attracted to Charles Hamilton, whom she considers unworthy of even the usual run-of-the-mill teasing. Instead, Scarlett wants to prove a point to herself and to everyone around her by marrying immediately after being rejected by the man of her dreams. Scarlett tells herself, "And if I married [Charles Hamilton] right away, it would show Ashley that I didn't care a rap—that I was only flirting with him." Wanting to reassure herself of her attractiveness, and longing for both self-control and revenge, Scarlett regards her future husband with calculated clarity, with a "coolness" that indicates her unwillingness to make herself vulnerable emotionally. "A frost lay over all her emotions and she thought that she would never feel anything warmly again," Mitchell tells us. Upon leaving Ashley, Scarlett considers the proposal from wealthy, unencumbered Hamilton (who is about to leave for the war anyway), and thinks, "Why not take this pretty, flushed boy? He was as good as anyone and she didn't care. No, she could never care for anything again, not if she lived to be ninety." Of course, we know that Scarlett is misjudging herself here, and lives to regret her marriage. In this, too, she is like many women who decide to marry a "second-choice husband."

According to researchers, the strategy often backfires. "The wife is pretty, impulsive, competitive with other women, and not very sexually interested in her husband," argue psychologists. When one partner is more attractive or sexually motivated than another, obviously the relationship becomes unstable. The woman who makes such a choice is hedging her bets, and basing her choice on fear, not love. She will come to resent her mate, and heap upon him her own feelings of inadequacy, self-punishment, and rage. Resentment will, in some cases, turn not only into contempt, but into hatred.

"On Women Who Hate Their Husbands," a paper originally read at the New Orleans Psychoanalytic Society, dealt with the phenomenon of women who married in order to "play it safe." Discussing patients

who married "second-choice husbands," Dr. David Freedman argued
that in each case the woman's "choice of mate had been based on the
specific defect of her own ego system implied by her inability to see
herself as a person of sufficient potential significance and ability to
hold a man she really admired." In effect, the women in question
believed that they were not worthy of fully desirable husbands, and so
chose mildly undesirable men instead. "She had chosen someone who
combined the contradictory, but for her safe, qualities of substantial
but not outstanding ability in his own professional sphere, and a
passive, dependent, and placatory orientation to the significant
female in his life." But this proved to make such women dreadfully
unhappy because "rather than satisfying, the relationship proved inevitably to be fraught with anxiety and frustration."

I knew one woman who, having resigned herself to marrying a
"second-choice husband," then made a career out of belittling any sign
of happiness between two other people. "Those love-birds are headed
for a fall," she'd cluck over any new couple, palpably longing for
disaster. She couldn't *stand* the idea that anyone might actually have a
relationship based on passion, fun, or even simply the promise of an
equal match between the partners. When her daughter wanted to
marry an interesting, handsome, and devoted man, this woman was
torn. She wanted her daughter to be happy, of course. But, on some
level, she was also tormented by seeing her own compromised and
diluted life pale in comparison to the promise held by her daughter's
union. If this was playing it safe, I thought to myself, I can't abide the
payoff.

This woman banked on the idea that her husband, short and portly
as a Dickens character, would never appeal to another woman. In
American Couples, Blumstein and Schwartz assert that "when it comes
to physical appearance, a fairly equal balance between partners seems
to be the best and most salutary arrangement." Not only might the less
attractive partner become increasingly possessive or territorial, but the
more attractive partner will lose the position of power in the relationship should he or she, for any reason, change his or her appearance.
So, too, might the once-passive husband decide not to "take it"
anymore, and find a woman who will indeed believe him to be a
first-choice rather than someone who is second-best. To marry a man

simply because he seems a "safe bet" is cheating: It cheats the woman out of actually working toward a real understanding of herself and what she needs, and it cheats a man out of being the real love object for a woman who believes he is truly desirable.

PLAYING HARD TO GET

When I was in my early twenties an older friend told me, "Always have more than you show, and that goes for love as well as for money." So much for the wisdom of the song "Tell Him," I thought. It was a revelation of sorts, this idea that the most effective strategy was to hide your emotions rather than display them. This advice, however, clearly echoed that which we had all heard in the maternal voice at one point or another: "Play hard to get."

"Play hard to get" was the standard-issue piece of advice handed out to girls along with their first tampon. The instructions for one were as perplexing as the instructions for the other. Remember what the little insert in the tampon box said? It went something like "Raise your left leg up over your right shoulder and bend forward while remaining upright and move your hand to the left—whatever is more comfortable and natural for you." That was the line that always got me— "whatever is more comfortable and natural for you"—because surely these contortions could never be either comfortable or natural to anyone. We all learned how to do it, however, and many of us also learned the contortions behind "playing hard to get."

Now, the trick with playing hard to get was that you had to seem to stay as far away from the boys you liked as the ones you didn't like—the more distant you were, everyone promised, the more they liked you. (Remember Jack Nicholson's line in *Carnal Knowledge*, "I'd almost marry you if you left me"?). We heard very much the same things as adults. We read Proust and learned that "an absence, the decline of a dinner invitation, an unintentional coldness, can accomplish more than all the cosmetics in the world." We heard from La Bruyere that "women grow attached to men through the favors they grant them; but men, through the same favors, are cured of their love." From a book called *Reading for Men* (which I can't help thinking sounds a little like "Bowling for Dollars"), there is a line that reads, "All girls will haggle like secondhand car dealers and expect a run for their money . . . Naturally an attitude of refusal can only make an object more desirable and, in this way, she contributes to your fuller pleasure ultimately." Refusal and denial were the most potent aphrodisiacs. Obviously men threw themselves at women who could walk away.

We read Anita Brookner's chilling dialogue in *The Debut*. "Now, for God's sake, Ruth, don't make a mess of this. Don't give in too easily," counsels a married friend of the heroine. "String him along. Take another lover. Keep him guessing. Break the odd appointment. How on earth do you think I got Brian after all these years?" The heroine asks sadly, "Is it all a game, then?" to which her friend sadly replies, "Only if you win. If you lose, it's far more serious." This is not just the "unrealistic" stuff of novels, however. We hear from the researchers behind *Marriage: Myth and Institution* that "how valuable a woman is as a love object to a man depends to a considerable extent on her apparent popularity with other men . . . A woman who readily gives proof of her affection to a man, therefore, provides presumptive evidence of her lack of popularity and thus tends to depreciate the value of her affect for him . . . To safeguard the value of her affection, a woman must be ungenerous in expressing it and make any evidence of her growing love a cherished prize that cannot easily be won." We heard it from research psychologists and then from popular psychologists—it's as if these men were on our mothers' payrolls, reiterating their advice.

When, for example, we bought *Smart Women, Foolish Choices* we were advised in no uncertain terms that "hard to get" was the way to go: "Your first step is to understand and master an important psychological law that smart women know—partial reinforcement. Partial reinforcement means rewarding a person for certain behavior some of the time but not all the time. If a laboratory rat is rewarded with a feed pellet every time he presses a bar, he will work quite hard. But he will work much harder at bar pressing if he is rewarded only at odd intervals." Many of us gulped at the equation of our dates with laboratory rats; even if they disappointed us in some ways, it seemed a pretty harsh comparison. But good doctors Cowan and Kinder pressed the point home by suggesting that the man in question "un-certainty also works with men. For example, a woman who breaks dates with a man a couple of times or comes home late and is slightly vague will drive him absolutely nuts. The uncertainty it stimulates in him would motivate him to reembark on romantic ventures."

Either that, of course, or he'll think you're a dishonest, man-ipulative, and controlling shrew and, unless he's insane or a maso-chist, he'll ignore you altogether. If he ignored you, you told yourself it was his loss. ("It's his loss," your friends would chorus. "He'll be sorry." "He was never good enough for you." "You're much better off without him." "Better to find out now than later.") If you were honest and open, then you were leaving yourself vulnerable.

A "GOOD ENOUGH" MAN?

Many women feel as if they have been told to reeducate themselves into being more accepting of men, and they resist this advice. As one of Terry McMillan's heroines explains in *Waiting to Exhale*, "Here I am all of thirty-six years old without so much as a prospect in sight; and on top of it, [a friend] said my swinging-singles life style doesn't amount to shit, that I run the gamut when it comes to stereotypes of buppiedom because I put too much energy into my career, that without a husband and children my life has no meaning . . . Sheila said I'm too choosy, that my standards are too high, and because they seem to be non-negotiable, she swears up and down that if I don't loosen up, the only person who'll ever meet my qualifications is God." What are her extraordinary qualifications for a man? "I just hope he's socialized, moderately charming, halfway articulate, and doesn't spend half the night trying to convince me how he got so goddamn wonderful." Some women learned to desensitize their instincts, to disassociate what they wanted from what they got, to numb their feelings, to the extent that they can't tell who they really like from who they don't like.

The upshot of this explains why a perfectly reasonable woman can be found at a café near her office at 8 P.M. wondering whether she should telephone the moody Russian artist who wants to move to L.A.

or, instead, call the newly divorced guy in her brother-in-law's bowling league. Deciding which man *she* wants to see appears at such a moment not as an awesome crossroad in her life but rather as an effort to decide which one of the men will want to hear from *her*. It is a situation in which many an otherwise sensible woman has lost her dignity, and no wonder. It's hard to keep your dignity when you've just decided to hang up if a woman answers.

But in such an arrangement, everybody loses. It's like a party game from hell: You try to compete with your potential partner to see who can be most detached, most uncaring, and most unavailable. You say you're busy when you're not, and let the answering machine pick up even when you're in so that he won't know that you're in and actually waiting for his call. Then you play the taped message he left over and over again, searching for hidden meanings in the phrase "I'll call you after eleven" as if you were deciphering the Dead Sea Scrolls. You call a girlfriend up and play his message to see what she thinks "I'll call you after eleven" really means. She tells you that it means he's having dinner with another woman and you should drop him. Or she tells you that you should have better things to do than play forty-second-long messages over and over again; don't you remember what happened when you saved your old boyfriend's last message for two months before getting up the strength to erase it—you promised that no such thing would ever happen again?

You call a male friend and he tells you that, given the fact that the caller didn't know you were playing the Girl from U.N.C.L.E. and spying on your own apartment while you were only pretending to be out, the caller no doubt meant to suggest that he would once again try telephoning after 11 P.M., Eastern Standard Time. To him it isn't a mystery. To anyone who actually knows better than to put herself through these paces, no doubt this seems like a farce. To the dozens upon dozens of women with whom I've discussed this phenomenon and who recognize it, this seems like the familiar and nearly unutterably embarrassing nightmare it really is. But apparently there is a reason some of us do this to ourselves, and it is called "The Principle of Least Interest." And for those of us who can only be "all-interest" or "no-interest" types, "least interest" can rarely be achieved; it can only be mimicked.

THE PRINCIPLE OF LEAST INTEREST

We pretend we're less involved or invested in a relationship than we are because we're trying to protect ourselves. Men talk about all the deals they have in the works that will take them to Tokyo and Munich not because they want to run away, necessarily, but because they want you to think that they're not wimpy home-boys. Women act aloof or disdainful not because they don't like men but because they're afraid of appearing to like them too much. Imagine a room full of hungry people at a banquet who won't sit down to eat because they're afraid that once they take their places, the food will immediately disappear. No one wants to look foolish, but we're like anorexics who starve themselves in the presence of sustenance because they are terrified of giving into what they believe to be the oceanic nature of their desires.

The reflex to protect oneself by remaining uninvolved draws heavily on the received wisdom that, as an old French proverb has it, "In a relationship there is always one who kisses, and one who offers the cheek." Who is the more powerful? The one who offers the cheek— the one who receives rather than initiates affection—is in ascendancy because he or she is less involved and therefore less invested in the outcome.

In *American Couples*, the writers delineate the connections between power, need, desire, and exclusive affection. "Power is the ability to enforce one's will even over the objections of others," explain Blumstein and Schwartz, who go on to claim that

> the less "needy" a person is, the more power he or she has. This was recognized more than forty years ago by sociologist Willard Waller, who wrote about the "principle of less interest." According to this principle, the person who loves less in a relationship has the upper hand because the other person will work harder and suffer more rather than let the relationship break up. This partner's greater commitment hands power to the person who cares less. When we evaluated our interview data, it seemed to us that when a partner was the less committed person, he or she was also more likely to be non-monogamous.

No wonder that many mothers want their daughters to remain free from the possible devastation of love; no wonder women were always counseled to be the aloof ones who "offered the cheek" rather than the needy ones offering the kiss.

"THEN THEY HATE YOU . . ."

What happens if you don't play hard to get? Then you risk feeling like the protagonist of Dorothy Parker's immortal short story "A Telephone Call," a monologue that should be included with every telephone bill (along with an option for "Call Thwarting," a mechanism that would automatically stop weepy calls made to men's apartments after 11 P.M.). Parker's unnamed character is waiting for the Call from the man she's been seeing. Although she is incredibly upset about the fact that he didn't ring when he said he would, she realizes that she can't let him know this because "they don't like you to tell them they've made you cry. They don't like you to tell them you're unhappy because of them. If you do, they think you're possessive and exacting. And then they hate you." We imagine her pausing for a deep breath, and then continuing, "They hate you whenever you say anything you really think. You always have to keep playing little games. Oh, I thought we didn't have to; I thought this was so big I could say whatever I meant. I guess you can't, ever, I guess there isn't ever anything big enough for that." The call has not yet come at the story's end, and she resumes counting to five hundred by fives.

DESIRING THE MAN

"The man's desire is for the woman; but the woman's desire is rarely other than for the desire of the man," wrote Coleridge. Most of us have been through the self-destruct cycle at least once or twice. We fall in love with a totally unsuitable man simply because he is unavailable, not in spite of the fact but *because* he is out of reach. It seems as if we love him for his faults rather than despite them. We adore him because he's one man we feel we can hardly hope to interest. We ignore the men who are interested in us in order to focus on the ones who aren't, much as Scarlett O'Hara ignored Rhett Butler to pursue Ashley Wilkes.

"Many women are taught by this culture to look for a man who will provide them with an identity," explains therapist Dr. Cynthia Adams, coauthor of *When Food Is a Four Letter Word* and a psychologist who specializes in marriage and family issues. She goes on to point out that "for these women, marriage allows them to form an identity which depends on their husbands' positions in the world rather than on who they are themselves. Obviously, the more prominent and elevated a man, the more difficult it is to secure his recognition so there is greater triumph in winning his affections. This gives women, especially insecure women, a sense that they are somebody. It's as if they are invisible until a man looks in their direction."

Many an administrative assistant sighs after the man giving her the assignments. Many a patient longs for a more personal relationship with her handsome—or not so handsome—shrink. (I remember telling a friend that I was relieved to find my therapist unattractive, a bulky man with thin lips. "Yeah," she said, "give it three months and you'll be talking about how terribly *adorable* his thin lips are.") But most women can recognize, after a certain point in the fantasy, that these relationships will not necessarily yield the real-life romance they're looking for. In many cases, the woman will eventually turn her affections to more realistic visions: the guy sitting next to her in class, the man working beside her in the office, a man who will listen to her without presenting a bill to send to Blue Cross. But some of us have trouble adjusting our sights to those more realistic visions and continue, often to our discomfort and disillusion, to want what we can't have. We get hooked on the fantasy and that takes up all the emotional time and space we have to offer so that, finally, we're left to hug our pillows at night instead of wishing a real live person lying next to us sweet dreams. Clearly, we're back to the idea of romance as a fetish, as a substitute for the real relationship, with marriage as a substitute for living one's own life.

WISHING FOR WHAT IS OUT OF REACH

The wish for what is out of reach seems to be a legacy from our first mother, Eve. Talk about eating disorders: Told that she could consume anything but the apple, it was the only food she craved. When you're on a no-starch diet, only pasta and bread look appealing. When you can't eat sugar, only candy bars call out to you from grocery store checkout lines. Enlarging on this theme, it is clear that when you're on a long business trip, you dream about sleeping in your own bed, but when you're stuck at home, you imagine the luxuries of a night in a hotel. When you're with your sweet, stable boyfriend, you long for a Lothario, and when you're hooked on a flirt, you long for the man who sits happily by the fireside. It's not so much that we don't want what we already have, but that what remains elusive appears to retain all its illusions and glamour. This is the same principle that dictates that the other line will always move faster than the one you're on, or that the woman going into the dressing room directly before you has the last sale dress in your size. What you have just missed looks better, generally, than what you just managed to get.

I, for one, fell in love with nearly every male teacher I ever had from seventh grade onward. They had a magical quality of being both available and distant at the same time. They were taboo—or should have been—since there was a sort of "intellectual" incest at work. Of course I did twice as well in their classes as in any others because I jumped through every hoop to get their attention. Nothing inspires like the desire for recognition from an opposite-sex authority figure who rarely pays attention to anyone. It provides a rush of excitement, of validation, and, most important, a sense of power. "He knows who I am!" you hooray in your head. "He knows my name even though he doesn't know anyone else! This means I'm really special." Remember, power is in proportion to the ability to give and withhold at will. It should come as no surprise, then, to hear that we learn to value masculine attention as children because it seems scarce, and because we learn early on to value what is scarce.

FALLING FOR "THE BOSS"

I wish I was only talking about falling in love with Bruce Springsteen here, since that is perfectly understandable and needs no explanation for most women. But the far more destructive habit of falling in love with bosses, teachers, priests, or any man who seems both far above you and out of reach is dangerous because you are likely to have fallen in love with the *idea* of the man rather than the man himself. If you're drawn to someone on the podium or behind the big desk and relying, metaphorically, on the furniture rather than the man, he's inevitably going to be disappointing once you see him in his socks and shorts stepping into your bathroom to brush his teeth. He's going to lose the glamour that kept you enthralled the first time he farts in bed. If you rely on someone's status to make him into a "real man," the first time that status is undermined (when a waiter raises an eyebrow at his mispronunciation of an item on the menu, or the first time he whines because he's too tired to go out and make a good impression on your friends) he's at risk of losing the very aspect that appealed to you most.

Fay Weldon offers an excellent example of a relationship along these lines her short story "Ind. Aff., or Falling Out of Love in Sarajevo." When the twenty-five-year-old unnamed narrator falls in love with her forty-six-year-old professor (who is already married and the father of three children), she falls in love with her idealized vision of him rather than falling in love with him as a man. The narrator, who tells her story from the perspective of one who has learned her lesson and is now simply imparting it, has come to understand that she confused "mere passing academic ambition with love," believing this man's assessment of the world and of herself ("He said I had a good mind but not a first class mind and somehow I didn't take it as an insult") when she should have been coming up with her own conclusions.

Weldon comments, in another story concerned with a young woman's infatuation with a much older man, that "it was not her desire that was stirred, it was her imagination. But how is she to know this?" She has to concentrate on how much of life he has seen in order to justify her love for him. She has to frame him a certain way, cropping the picture of him in her mind so as to mask the unattractive qualities, in order to feel a sense of desire. What the narrator wishes to believe about her lover—that this is "not just any old professor-student romance"—and what she actually feels about him are two different things.

In "Ind. Aff.," Peter Piper is a Cambridge professor who has been married to a swimming coach for twenty-four years. He likes to "luxuriate in guilt and indecision," and has taken his student mistress with him on a holiday to see whether they are "really, truly suited," to make sure that it is "the Real Thing" before they "shack up, as he put it." The narrator is desperately drawn to her teacher even though he represents much more than he actually offers. To maintain her affection for Peter, she overlooks his stinginess ("Peter felt it was less confusing if we each paid our own way"), his whining ("I noticed I had become used to his complaining. I supposed that when you had been married a little you simply wouldn't hear it"), the fact that often when she spoke "he wasn't listening," the fact that he might not want her to go topless at the beach ("this might be the area where age differences showed"), as well as overlooking his "thinning hair" because he seems authoritative (speaking in "quasi-Serbo-Croatian") and powerful. He "liked to be asked questions," and obviously adores the adoration of his student. She loves him with "Inordinate Affection," she claims. "Your Ind Aff is my wife's sorrow," Peter moans, blaming this girl, who was born the first year of his marriage, for his wife's unhappiness, thereby absolving himself of any blame.

The question of whether particular events happen because of the inevitable buildup of insurmountable forces or, instead, because of a series of particular moments that might have been avoided with care, caution, or consideration is brought to bear not only on the narrator's relationship with Peter but on the question of World War I. With the background material effortlessly supplied by Weldon, even readers unfamiliar with the story of the assassination of the archduke will be able to see the way the assassin's tale parallels that of the narrator. Was the war inevitable? Was it, as Peter Piper claimed, bound to "start sooner or later," because of the "social and economic tensions" that had to find "some release"? Along the same lines of reasoning, was the twenty-four-year marriage between Peter and the woman who is known only as Mrs. Piper doomed to failure, or was it instead pressured into failure by the husband's infidelity? Was it, as the narrator's sister Clare (herself married to a much older professor) claims, a fact that "if you can unhinge a marriage, it's ripe for unhinging, it would happen sooner or later, it might as well be you"? Is it, in other words, the narrator who is assassinating the Piper marriage?

The climax of the story occurs when the narrator and Peter are waiting to be served wild boar in a private restaurant. She notices a waiter whom she describes as "about my age" (showing her keenly felt awareness of the difference in age between herself and Peter). She has felt desire for Peter in her mind, and has learned to feel "a pain in the heart" as an "erotic sensation," but in looking at the virile, handsome man her own age, she feels "quite violently, an associated yet different pang which got my lower stomach." She describes this desire as the "true, the real pain of Ind Aff!" Her desire for the waiter has nothing to do with his position, his authority, or his power. It has to do with his "flashing eyes, hooked nose, luxuriant black hair, sensuous mouth." She thinks to herself in a moment of clear vision, "What was I doing with this man with thinning hair?" She thinks to herself, when she automatically tells Peter that she loves him, "how much I lied." She has freed herself from the confines of his authority, and declares in opposition to his theory that "if Princip hadn't shot the archduke, something else, some undisclosed, unsuspected variable, might have come along and defused the whole political/military situation, and neither World War I nor II would ever have happened." She then gets up to go "home."

"This is how I fell out of love with my professor," declares the narrator, describing their affair as "a silly, sad episode, which I regret." She sees herself as silly for having confused her career ambitions with desire, and silly for trying to "outdo my sister Clare," who had married her professor (but has to live in Brussels as a sort of cosmic penance). Piper eventually proved spiteful and tried to refuse the narrator's thesis, but she won her appeal and, delightfully, can confirm for herself that she does indeed have a "first-class mind" after all. She feels, finally, a connection to poor Princip, who should have "hung on a bit, there in Sarajevo" because he might have "come to his senses. People do, sometimes quite quickly." In many ways, the heroine's ability to distinguish between the erotics of power and the true erotics of sexual attraction resembles the way a spell is broken in a fairy tale. The heroine wakes as if out of a deep sleep to see what is really going on around her. She can then get on with her life, having left the spell of power behind her.

FALLING FOR THE MARRIED MAN

One of the ultimate ways for a woman to torment herself emotionally with a man who is out of reach is to fall in love with a married man. There is the paradoxical appeal of the already-married man. In *The Seven Year Itch*, Marilyn Monroe smiles as she explains to her entranced neighbor, "I wouldn't be lying on some man's floor in the middle of the night drinking champagne if he wasn't married." Monroe's character feels "safe" with the married man, since nothing can get "drastic" and since, as she explains, a married man can't possibly ask you to marry him. For the woman who wants a man who'll stay out of reach, nothing could be more perfect.

UNFAITHFULLY YOURS

As one friend of mine put it, one of the sexiest things a man can say during an amorous overture to another woman is, "I'm really a very good husband," even as he is about to disprove that theory. If he were a good husband, he wouldn't be trying to get another woman into bed, after all. Ditto for the line "I love my wife, but I'm not *in* love with her." If the number of people who have heard (or said) that line were laid end to end, I wouldn't be a bit surprised. "I love my wife, but I'm not *in* love with her" usually translates into the following: "I'm attracted to you sexually and would like to begin a relationship. But you must understand that our affair—and make no mistake about it, it will be an affair and not the beginning of a primary relationship—will have to remain clandestine, be short-termed, and run completely according to my schedule. Okay?"

"I love my wife, but I'm not *in* love with her" means that the man involved will almost inevitably see himself as a victim of his passions. Since he regards himself as the one upon whom demands are made, rather than as a man making impossible demands on two women, he will almost inevitably be unable to make himself or either of his partners happy. He'll feel sorry for himself and feel defiant about his right to say "no" to either woman when he wishes—when he starts to feel guilty or nervous, for example. He will feel put upon by both the woman he loves and the one with whom he is in love. They'll both want him to call if he'll be late; they'll both want him to pay special attention to them at parties; and they'll both become deeply concerned if he's laconic sexually.

In the novel *Babbitt*, by Sinclair Lewis, George has become involved with the attractive and divorced Tanis because his wife has for years been bored by anything more than a morning kiss. He is "faithful" to his lover Tanis (in part out of a sense of loyalty to his mistress, but also in part because he is bothered by the weight that his wife has gained). Yet at a certain juncture he recognizes that Tanis has become as tedious as his wife, to whom he returns. A man might well feel that if a woman is going to make demands upon him, insist on sexual fidelity, and assume a long-term intimacy, that woman might as well be his wife. "You can become as sated with your lover as with your wife," sighed a man in his fifties, "and rediscover in adultery all the boredom of marriage."

Babbitt wants out of his affair, and manages to convince his wife that she drove him to having an affair, practically against his will. "With true masculine wiles he not only convinced himself that she had injured him but, by the loudness of his voice and the brutality of his attack, he convinced her also, and presently he had her apologizing for his having spent the evening with Tanis. He went up to bed well pleased, not only the master but the martyr of the household."

Being both master and martyr is the hallmark of the adulterous husband, especially one who has decided that he no longer wishes to continue seeing a particular lover. He might well "let" his wife discover his affair in order to get himself out of the other relationship. Such is the case with Babbitt, who tells himself, if not his wife, that he intends to "keep free. Of her and Tanis and the fellows at the club and everybody. I'm going to run my own life!" Statistically, the married man who has an affair is unlikely to marry his partner in adultery even if he gets divorced, in part because he has come to associate a marital sense of obligation and pressure with his adulterous affair. When he decides he wants out, it is likely that he'll want out of *everything* he sees as belonging to his old life.

Why do the wives of unfaithful husbands remain married to them? There are many reasons, of course, and first among them are the practical concerns of wanting to remain a family if there are children involved. But there are also less obvious reasons. Do the wives of chronically adulterous men think along the lines of Jane Welsh Carlyle, wife of historian and writer Thomas Carlyle, who, when she was asked about her husband's affections for another woman, responded, "People who are so dreadfully devoted to their wives are apt, from mere habit, to get devoted to other people's wives as well"? Or do women think, as I once thought about a man to whom I was not married but with whom I was deeply involved, that sleeping with another woman was his way of trying to get my attention? Like Babbitt's wife, many women justify their mate's infidelity by turning his problem into their problem, which will at least give the woman a sense of having some control over her life.

Husbands are often allowed to bounce back into the family game after going offside, and then the "other woman" appears to be to blame. After all, Anne Archer fights for Michael Douglas at the end of *Fatal Attraction,* and in Scott Turow's best-seller, *Presumed Innocent,* the wife murders the girlfriend but leaves her husband intact. Plots such as these position the husband as a naive and unwitting dupe of the sophisticated connivings of a desperate single woman who has realized too late that she gave up love for success. Of course she has to be shot by the sweet stay-at-home wife.

There's an old joke that goes something like this: A man is standing on the bank of a river that suddenly begins to flood. His wife and his mistress are both being swept away. Who should he save? One answer says that he should save his wife, since his mistress will, of course, understand. That punchline relies on the husband's assumption that his mistress will always forgive his putting his wife first; the mistress is "stronger" and so can be sacrificed. Another punchline has it that he should save his mistress, because his wife will never understand. This punchline, in contrast, depends on the fact that this mistress has a fuller and truer knowledge of the man's life than his wife. The implication is that the man's wife will only give him hell even if he saves her, since the wife will begin asking, "Who was that other woman calling your name while she was drowning?" It seems easier to let the wife drown than to explain anything to her. A third punchline was suggested to me over lunch recently by a woman who has herself been a married man's lover: "The two women should save each other and drown the bastard who can't make up his mind."

Part of the enormous difficulty in becoming involved with a married man is that men are also "likely to have a different conception of the meaning of an affair," according to researchers Blumstein and Schwartz. "In interviews, they were likely to speak of an affair as a short period of intense romance that would eventually disappear, leaving the original relationship intact." That "original relationship" with his wife will offer the adulterous husband all-season emotional protection against true intimacy with a lover.

The woman who becomes involved with a series of married men may well want to examine what attracts her about a triangle: The most expedient, and no doubt reductive, explanation argues that such a woman is replaying her unconscious childhood fantasy of trying to win Dad away from Mom, only this time she has a better shot at being able to achieve her goals. A woman I knew for years, who was otherwise a kind and stable woman, had what amounted to a fixation about married men. She would fall passionately in love with a man who seemed to be "happily married"—it was important to her that he did not have a history of affairs—and he would almost inevitably respond. Everything would go according to plan unless or until he started to talk about the possibility of leaving his marriage. Then this woman would flee from *him*. She wanted, it became clear, a man who would stay within his domestic sphere and allow her to be involved without the thought of a future together. She also had a great deal of anger toward her mother, an attractive and dynamic woman even in her seventies. My friend was clearly acting out her wish to hurt the wife in any couple (much as she might have wished to compete with her mother when she was a child), but she also lived in deep fear of actually breaking up the primary relationship (as a child, she wouldn't have really wanted to lose her mother). Until she began an extensive course of therapy, she repeated this pattern compulsively. Fortunately, being aware of the hidden dynamics, she was able to exercise some control over them, and has now begun a relationship with a single man. He seems interested in making a real life with her instead of letting her "borrow" time that belongs to someone else.

Not only do men and woman have different conceptions of what an affair means or why they see themselves as having them—they also manifest responses to jealousy very differently. In *American Couples: Money, Work, Sex*, Blumstein and Schwartz point out that jealousy is often used to gauge levels of involvement and commitment. "People may test their partners' real feelings by attempting to arouse jealousy . . . For example, a wife seeking confirmation of her worth to her husband and assurance of his steadfastness may flirt with another man at a party, hoping to get a rise from her husband. If he reacts in the way she wants, she may relax, believing he is committed to her." In other words, if he becomes angry and possessive, she thinks, like the girl in the song "Johnny Get Angry," that he really cares after all. "However," warn the researchers, "our data tell us that he may or may *not* be committed in this case. What she may in fact be observing is his need for control over her actions. These women would be surprised if their husbands were to leave them, since they have relied on scenes like this to define the state of their marriage." Apparently men are jealous when other men pay attention to "their" women whether they are still in love with that woman or not.

For example, a woman who flirts with another man at a party may read her husband's outrage at her behavior as a sign of his own fidelity. "If he was having an affair, he wouldn't dare act so possessive," she might think. She would be wrong. She is judging a male response by a female standard: When women are no longer deeply involved, they are no longer jealous. A woman who is herself having an affair would, according to research, be unlikely to "call" her husband on his misbehavior. But a husband, in contrast, will exhibit the same level of jealousy about his wife's behavior even if he intends to abandon her the next day. He will, by the way, behave the same way about his lover. If he appears to be jealous of her independence, or her possible availability to other men, it does not mean he is committed to the relationship. In the end, when a man is jealous—it means he's jealous. That's all.

But why do women want men who are above them or out of reach in the first place? In *Psychoanalysis and Women: Contemporary Reappraisals*, Judith L. Alpert underscores the importance of childhood experience in the formation of adult desires. Alpert argues that "in a family structure in which one parent is primary and the other is secondary, disappointment is likely to be associated with the primary caregiver; reassurance and compensation, with the one who is secondary. To some extent this is true irrespective of what the parents actually do. Since usually the primary caregiver is a woman, gender asymmetry of parenting contributes to initially differential attributions to the parents and, more specifically, to their respective genders." To put it another way, both boys and girls regard their mother's attention as something to which they are entitled. In contrast, they have to "win" their father's attention through achievement. They must "distinguish" themselves in some manner in order to receive his stamp of approval, because unlike Mom, he's not very easy to please.

The little girl learns to be "feminine" in order to win the father's approval, according to psychologists. Helene Deutsch, an early prominent psychiatric researcher whose work on women's roles has come under recent criticism, argued that "the bribe offered to the little girl by the father is love and tenderness . . . For its sake, she renounces any further intensification of her activities, particularly of her aggressions." Little girls, argued Deutsch rather damningly, are "happiest" in the role of "collaborator" and, she continues, young women "seem to be easily influenceable and adapt themselves to their companions and understand them. They are the loveliest and most unaggressive of helpmates and they want to remain in that role; they do not insist on their own rights—quite the contrary. They are easy to handle in every way—if one only loves them." It makes women sound like the perfect household pets—it certainly doesn't make them sound like complete human beings.

Deutsch, who published her remarks in 1944, provides a blueprint for the misery of women everywhere: "If gifted in any direction they preserve the capacity for being original and productive, but without entering into competitive struggles. They are always willing to renounce their own achievements without feeling that they are sacrificing anything, and they rejoice in the achievements of their companions." The girls learn to win affection not by going out and doing something, but by mastering the game of femininity.

In part this pattern for passivity is influential because the girl's father appears, in her eyes at least, to be most accepting of her when she is quiet, well-behaved, neat, and pretty. This idea of the father is similar to the concept of the "ideal" marriage, insofar as it is something that a child understands in a larger cultural sense whether or not the child's own experience mirrors it exactly. In those instances where a child is brought up by a single mother, for example, validation from a male adult might become even more desirable because it is even more elusive.

The masculine model becomes, through this process, the admirable model. In other words, we love our mothers, but we admire our fathers. "Knowing one is valued and understood by an admirable person is far more reassuring than similar demonstrations of love from a person whom the child does not admire," explains Alpert, and "conversely, doubts that one is valued and understood by a person whom one admires are far more distressing than similar doubts about a person for whom one has little admiration." We are encouraged to look toward others for validation, and we are more likely to believe in our own value if someone we respect seems to grant us their attention. We learn to value ourselves through their valuing of us.

Too often, however, this pattern continues into the adult lives of many women. We are stuck in a habitual search for a positive reflection of ourselves, looking for romance like a narcotic that will simply dull the pain of our low self-esteem or lack of power over our own lives. Louise J. Kaplan writes in *Female Perversions* of "a woman, dissatisfied and disillusioned with everything the real world has offered to her, is possessed by the idea that a certain kind of person does have the power to fix her—a father, a priest, a husband, a teacher, a lover, a hairdresser, a toreador . . . [can] bring her illusions to life and satisfy all her frustrated desires." The belief operating here is that men can do anything if they choose: It is a distorting and distorted view of the male as omnipotent and the woman as flawed. If he will fix her, then she will be fine. But then she must be damaged in a way that will call attention to her plight and permit her to be fixed, to be made whole by a man. She has to be wounded, but bravely wounded; she has to be needy, but not desperate. In the eighteenth century, she would drop a handkerchief for the gallant gentleman to pick up; in the twentieth century she is told to ask for instructions on how to fix her car/stereo/ computer even if there's nothing wrong with it. (Ever notice how many times women are advised by magazines to go to a "do-it-yourself" shop to find a man who will do it *for* them? If she actually does it herself, then she'll scare him off.) "Make him feel useful," we're told, but if we do this for real, then we end up being less and less able to do anything for ourselves. Instead, we seem to be most powerful when we're most useless, and most controlling when we're out of control.

As Dr. Alexandra Symonds writes, girls were brought up believing that they are "not allowed to fight for themselves on the basis of strength, since this was not feminine, but instead learned to fight on the basis of weakness. They learned that men will do things for women because they are too weak and helpless to do them for themselves." This is one reason, for example, why women are encouraged, oddly enough, to equate passivity with power. "All good things come to those who wait," we've been told, but unless you equate all good things with monthly bills, IRS forms, and correspondence marked "Occupant," very little actually comes to those who wait.

As Dr. Martin Symonds (husband of Alexandra Symonds mentioned above) frames it in his article on the "Psychodynamics of Aggression in Women," women are so well-versed in passivity that they will go to great lengths to preserve this image of themselves. In an example almost too perfect to be true, Martin Symonds describes a woman who "told me of her experience with an encounter group. She was told with the others to line up in order of aggressivity. The most aggressive was to be first on line and the most passive at the end. She said to me in utter seriousness: 'You know, I had to fight for last place.' "

CHAPTER TEN

MATING IN
CAPTIVITY

Sexual Scripts and Cultural Climaxes

WE HAVE SEEN that the conventional hero in our culture is a man who wants above all to be free: The conventional heroine is the woman who can make him curtail that dream of freedom. The question is, will either of them value what is left over after the man has been extracted from the husband? Does a man lose his identity once he marries? Is one husband basically the same as another?

A popular bumper sticker proclaims, "Divorce Is Nature's Way of Recycling Husbands," as if to underscore the validity of such an argument. The basic interchangeability of husbands is suggested by a powerfully ironic chain letter, recently discussed in the *New York Times,* the prototype of which reads as follows: "This chain letter was started by a woman like yourself in hopes of bringing relief to tired, discontented women. Unlike most chain letters, this does not cost anything. Just send a copy to five of your female friends who are equally tired, then bundle up your husband and send him to the woman at the top of the list. Then add your name to the bottom. When your name comes to the top, you will receive 16,748 men, and some of them are dandies, I assure you." Trying someone else's husband on for size seems no more scandalous than exchanging recipes. Are husbands really such neutered creatures, "fixed" into position?

Occasionally, the husband is portrayed as devoted and true. But at these moments, he is often framed as a dope and a sucker—nervously annoying at best, horrifyingly pathetic at worst. Rodney Dangerfield does a routine about how his wife has cut him down to having sex only once a month, but, he explains while pulling on his tie, it's not so bad because "Hey, I know two guys she cut out altogether." He also does a routine about how he finally told his wife the truth, that he was seeing a psychologist. "Then she told me the truth. She was seeing a psychologist, two accountants, and a mechanic." Good husbands occasionally end up looking like James Dean's father in *Rebel Without a Cause*, painfully emasculated, wearing an apron, and picking up the broken dishes.

THAT'S NO MAN, THAT'S MY HUSBAND

In other words, while it is has been a standard joke to say, "That's no lady, that's my wife," the opposite remains unspoken although powerfully poignant. The phrase "That's no man, that's my husband" is perhaps taboo because it is too true to be spoken: A man, in terms of Western culture, is unmanned when he marries. He becomes a husband instead of being a man; marriage is a process whereby masculinity is replaced by domesticity. If becoming a bride is the culmination of socially sanctioned rituals validating femininity, if becoming a bride is the crowning achievement of traditional rites of womanhood, then becoming a husband is the negation of masculine sexuality, the ritualized domestication of that which—according to every encoded pattern—is meant to be "free."

The very question of "freedom" is at the center of the discussion of the masculine privileging of the exotic over the domestic. Both women and men seem to prefer men who are free from the yoke of marriage; in a study compiled by sociologists in 1988, the results indicated that married men were rated lower than single men in terms of "absolute masculinity," "intellectual achievement," "emotional stimulation," and "creativity" by both male and female subjects. What is true of sociological data is true of the narratives available in everyday life: The married man, in texts generated by and for women as well as those created by and for men, is devalued, the assumption being that what is exotic is worth pursuit; what is domestic is barely worth the bother of cultivation.

THE GOOD HUSBAND AS FAILED LOVER

In Gustave Flaubert's nineteenth-century novel *Madame Bovary*, the author presents us with a remarkable portrait of the good-husband-as-failed-lover when he shows us Charles Bovary, the heroine Emma's husband. In first meeting Charles, Emma's father thinks that "Charles [is] rather a wisp of a man, to be sure, not quite the son-in-law he could have wished for. But he was said to be steady and thrifty, and well-educated," and following the old adage that you should marry your son when you will but your daughter when you can, he accepts Charles's proposal to marry his daughter.

Initially, Emma is very pleased with married life, but then subtly things change. Flaubert tells us that Emma can "hardly persuade herself that the quietness of her present life was the happiness of her dreams." In one particular respect especially Flaubert captures the essence of the doomed relationship: The more devoted to his wife Charles becomes, the less respect she has for him. This is a reversal of the pattern we saw applied to women; in this relationship, the husband is the one who kisses and it is the wife who offers the cheek. Charles would give Emma "great smacking kisses on the cheek, sometimes a chain of little ones all the way up her arm from finger-tip to shoulder. And she pushed him away with a weary half-smile, as you do a child that hangs on to you. Before the wedding, she had believed herself in love. But not having obtained the happiness that should have resulted from that love, she now fancied that she must have been mistaken. And Emma wondered exactly what was meant in life by the words 'bliss', 'passion', 'ecstasy', which had looked so beautiful in books." She is disappointed in her husband because he is not everything she imagined a man should be, since Charles "couldn't swim, or fence, or fire a pistol, and was unable to explain a riding term she came across in a novel one day. Whereas a man, surely, should know about everything; excel in a multitude of activities, introduce you to passion in all its force, to life in all its grace, initiate you into all mysteries! But this one had nothing to teach; knew nothing, wanted nothing."

In short, Emma is angered that she cannot look up to her husband. The thing that most infuriates her, however, is that "he thought she was happy; and she hated him for that placid immobility, that stolid serenity of his, for that very happiness which she herself brought him." If she is enough to make him happy, her reasoning goes, then he can't be all that wonderful. So instead Emma turns to romantic fantasies the way that young men might turn to pornography in order to satisfy a craving for the unrealistic, if not for the downright impossible.

Emma feeds her imagination on novels, the way a young woman today might become addicted to soap operas. Her favorite books are

> all about love and lovers, damsels in distress swooning in lonely lodges, postilions slaughtered all along the road, horses ridden to death on every page . . . rowing-boats in the moonlight, nightingales in the grove, gentlemen brave as lions and gentle as lambs . . . invariably well-dressed, and weeping like fountains . . . She would have liked to live in some old manor house . . . leaning on the parapet, chin in hand, watching a cavalier with a white plume galloping out of the distant countryside on a black charger. She was at this time a worshiper of Mary Queen of Scots, and had an enthusiastic veneration for all illustrious or ill-fated women.

The images are still familiar; anyone who has read a contemporary romance novel will recognize all the likely suspects rounded up here.

The romance writer of today is advised, by specific guidelines issued through the various publishing houses, to "create a heartwarming and exciting love story. The writer's job is to get the heroine and hero together, keep them together, make sparks fly, put obstacles in the path of true love, and finally resolve the complications and end the story on a high note with a satisfying ending." In addition, the romance novelist must provide for the heroine—and, by extension, for the reader who identifies with the heroine—a male protagonist who is "virile, masterful, and attractive . . . He is tender and sensitive . . . While he need not be rich, he must be successful at whatever he does." Clearly these texts are supposed to provide an escape into fantasy for the reader, and allow her into a world where the men are powerful, tender, adoring, and available. The reader is freed from the cares of a humdrum daily life and better for her flight into fancy.

But instead of giving Emma a way out of her tedium, these texts only reinforce it. Given a dose of adventure by these books the way a physician might administer a dose of methadone in order to keep an addict stable, Emma uses romance as a drug to alter her consciousness. As we discussed earlier, romance can be a form of narcotic for a certain kind of woman, and Emma is the embodiment of the woman whose life can be shattered by too heavy a dependence on fantasy.

ROMANCE WRITES CHECKS THAT REALITY CAN'T CASH

The damage done by Emma's addiction to romance is fatal to her. But the emotional aftershocks of the romantic tradition are felt even by those who grew up only overhearing, instead of actively seeking out, such tales. As we've seen, the images we carry with us from our childhoods concerning love, marriage, and romance (not necessarily in that order) stay with us, in shadow or in substance, well into our adult lives. Sometimes the earliest stories we hear remain the most powerful.

Consider the central character of Anita Brookner's novel *The Debut*. The heroine believes that her fairly unhappy sexual life can be "put . . . down to her faulty moral education, which dictated, through the conflicting but in this one instance united agencies of her mother and father, that she ponder the careers of Anna Karenina and Emma Bovary, but that she emulate those of David Copperfield and Little Dorrit. But really it had started much earlier than that, when, at a faintly remembered moment in her early childhood, she had fallen asleep, enraptured, as her nurse breathed the words 'Cinderella *shall* go to the ball.' The ball had never materialized."

Brookner's progression of texts is telling. Starting with the bedtime stories of Cinderella, who will be found to be the perfect princess once she appears at the ball in an extravagant gown which was paw-made by local mice (if you follow the Disney version), Brookner then moves on to Anna Karenina and Emma Bovary, who think they are princesses but turn out to be less lucky, and ends anticlimactically with Dickens's tedious, didactic, and unappealing characters. Cinderella, Anna Karenina, Little Dorrit: It starts out with enormous promise, but turns out either tragically or stupifyingly dull. The pull of the voice promising that "Cinderella *shall* go to the ball" maintains its hold over feminine imaginations of both the young and the old.

Disney's new version of the woman-who-must-be-saved (not the one with the hooker, *Pretty Woman*, the one with the fish, *The Little Mermaid*) still promises that when a female loses her voice, keeps her hair long, and sacrifices everything in her life for him, her prince will fall in love with her. But in the original Hans Christian Andersen fairy tale, the little mermaid replaces her tail with feet, only to find that every step she takes feels as if she is walking on knives, and the prince marries a human princess anyway and the little erstwhile mermaid (who has forfeited her immortality in the process) is left alone. Disney didn't do that version, but somebody should. (Maybe NOW, for example, could subcontract it to a female director.) What we hear whispered to us is the promise of a future where if only we change ourselves enough (get rid of our fins and gills, or for those of us on land, get rid of our hips and excess upper-arm fat), then someone will love us. Not only will they love us, which of course would be quite nice (although what happens if your hips or gills start to reappear?), but we will live happily ever after.

We think of ourselves as going to the chapel and getting married so that we'll never be lonely anymore. The last part of that lyric is what causes trouble, like the last part of the Beach Boys song "Wouldn't It Be Nice?" which says that when you get married then you'll be happy. The trouble is that life is not a text—not a fairy tale, not a novel, not a song—with an "ending," and the catch is that you can't have happy endings in the middle. Life means risking trouble. As George Bernard Shaw writes in *Pygmalion*, "Making life means making trouble. There's only one way of escaping trouble; and that's killing things. Cowards,

you notice, are always shrieking to have troublesome people killed."
As long as we're all alive from day to day, you can't look for a happy
ending that means nothing will ever change again. The happy endings
we were promised—men and women alike—are checks that reality
can't cash.

The lure of the Cinderella story has kept women enthralled for
centuries, and it has led to the disturbing belief that if you wait long
enough and keep your fingernails clean (and your virginity intact)
then the right man will come along and save you from having to fill
out all your own federal income tax forms. Emma Bovary wants
someone to give her a life, for example, because she does not have
available to her the option of creating one for herself while remaining
a "lady."

Interestingly, the resistance movement against romance did not
coincide with the demand for the vote for women, or even with the
advent of the pantsuit. The diatribe against romantic novels put forth
by the protofeminist protagonist of Victorian author George Gissing's
1893 novel, *The Odd Women,* gives us insight into the perpetual
nature of this struggle against the seductions of romance.

Gissing presents us with the world of England in 1887, where, as
one character puts it, "there are half a million more women than men
in this happy country of ours." The novel centers on the choices
women have available to them: living single, being married, or even
living together without marriage. Most significantly for our present
argument is the declaration given by one of the "older" women in her
thirties concerning the influence of romantic novels on the notions of
the younger women around her.

Rhoda declares that "if every novelist could be strangled and
thrown into the sea we should have some chance of reforming women
. . . Love—love—love; a sickening sameness of vulgarity. What is
more vulgar than the ideal of novelists? They won't represent the
actual world; it would be too dull for their readers. In real life, how
many men and women *fall in love?* Not one in every ten thousand, I
am convinced." Rhoda presses home her point that "not one married
pair in ten thousand have felt for each other as two or three couples do
in every novel . . . When [a "fallen" young woman] rushed off to
perdition, ten to one she had in mind some idiot heroine of a book."

Angry at what she sees as the enslavement of women's minds by the poisons of sentimental fiction, Rhoda fights against romance the way a temperance worker fights against alcohol.

If it were possible to mention every novelist who lists the dangers presented by lesser novelists, this would no longer be a book of reasonable size, but it is a fascinating and tellingly gender-specific pattern. When the girl who is the object of Rhoda's concern dies, Gissing allows his readers to sentimentalize her death as the inevitable outcome of a girl who married the wrong man. Margaret Drabble writes that "in the past, in old novels, the price of love was death, a price which virtuous women paid in childbirth," and that is exactly the fate allotted by Gissing.

ENABLING FICTIONS

The sort of idea that suggests that even death can be a woman's friend since it allows her to escape pain can be called an "enabling fiction." What is an enabling fiction? Enabling fictions are the stories we tell ourselves to maintain equilibrium. Enabling fictions are as complex and subtle as the reasoning behind a murder mystery: Their narratives try to tell you why the person holding the smoking gun isn't the murderer—in other words, why the obvious isn't true.

Enabling fictions are the internal monologues we rehearse and the silent arias we sing to tell ourselves that we live in the best of all possible worlds. They are the narratives we create for our own lives so that we won't have to confront our anger, or disappointment, or unhappiness. Dr. Mary Ann Caws, distinguished professor of Comparative Literature, English, and French at the City University of New York, researched this idea and applied it to literature and developed the term *enabling fictions* to describe the story created by the character, which works inside the larger story created by the author.

The idea of the "enabler" is originally drawn from psychologists' work with the families of alcoholic and substance-addicted adults. There is always a family member who can be identified as the "enabler"—the one who is primarily responsible for keeping the household going, keeping it stable. Except, of course, that the household doesn't "go," and isn't "stable." The enabler creates the fiction, the false appearance, of these elements in the family so that an acceptable front can be presented to the outside world to allow the status quo to continue without disruption. The enabler cleans up the morning after, calls the boss to say that the substance abuser is "legitimately" sick or was called away on urgent family business. The enabler supports and forgives and replaces the chaos caused by the abuser with a semblance of order. The enabler is the first to comfort the abuser, agreeing that "this is the last time this will ever happen" (not mentioning that this promise has been given weekly for ten years). The enabler spends a great deal of time reassuring herself and the other members of the family that "everything is all right" and "will be fine" when it is clear that neither of these is true.

Women whose husbands use violence against them or their children are often enablers, choosing perpetual forgiveness over the possibility of change. The enabler gets her name by "enabling" the alcoholic to continue drinking, although the very thought is against her deepest wishes. She refuses to see that she is conspiring against her own desire for the substance abuse to stop by permitting the façade of normalcy to be erected and kept intact. She is fierce in rejecting the very idea of "enabling" until it suddenly becomes too clear, too poignantly obvious even to her, that she is allowing the situation to continue by creating a fiction that keeps the family afloat. The story loses its power and she must confront the reality of her situation. Then she can begin to change it.

Enabling fictions can be created by anyone who wishes to avoid having to face the cracks in the façade of their false sense of security. For example, a young couple in Virginia Woolf's story "Lapin and Lapinova" come to depend increasingly on a fantasy world inhabited by woodland creatures representing their inner selves. When one of the partners, tired after a long day at work, refuses to participate in this emotional game, their entire world collapses. Woolf believes the relationship between the young couple to be entirely dependent on their fantasy world of being two little bunnies in the vast meadows and forests of their imagination. When the husband announces that his character has died—thereby ruining the enabling fiction—Woolf ends the story abruptly with the single line "That was the end of that marriage." Nothing had actually changed in the "real world"; their circumstances remained unaltered. Nevertheless, nothing looked the same anymore.

One or two words can change a relationship irrevocably. Picture a hundred-ton freighter on the ocean, and picture the small rudder that need only move a fraction of an inch for the hundred tons of steel to change direction. Like the movement of that rudder, the course of these lives is irrevocably changed by the moment of awareness in these stories and in relationships. The smallest motion has an enormous effect. Words withheld can have as much impact as words spoken.

LIVING WITHOUT HEARING "I LOVE YOU"

Can you imagine living for three years, for example, with a man who never says, "I love you"? This question assumed more than an academic place in my life, since I was once involved with a man who had a sort of hysterical inability to make this most obvious declaration of affection. I spent a long time thinking about this: How, in short, do you manage to live without what you want?

If you're like me, you convince yourself that he simply cannot say three short words, despite the fact that he inevitably has recourse to the first and second (and even uses the L word) in daily conversation. ("I'll be home for dinner, and I'd love to have lasagna.") You tell yourself that he is just not the kind of man to show affection openly; you tell yourself that words are cheap, throwaway things, that the real, genuine love between you is beyond language. You tell yourself that anyone from his: (1) under- (or over-) privileged background; (2) distant (or smothering) family; (3) over- (or under-) pressured work situation could never be expected to live up to the romantic fantasies you created during your ridiculous adolescence. You convince yourself that you are to blame for wanting such absurd declarations. You allow yourself to stay in a situation by avoiding confrontation with your own dissatisfaction.

Your "enabling fiction" will then permit you to live three years with a man who does not say, "I love you," because you have convinced yourself that he *cannot* say, "I love," rather than (as you do know somewhere inside you and all your friends know rather more definitely) that he *will* not say, "I love you." It wasn't until a year later, when I was in a different relationship and became the one "unable" to say the three magic words, that I finally understood: I couldn't say it because I didn't feel it. Bingo, the light bulb appeared over my head like in a cartoon. The person who doesn't say, "I love you" probably doesn't love you. That's what is so impossible to face, but easy to see once you get some perspective.

WHY BOTHER CHANGING?

Enabling fictions tell us there are no good jobs (so why bother looking), no good apartments (ditto), no better men (so stick with the one you've got), no way to change anything because that's the way the world works (and always will). Enabling fictions tell you that he needs to take a holiday on his own because he is, after all, a man who needs solitude to create his: (1) art; (2) music; (3) critical theory; (4) financial game plan; (5) pottery. Or get away from his office, practice, classroom. Not that he wants to get away from you. No, no, no. Anyone who suggests that simply doesn't understand the way your relationship works, doesn't understand that he will appreciate your relationship even more after he returns, will be more affectionate and receptive.

Along the same lines, we can see enabling fictions working through Fay Weldon's novel *The Life and Loves of a She-Devil.* The enabling fiction of the bulky, unhappy protagonist Ruth at first appears in the guise of "the litany of the good wife" where she recites the attributes listed in anachronistic "guides to a good marriage": not making demands; not asking for sex; taking the backseat always; forgiving infidelity; and understanding her own insignificance. To be a good wife is to be unimportant, declares Ruth's early enabling fiction. She bought the entire package until the moment she confronted her own inability to continue the ritual. Her second enabling fiction becomes the obsession to look like, to become, her husband's mistress, the tiny, successful romance writer Mary Fisher. Ruth believes that if she can reduce herself and "look up to men," literally as well as figuratively, then she'll be happy. She replaces one enabling fiction with another. She cannot therefore ever be happy; she can win (and she does, with a vengeance!), but happiness must elude her. She replaces the "guide to good marriages" with a "romance novel," but the trouble with all formulaic plots is that they cannot and do not reflect life.

Does the same work with bouts of infidelity? The reason he thinks it's all right to sleep with another woman is because he loves you so much ("Honey, I'm so secure in our relationship that I know it can withstand some silly little affair that means nothing, absolutely nothing, not compared to what you and I have together. So, really, this shows how much I believe in us. I know that nobody can come between us, so don't let this get to you, okay? You're the only one for me. She doesn't count"). The complexity involved in creating this argument is worthy of the most subtle murder mystery, only the evidence is far too clear. That man standing over the body with a gun? No, Officer, he just happened to walk into the room after shooting a pesky crow and that's why the gun is smoking and nobody knows who the girl was anyway.

We'll do anything to dance around the obvious.

Because they blind us to the real causes behind our disillusionment, and because we conveniently abandon trying to chart the course of our own lives if we believe that "things just are the way they are," enabling fictions are one reason change is difficult. In a recent issue of *Brides* magazine, in a section titled "How Can Couples Reach a Balance Between Feeling Loved and Autonomous?" we read that "finding out how much 'space' each partner requires is a matter of trial and error," which seems like quite a reasonable statement to make to a newly married couple. Then we hear from a newly married man who is apparently considered an average gem of a husband by the magazine that quotes him: " 'Before marriage, I played a lot of sports,' " says "Dean, 27, a chemist from Naugatuck, CT, married to Mary-Ellen, 23, a teacher, since September of 1990." So how does he work things out now that he's married to a woman who doesn't share any of his interests?

What kind of compromise do they reach so that both their needs are met? " 'I spent this past Sunday playing tennis competitively; my wife stayed home. It left me feeling a little guilty. So we're trying to incorporate some of my interests into our marriage,' continues Dean. 'For example, I've taught Mary-Ellen how to ski and snorkel. I'm still doing my own thing, but now I have a great partner.' " So, in other words, now his wife does what he wants to do. He's doing his "own thing" and now she's doing "his own thing" too. The enabling fiction at work here says that he is being generous and understanding instead of selfish. At some point, his wife is likely to attempt or at least wish to keep his head under wanter longer than he might like.

Enabling fictions, by the way, aren't limited to love affairs, although these are the places they appear most clearly when looking at other people's lives. They also work on a philosophical scale: An enabling fiction tells us that we should put up with misery and oppression in this life because the next one will be better, or, conversely, that we are miserable and oppressed in this life because we didn't behave ourselves in the last. Either way they keep us treading water, running in place.

Enabling fictions are more than just "excuses"; they are intricately wrought patterns of experience that evolve over a number of years. Sometimes they literally become our life stories. If, in childhood, we were told that good girls sacrifice their own wishes for the wishes of others, we will probably grow up believing that each act of self-sacrifice makes us "even better." We sacrifice our wishes at our own peril, however, because too often we end up not being able to read ourselves. We become unable to identify our own desires and hopes because we are eager to sublimate them in order to make someone else happy. If we believe that "you only hurt the ones you love" then we are likely to incorporate that pattern into our relationships by equating love with pain, metaphorical or even physical. We are likely to believe that the more we fear loss, the more we feel hurt, the greater is our passion. If we believe that the "course of true love never did run smooth" then we are likely to stay in an unworkable relationship beyond the period of any possible reconciliation. These horrific fictions work brilliantly well.

LACKING THE WORDS,
LACKING THE COURAGE

As we've seen, Emma Bovary has her own set of enabling fictions. She believes that she deserves to be treated like the heroine of a novel, so she indulges every whim. She convinces herself that her husband is unworthy of her, so she justifies her adulterous liaisons by telling herself that he is unaffected by her behavior. She convinces herself that she has every right to go into debt since she'll "figure out" a way to repay her creditors when the time comes. Many of Emma's most dangerous enabling fictions are cribbed from the novels to which she is a slave.

Emma is susceptible to novels in part because she is a middle-class country girl (the subtitle of the novel is *A Story of Provincial Life*) without much experience of the world, and so she is without a vocabulary or grammar for her unhappiness. Without a name for her sense of disappointment, Emma is unable to understand her unhappiness and therefore unable to change her situation: "She would have been glad of someone in whom to confide all this; but how to describe an intangible unease, that shifts like the clouds and eddies like the wind? Lacking the words, she had neither the opportunity nor the courage."

Like the women described by Simone de Beauvoir in 1948, Emma sees herself as tightly bound by the shackles of femininity. De Beauvoir discusses a world where men are considered full human beings, while women are regarded as second-class citizens, defined by their gender alone. She describes a woman's existence in vivid and terrifying terms: "Whereas man is impetuous, woman is only impatient; her expectation can become ardent without ceasing to be passive; man dives upon his prey like the eagle and the hawk; woman lies in wait like the carnivorous plant, the bog, in which insects and children are swallowed up. She is absorption, suction, humus, pitch and glue, a passive influx, insinuating and viscous: thus, at least, she vaguely feels herself to be." This is not the language used by women in everyday life, but that does not make de Beauvoir's observations any less salient. If anything, the effect of her sentiments is heightened by the choice of her words and she drives home the point that women see themselves as the entrapped and the entrapper.

In 1963, Betty Friedan built on de Beauvoir's legacy, and once again the issues facing Emma Bovary were transposed onto the modern woman, this time the American housewife. In her book's title, Friedan termed the gnawing inner malaise "The Feminine Mystique." Friedan argues that apart from the prescribed role as suburban, stay-at-home housewife, "no other road to fulfillment was offered to the American woman in the middle of the twentieth-century." She goes on to say that "most adjusted to their role and suffered or ignored the problem that has no name. It can be less painful for a woman, not to hear the strange, dissatisfied voice stirring within her." Emma would have recognized this voice and, like the housewives to whom Friedan spoke, she would have been enormously relieved to find out that she was not alone.

NOT A SAFETY NET, BUT A SNARE

Women who were depressed by their lives sought—and found—in Friedan's book a mirror of their own situation. They discovered that they were not alone, that they were not at fault, and they found suggestions concerning ways to make their lives better. Friedan suggested that women gain a sense of control over their own lives by refusing to be full-time housewives, by refusing to follow a script that tells them to bend their will to another's, and by seeing that the problems they thought of as personal were really political in nature. They, in effect, woke up to the idea that they should play against the house, that what they had believed were rules and regulations set up to nourish and protect them had the opposite effect. The house wasn't a web of safety woven around them; it was, instead, a net, a snare, and a trap.

How is a housewife's feeling of isolation representative of a larger political issue? It is a matter of gender politics, not a matter of political parties. Instead, if we see women as a group whose power is diffuse and therefore weak, we get the sense that women are caught in a sort of cultural loop that prevents them from making significant headway. Anthropologist Elizabeth Janeway, author of *The Powers of the Weak*, argues that a "deep sense of isolation from others" is one of the conditions that strengthens the powerful without their having to conspire against "the weak." She goes on to point out that what she calls "the trivialization of life" convinces those outside the center of power that nothing they do or feel can be very important, "so why insist on having one's way in the fact of opposition? It isn't worth it." In addition, chronic "self-doubt and lack of confidence" persuade them that any action they take against the status quo is useless because those with authority seem "magically to authenticate their legitimate possession of it." Janeway concludes that "these unhappy convictions feed on each other: if you are sure that you can't achieve your ends, you will try very hard not to want them passionately." You will not, in other words, bother to define what is wrong since you will consider yourself powerless to change it.

DEPRESSION AFTER MARRIAGE

Does this seem out of date? Have women moved beyond such name-less sadness and despair? While I would love to say "yes, isn't it wonderful that nobody feels this way anymore," such a declaration is impossible. There is still enough post-wedding depression among women that a 1991 issue of *Brides* magazine devoted several articles to "how to cope" strategies for surviving *marriage* (let alone surviving the wedding). Perhaps we should all remember what Goethe wrote nearly one hundred years ago: "One should only celebrate a happy ending; celebrations at the outset exhaust the joy and energy needed to urge us forward and sustain us in the long struggle. And of all celebrations a wedding is the worst; no day should be kept more quietly and hum-bly." When it comes to advice on how to survive the wedding itself, it seems you're supposed to get a facial and watch what you eat. Period.

To survive the marriage, even in the era that embraces *Thelma and Louise, Backlash,* and "Murphy Brown," the tricks of the mind that women are supposed to put themselves through are more anachronis-tic, complicated—and chilling.

Consider the following scenario presented by *Brides:*

> After months of planning, endless phone calls, and entertaining rela-
> tives from out of town, the big day was all over. Rather than feeling

relieved, as she'd anticipated, [the bride] was depressed. "I'd put my heart into it, and it was like someone had just died," she recalls. It might have helped [her] to know that such feelings are not only normal, but healthy, according to Professor Edward Bader, M.A., of the department of family and community medicine at the University of Toronto. "Any event has some letdown, because you've channeled your energy in that direction. Afterward, there has to be some recouping of emotions."

It is not for nothing that this unfortunate young woman compares her wedding to a funeral, since the death of her analogy might well be the romantic illusions she was raised on. When you've looked forward to one event your whole life, how on earth are you supposed to be glad to see that moment pass? Studies show that conservative young women are particularly vulnerable to depression following their weddings.

COURTSHIP VS. MARRIAGE

In *American Couples: Money, Work, Sex*, Blumstein and Schwartz explore the difference in behavior during the "courtship" period and after marriage: "Courtship is usually a time for sharing activities, intense conversations, and emotional intimacy. The experience can confirm a woman's romantic hopes of what a companionate relationship will be like. But these women may be in for a disappointment. After their marriage, or when they move in together, men soon return to their previous routines, occupying themselves with the mundane but necessary task of making a living. Intense conversations and time alone together may become scarcer commodities for the couple." The researchers provide reasons why this change in patterns of intimacy should not surprise the bride, but if she was brought up to believe the "I'll never be lonely anymore" refrain, she won't be very reassured.

It is true that *Brides* magazine does counsel their readers that "too often, the bride expects the fantasy to last forever. 'Since you're young, you have this dream of getting married, and you expect to be on a continual high.' " However, given that this publication itself is swamped by ads for everything from silverware to toilet paper, all of which promise to help the married couple keep the post-wedding high, the advice from the expert gets washed away by the tidal wave of preventative shopping. The practical solutions offered by *Brides*, called "Pick-Me-Ups to Beat the Blues," suggest, for example, that the young wife "set a time frame for your negative feelings (say, two weeks). Then, vow to start a new project (wallpapering the kitchen?)."

In this day and age, for wallpapering the kitchen to be offered as a method of alleviating feelings of depression and disillusionment is really quite astonishing. The article in *Brides* goes on to ask the reader to soothe possible feelings of fear and isolation by suggesting that she "look at your depression in a positive light. Says [one newlywed], 'Feeling down after my wedding made me realize the importance of the day and that I'll only be getting married once.' " She is, in other words, told to align her feelings of depression with her new role as a wife. Perhaps because women are told that they will be fulfilled by marriage, that this is what they have been waiting for their whole lives, they look exclusively to this transition for fulfillment, in contrast to their young husbands, who realize that they have to get back to "real life" after the wedding bells stop ringing. Under another heading, titled, boldly, "Depression Prevention," is the recommendation that the young wife assuage her despair by buying "new clothes for returning to work, going out," because "they help increase self-esteem."

It seems the right moment to mention that Emma Bovary is brought to her lowest point, neither because of her disillusionment with her husband, Charles, nor because of her devastating affairs with Rodolphe and Leon but instead because of her debt to the shopkeeper L'Heureux. Emma, you see, cannot stop buying trinkets, clothes, and furniture as a way of trying to fill up the void in her life. She tries to find the "thing," the fetish, that will guarantee her happiness, whether it is a dress, a piece of lace, or a handsome man. And it should be noted that while Emma does not wallpaper the kitchen, she does try reupholstering the living room furniture in order to regain a sense of purpose and control over her life. It did not work then, and I would not recommend it now.

As Flaubert ends her story, Emma dies of rage, heartbreak, and disillusionment. Her husband goes bankrupt trying to pay off her debts. Charles is miserable, but still devoted to the image of his wife—until, years after her death, he discovers packets of letters from her lovers. Flaubert refuses to allow Charles Bovary to keep his romantic illusions any more than he will permit Emma to keep hers. Unlike Emily Brontë's treatment of Cathy, however, Flaubert refuses to provide an ending that will allow for a romantic, gentle slipping away of the heroine. Instead, Emma kills herself by taking arsenic, and she dies in gruesome, ugly, and highly unromantic agony. In this way, as well as in many others, Flaubert rewrites romance into realism.

Neither death nor love are as pleasurable, sweet, or welcome as romance would have us believe. And no one who does not live between the pages of a book can exist, full-time, inside a romance.

CHAPTER ELEVEN

HUSBANDS AND OTHER STRANGERS

Who Is that Emotionally Masked Man?

IF LIFE WERE an SAT exam, the conventional wisdom would have us believe that "lover is to wilderness" as "husband is to garden," or that "lover is to wolf" what "husband is to one of those miniature dogs that looks like a pair of false eyelashes on a leash." The static and undifferentiated image of the husband makes him nearly invisible in the texts of both popular and high culture. Heathcliff from *Wuthering Heights*, Rick from *Casablanca*, and the younger brother from *Moonstruck* are all high-profile romantic heroes who are cast in direct opposition to those humdrum characters who make for "good" husbands.

"A MAN IS INCOMPLETE UNTIL MARRIAGE— THEN HE'S FINISHED"

Helen Rowland, author of the *The Rubaiyat of a Bachelor*, which was published early in the century, wrote rather unkindly that "a husband is what's left of a man after the nerve has been extracted." Rowland's remark comes straight out of an even older joke that claims that "a man is incomplete until he is married—then he's finished."

The term *good husband* almost seems to be paradoxical since a husband who appears too devoted risks losing his appeal as "Other" to his wife; and if he is too sweet, he risks losing his definition as a man. The "good" man seems destined to end up as a "second-choice husband." So we return to the question: Why are these the only images we see? What images come to mind when men think of themselves as husbands? What do women want?

Women's emotional lives, for all the apparently monumental changes in educational and professional possibilities, have not changed much between the days of Emma Bovary and those of Donna Reed, Claire Huxtable, or Murphy Brown. Sure, women can now attend nearly any university in the country (although the odds are that they will be taught primarily by male instructors), they can assume positions of leadership (although the higher they get on the corporate ladder, the fewer women they'll see), and they can hold public office (but if they are married and have children, they will be accused of lacking appropriate family values). But even those of us who've never allowed anybody but Mom to call us "Baby" haven't come a long way. As women, most of us are still questioning our lives and the relationship between what we *think* we want, what we *really* want, and what we're *likely* to get.

In the early 1960s it was Betty Friedan again who posed a question American women continue to ask: What is wrong with my life? Freud framed the question differently: "The great question that has never been answered, and which I have not yet been able to answer despite my thirty years of research into the feminine soul, is: What does a woman want?" Many years have passed since Freud wrote those lines, but the question remains basically the same: What is it that women really want? Humorist Mimi Ponds says the answer is "shoes," but if we look to examples provided by women from Emma Bovary to Imelda Marcos, we must admit that even a great pair of shoes does not offer the perfect solution.

DO WOMEN SIMPLY WANT TO MARRY?

Do women simply want to marry? A woman's life is validated in several ways once she can produce a marriage certificate. In a recent issue of *Lear's*, for example, a much-married Lou Saathoff says that she "married because I was angry, because it seemed the thing to do, because I was broke, because I was bored, because I didn't want to work, because I wanted good genes, because I thought I was in love, and because I truly was in love." There are many reasons to marry, but unless you're going to tie the knot so many times it looks like you're doing macrame, you'll have to figure out the reasons—specifically— why marriage is desirable.

Consider Bathsheba from Thomas Hardy's novel *Far From the Madding Crowd*. Bathsheba is enormously marriageable but hesitates, thinking that "a marriage would be very nice in one sense. People would talk about me and think I had won my battle, and I should feel triumphant, and all that. But a husband . . . He'd always be there, as you say; whenever I looked up, there he'd be . . . What I mean is that I shouldn't mind being a bride at a wedding, if I could be one without having a husband. But since a woman can't show off in that way by herself, I shan't marry—at least yet." Honest in her desire for attention, Hardy's heroine wants to stay the focus of her own story instead of handing herself over to be submerged in someone else's life. She is bound, within the conventions of the nineteenth-century novel, to be headed for trouble.

"I WANT SOMEBODY TO TAME ME"

Bathsheba refuses, at several points, a proposal from the man who will ultimately be her third and final husband. She turns him down because she admits that "I want somebody to tame me; I am too

independent; and you would never be able to, I know." Terrified of
her own appetites and demanding nature, Bathsheba wants a man who
will have more "voltage" than she does and who will be able to
outperform her. Her first marriage is to one of the original Bad Boys of
literature, Sargent Troy.

Bathsheba becomes literally "hooked" on Troy when her dress gets
tangled in his military gear during a walk down a dark path: "His
sudden appearance was to darkness what the sound of a trumpet is to
silence." This dangerous man is the one she chooses to tame her, and
tame her he does, in part because he can dissimulate so well that "he
could . . . be one thing and seem another; for instance, he could speak
of love and think of dinner; call on the husband to look at the wife
. . ." Troy expertly handles Bathsheba and breaks her spirit the way a
circus trainer breaks the will of a creature more powerful than himself:
By wearing down her usual defenses, he makes her dependent upon
him. He breaks her spirit and delights in her subjection, transforming
respect into contempt to the extent that he comes to despise her. Her
dependence upon Troy is her undoing.

The example of Bathsheba is interesting to the modern woman
because in many ways she is a predecessor of the heroine with some
independence of spirit. She also serves as a reminder of the way even
the most independent of women can lose that faculty when confronted with a certain kind of man. "Bathsheba loved Troy in the way
that only self-reliant women love when they abandon their self-
reliance." Hardy cautions his readers that "a strong woman recklessly
throws away her strength . . . She has never had practice in making
the best of such a condition. Weakness is doubly weak by being new."
Bathsheba has an enormous amount of self-reliance, and therefore an
enormous amount of self-reliance to lose, but lose it she does. She
wants to submit to a man in much the same way that Jessica Benjamin
explained the process earlier in this book; she wants a man who will
"make" her want to give in.

I know a woman who could be Bathsheba's contemporary counterpart. She possesses a remarkable combination of traits: She is intelligent but with a gift for silliness, powerful in her professional life
but vulnerable in her emotional life, and sexy without being classically
beautiful. When I asked whether I could describe her life, she agreed

with the stipulation that she be called "Sophia" because it was the name she longed for as a child. Sophia is a terrific person—the kind of woman women love and admire and the kind that men pay attention to and adore. Why shouldn't we all simply go green with envy and leave her story alone? Because she has never been able to find a man who will "tame" her and then stay around long enough to see the effect.

"I can almost sense when it's starting to fall apart, even though I can't stop it," claims Sophia. "The man in question will spend a lot of time trying to convince me to take our relationship seriously. I get pretty wild and demanding after I'm on my own for a while, and I bridle at any attempt to fence me in. I keep my own hours, don't tell anyone about my personal life, and promise myself that I'll never get heavily involved again. I'll resist, and he'll keep at it. In this last round, for example, I left town on business for two weeks and he showed up with flowers and champagne at the hotel in Chicago. I dated other men despite the fact that I really did like him best. He would come to my favorite restaurant and eat alone at a separate table, trying to catch my eye and make me laugh. I told him that I was genuinely uncertain and he was so convincing that I figured, okay, this is really it. I began seeing him exclusively, telling him I loved him."

So did this plot for a romance novel produce a happy ending? "It was great for about a month. Then he started leaving messages on my answering machine saying he had to go out of town. So I figured I'd take a leaf from his book, and I tracked him down at his hotel, champagne in hand. He was so aloof, it was like I had violated his trust. When I'd spend the night at his apartment—something I don't like doing at the best of times, I like my own turf—he'd say, 'Please don't pick up the phone while you're here. I'll answer it.' He'd get furious if I looked through the mail sitting on the counter even though he regularly looked at mine. I started calling at all hours to see whether he was home. If he answered I hung up. If his machine picked up, I never left a message, but I would call several times in succession, figuring that I'd annoy him into answering the phone if he was there. It was awful. He drew further away and I couldn't figure out who I hated more—him or myself for having lost my dignity."

This is not the first time Sophia has been through this pattern, and she has become, with good reason, suspicious about her own motives in choosing such men. "I suppose I like a man who will override my reluctance to get involved, so I choose men who are nice enough superficially, but who are actually daring, selfish, and controlling. They are attracted to me as long as I'm not available, and as long as there's some 'sport' involved, and then when they 'win' me they go on to the next conquest, I guess."

What's the solution? Perhaps since Sophia can see that there is a pattern, she can begin to control her responses to it. She has, in her kitchen, a small slip of paper with Edna St. Vincent Millay's dictum on it: "Pity me the heart that is slow to learn/What the quick mind sees at every turn." She sees herself as learning to connect her quick heart and quick mind. Perhaps, too, Sophia can see that a man who wants to take over her life may not be the best partner under any circumstances. A man who spends his time "taming" women won't want one after she's "broken in" any more than the man who longs to deflower virgins will be happy with a woman whose hymen he has already pierced, despite his protestations to the contrary.

If a man's desire is based on the knowledge that his partner is desired by a great number of men and titillated by the thought that he has to fend off her other suitors, then he will become less interested in her when there are no longer other men seeking her favors. This is likely to happen once his partner no longer sends out signals saying she's available—like when she puts on a wedding ring. This is, clearly, a recipe for disaster.

When women look for a man who is interested primarily in "taming" her, she should remind herself that *The Taming of the Shrew* is a comedy with what we would now read as an uncharacteristically *unhappy* ending. Shakespeare's Kate has a husband who plans to "kill a wife with kindness," and he manages to do this—to a certain extent. Parroting back her husband's words, by the end of the play, Kate sounds either like a brainwashed member of a bizarre religious cult or a Stepford wife, a woman whose personality has been wiped out and replaced by one more acceptable to her husband. She has been so completely transformed by her "taming" that she has lost herself in the process.

"THE SHAPE OF THE MAN"

In contrast to the woman who wants a man to tame her is the woman who appears to want a man whom she can "tame." Do women want a malleable man who will not disturb their lives? Near the turn of the century, Oliver Wendell Holmes wrote in *The Professor at the Breakfast Table*: "I should like to see any kind of a man, distinguishable from a gorilla, that some good and even pretty woman could not shape a husband out of." This leads us to question the shape that a husband is expected to assume, and focuses our attention on the weakness of the husband rather than on the strength of the wife. If a man is supposed to be simply a bit player to his wife's leading role, then it is no surprise that neither women nor men have very much respect for the position. Almost anyone who auditions for the part could play it adequately.

If, as the conventional cultural vision has it, a husband can be made out of anyone harmless and willing, then it seems as if the job description has pretty low entry-level requirements. It sounds like a position that pays "minimum wage" in terms of emotion, a position that anyone can fill if he wants a steady but uneventful life. There are benefits, of course, but little room for promotion.

Along the same lines, there is a T-shirt, sold in the hip flea markets of London and New York, that has a Lichtenstein-esque cartoon of a bride embracing her groom. The thought bubble over her head reads, "I'm so glad to be married! Someday soon I must find out what his name is." This is the sort of woman personified by Charlotte in Jane Austen's *Pride and Prejudice*, who marries a man "favored with stupidity" by nature because "without thinking highly either of men or of matrimony, marriage had always been her object." Charlotte declares that she accepts her suitor "solely from the pure and disinterested desire of an establishment" and argues that "I am convinced that my chance of happiness with him is as fair as most people can boast on entering the marriage state." Charlotte remains the prototype for the woman who wants to marry the man who is most ready and willing to marry her, irrespective of her own desires beyond the attainment of the married state. Like the auctioneer who wants to move the goods off the table as soon as possible, she sells herself to the highest bidder in the room, unwilling to wait for someone to meet a price she has set independent of the market.

THE APPEAL OF THE ABSENT HUSBAND

Or do women want, for example, an absent husband? Do they want a husband in theory, but not in practice? Charlotte in *Pride and Prejudice* certainly wants an absent husband: Her spouse causes her the most joy when he is out of the room and can be "forgotten." Once they have achieved marriage, some women then want their husbands to disappear into the backgrounds of their lives. They encourage their husbands to "get out of the house" as often as possible, and are responsible for the sort of attitude summed up by the often-quoted line "I married him for better or worse, but not for lunch."

An absent husband also frees up his wife for other adventures, both sexual and nonsexual. A husband who is rarely present can still afford his wife the legitimacy of married life while allowing her to act with all the freedom she had while single. I remember vividly the appeal of the relationship between the two spies in the British television series "The Avengers."

Emma Peel, played brilliantly by Diana Rigg, was usually referred to as "Mrs. Peel" by her partner in anti-espionage and crime prevention. She called him, quite simply "Steed." Played by the urbane and witty Patrick MacNee, Steed was an upper-class English gentleman, with a signature bowler hat and a tightly rolled umbrella. Mrs. Peel, in contrast, would often appear in a black leather jumpsuit, looking more like an S&M dominatrix than a lady of good breeding. But Mrs. Peel was magnificent: In a sixties world that offered Gidget in Hawaii as the height of adventure, Diana Rigg presented an intelligent, strong, self-sufficient woman who was not afraid to kick an Eastern-bloc enemy in the shoulder (Rigg is very tall and they did nothing to diminish her height; indeed, she often fought off Steed's attackers as well as her own).

But looking back on the series, which ran almost ten years in total and is now in syndication, it is interesting to note that Emma Peel was a married woman. She was not married to her partner, Steed, but to the shadowy Mr. Peel, who was never mentioned. He was away, possibly lost forever. This permitted a certain margin of implicit eroticism, but nevertheless provided boundaries that kept the relationship between Peel and Steed from becoming a typical, and therefore uninteresting, romance. Instead, the chemistry between the two was complex and enormously erotic, despite the fact that they never touched unless it was to cut each other loose from chains or to offer a helping hand over a cliff. No doubt this increased the electricity of the relationship: The dialogue crackles with innuendo and genuine wit of the sort that later programs such as "Moonlighting," "L.A. Law," and "Northern Exposure" could only weakly imitate.

Mrs. Peel had the advantages of the married woman, namely that she could spend her time exploring the castles of eccentric Scottish millionaires who were hiding secret submarine stations instead of looking for a date or explaining why she was in her thirties and not married. She could have an unconventional relationship with Steed without being thought of as a tramp. We saw her husband only once, in the last moments of the final program. Mr. Peel, seen only from behind and from a distance, is wearing the same bowler hat as Steed and looks like his replica. Mrs. Peel's absent husband allowed her to seize adventure, freedom, aggression, and self-confidence without being accused of being either masculine or anti-male. He was a safety device, a talisman that kept criticism away from Emma and provided implicit and acceptable answers to any unspoken questions concerning impropriety. So do women want the institution of marriage, but not the man himself?

A husband, of course, provides one absolutely basic function in most societies: He legitimizes a woman's children, who might otherwise be shut out of the community. As one author put it, that paternity is merely a legal fiction has been the nightmare of many men. We hear from one source that Julia, daughter of the Roman Emperor Augustus, was renowned for her immoral behavior. She was so outrageous that her father banished her from Rome. Her five children, however, all bore a striking resemblance to their legal father. When questioned about them, she explained, "That is because passengers are never allowed on board until the hold is full." A husband provides legitimacy for his wife's children and also "allows" her to legitimize her life as a wife and mother. Traditionally, a husband is usually responsible for "taking care" of his family in such a way that they do not have to participate in the world themselves, and can remain free of its harsh, uncomfortable, and possibly corrupting influences. In other words, a husband is supposed to deal with reality so that his family will not have to face it. This had the effect of shutting women off from "reality," and therefore isolating them even more. If they were too fragile to handle it alone, then how could they expect to have any say?

BEING "TAKEN CARE OF" VS. "BEING TAKEN"

Men think that they compensate women for their lack of participation in the world of work, and being kept out of the corridors of power, by "taking care of" them. "See?" men would say. "You don't have to worry your pretty little heads about it, it's all taken care of." What was taken care of was the future. If men felt straitjacketed by the necessity to script and provide funds for another adult, women felt equally bound by rules not of their own making. If a man felt resentment at having to provide financially for his wife, he would often feel justified in "correcting" the balance of power by taking something away from her—like his sexual fidelity. If a man feels like he's giving himself away to his wife every day of their marriage without getting very much back, then he will reward himself. Sometimes he will do this by the overt "balancing act" of giving himself an obvious present: season tickets to the game, a two-seater sports car, or a regular poker game where he can win—or lose—money without accounting for it.

If he feels guilty about rewarding himself, or feels as if he needs to hide the balancing act from his wife (perhaps worrying that she won't think he's particularly deserving), then he might resort to more surreptitious forms of self-recompense. He might think, "I'm tired of behaving like a well-trained workhorse," and so allow himself to "balance" his feelings of oppression by acting out scenes of freedom that are actually disguised acts of revenge. He will "steal" things from her emotionally by not telling her his best stories, but saving them for colleagues or friends. Innumerable women have asked me why

their husbands will come in the door morose and withdrawn, replying in monosyllabic terms when asked about their day, only to
become engaged and energetic if a friend calls or drops by. "Why
couldn't he tell me about the water cooler exploding?" the wife will
wonder. "He told this hilarious story about his day at work, but the
only way that I got wind of it was by overhearing him tell his old
roommate about it over the phone." The husband in such a case is
evening the score with his wife in a covert, probably unconscious,
manner.

Having an illicit affair might also restore some balance in his mind
by removing some power from his wife if he feels overwhelmed by her
or her demands. An affair is like an education: Nobody can take it
away from you once you've had it. A secret affair—as most adultery
is—doubles the "score" by being both secret and rebellious. The
adulterous husband breaks the rules and the bonds of marriage, and
forges a fidelity the way an embezzler might draw illicit checks from
the company's account. His retribution—even if he might not think
of it in such terms—is rationed out according to what he perceives as
the unreasonable demands made upon him. One husband, who began
counseling after realizing that his patterns of behavior were destructive
to himself as well as to everyone around him, told me that he called
his lover nearly every time he hung up the phone on his wife. "My
wife kept calling me at work, asking me to do stuff on the way home,
to call the bank and get information, to call the vet and ask about the
dog's medication—and after I'd get off the line with her I'd call the
other woman in my life and she'd be delightful. I'd think as I dialed,
'There's another nail in your coffin,' to my wife. I kept a ledger in my
head. Every time I did something for my wife, I did something
surreptitious for myself to make up for it."

Interestingly, at least one researcher has argued recently that "thet-
raditional woman who defines her husband's role as mainly that of the
breadwinner and authority figure to whom she must submit is not
generally affected greatly by her husband's infidelity as long as he
fulfills his financial responsibilities toward his family and does not
become violent." Here the man is reduced, in his home, to a mere
functionary. He is there to "provide" for his family, and that appears
to be enough. It sounds as if the old maxim has been amended to say

that if he doesn't drink, gamble, or hit you, maybe he *is* allowed to run around with other women—this hardly looks like progress. He might well congratulate himself on being able to "satisfy" two women's needs—emotional, sexual, and in some cases, even financial. It can be seen as a mark of masculinity to be the central man in the lives of two women. This is especially the case for men who feel as if they are less than successful in other areas of their lives.

Some men feel that an affair keeps them vigorous, which helps their marriage by shoring up their masculinity. Oscar Wilde pointed out that "men are horribly tedious when they are good husbands, and abominably conceited when they are not." Better the joys of conceit, a man might think, rather than the horrors of tedium. And, surprisingly, a wife might concur. She herself might be unaware of the dynamic at work, but she is nevertheless prey to it. I know a woman who made no secret of her contempt for her husband, a journalist who was only moderately successful in his freelance career, until she suspected that he might be seeing another woman. It was clear that her estimation of him increased in proportion to the value she thought some other woman placed on him. She played into his hands, in one respect, by becoming more interested in him as he became less interested in her. She worried about whether he would be home on time, and after years of never even thinking about where he was, she found herself happy to see him. He transformed himself from the domestic into the exotic before her very eyes. The husband in this case, however, was already so weary of his wife's contempt that he left her despite her renewed appreciation of him. "If she's only interested in me when I'm acting like a cad," he told a mutual friend, "I'm better off alone. I can be a more honest man if I'm not married to a woman on whom I must cheat."

MARRYING A CAD

There are, of course, women who marry men with the unspoken but certain knowledge that the man is a cad. In such cases, it can be argued, a woman marries a man who remains exotic. He remains elusive, an enigma, as fascinating as another woman's husband. Indeed, she may well fall in love with him because he is or has been another woman's husband, which compounds his desirability in her eyes. For a woman who wants the exotic man, however, very little will be relaxing or, in the long run, secure or happy.

Henry James presents us with such a woman in *Portrait of a Lady*, published in 1881. Isabel Archer, a young American woman who comes into some money, is attractive, intelligent, honest, and self-reliant. Although "not without a collection of views on the subject of marriage" Isabel is convinced that the "first on the list was a conviction of the vulgarity of thinking too much of it." She wants to resist the seductions of the easy, domestic, and conventional life and refuses to be one of the women who are "more or less gracefully passive" as they "wait for a man to come that way and furnish them with a destiny."

Isabel is enormously marriageable, but she turns down several likely suitors. When a handsome and powerful English lord is smitten with her—something out of a Cartland romance, but without the requisite bad temper—"she would have given her little finger at that moment to feel strongly and simply the impulse to answer: 'Lord Warburton, it's impossible for me to do better in this wonderful world, I think, than commit myself, very gratefully, to your loyalty.' But though she was lost in admiration of her opportunity she managed to move back into the deepest shade of it, even as some wild, caught creature in a vast cage. The 'splendid' security so offended her was not the greatest she could conceive." Isabel wants something besides "the very brilliant" career of marriage offered her by Lord Warburton because her life would "be a little prosaic. It would be definitely marked out in advance; it would be wanting in the unexpected."

When her suitor offers to allow her to "keep" her independence, Isabel understands that true independence rules out the idea that another person can award it; if someone "allows" you your in-dependence, you are no longer independent. "Who would wish less tocurtail your liberty than I? What can give me greater pleasure than to see you perfectly independent—doing whatever you like?" asks Lord Warburton, because "It's to make you independent that I want to marry you.

" 'That's a beautiful sophism,' said the girl with a smile more beautiful still." When Isabel turns down Warburton she is pleased with her gesture.

The shine is taken off of the triumphant moment, however, when an older, more experienced female friend, Madame Merle, tells Isabel she should not consider her refusal of a good proposal as so important or creative: "We've all had the young man with the moustache. He's the inevitable young man; he doesn't count." Every attractive young woman with money has refused offers, she implies, and Isabel should set her sights higher when looking for triumph.

NO CAREER, NO NAME, NO POSITION

As the novel progresses, Isabel becomes deeply attracted to Gilbert Osmond, who is introduced by Madame Merle as a man having "no career, no name, no position, no fortune, no past, no future, no anything. Oh yes, he paints, if you please . . . His painting's pretty bad." Osmond, like Dracula, sleeps much of the day, has no employment, but still manages to make people around him "feel he might do something if he'd only rise early." Why does Isabel, who has been loved by such good men, turn to one who is so unlike them and who is so unlikely a candidate as a husband?

What James tells us harks back to what we saw in *Wuthering Heights, Casablanca,* and *Smart Women, Foolish Choices:* "It was not so much what he said and did, but rather what he withheld, that marked him for her . . . he was an original without being an eccentric." Isabel, then, turns away the traditional and nice men who want her and finds someone whom she wants, someone she thinks of herself as choosing. In marrying Gilbert Osmond, and in rejecting the men who offered her easier lives, Isabel believes she is carving out her own destiny. She sees herself as a sort of heroine. What is the outcome?

Apparently, according to James, when you marry someone who seems to be withholding, diffident, and aloof, he stays withholding, diffident, and aloof. He does not change the way Barbara Cartland's heroes do, suddenly becoming nice men once they are married. To attract Osmond in the first place, Isabel "had effaced herself when he first knew her; she had made herself small, pretending there was less of her than there really was. It was because she had been under the extraordinary charm that he, on his side, had taken pains to put forth." In a way, therefore, she was disingenuous. She pretended to be more "feminine" insofar as she pretended to be more submissive, more compliant, less intelligent, and to have less integrity than she actually possessed. As for Osmond, "he was not changed; he had not disguised himself, during the year of his courtship . . . But she had seen only half his nature then, as one saw the disk of the moon when it was partly masked by the shadow of the earth. She saw the full moon now—she saw the whole man . . . she had mistaken a part for the whole." She had fallen in love with Gilbert Osmond in part because Madame Merle had encouraged her to do so. We find out only later that Madame Merle was herself Osmond's lover.

When you marry a man who seems to have a sneering disdain for the rest of the world, chances are he'll stay that way. Why doesn't she just leave? When a friend asks the same question, Isabel replies, "I'm extremely struck . . . with the off-hand way in which you speak of a woman's leaving her husband. It's easy to see you've never had one!" When her earlier nice-guy suitors try to rescue her from her unhappy marriage, she refuses their chivalry.

The aloof, terrifyingly cold, and unhappy man still exerts an attraction, it is true. Perhaps, as the old adage goes, a wise woman prefers the man who has no passion for her to a devoted lover, for one day he may be in love with her, whereas one day, the lover may not. *Portrait of a Lady* is, in its own way, a terrifying book for both women and men because it is relentless in exposing the mechanism of a woman's attraction to a man with whom she will be unhappy and from whom she can expect no support.

"WHO ARE THESE GUYS IN REAL LIFE?"

Humorist Merrill Markoe suggests that we reconsider our longing for the aloof, mean, distant man. Listing men from James Dean to Johnny Depp, she asks, "Who are these wounded, brooding guys in real life?" and comes to the conclusion that they are "the emotionally crippled, paranoid, narcissistic guys with drug and alcohol problems who drove the woman of the Eighties into a frenzy."

They don't have to have substance abuse problems to drive you crazy, either. Sometimes the substance they abuse is *you*. My friend Kitty, while living far from the glamorous life of James's novel, shares some of Isabel's traits. Kitty married the "exotic man" of her dreams, a charmingly intelligent actor who'd broken the hearts of women on both coasts without so much as breaking a promise. (When, as happened for months after he moved in with Kitty, an old flame would call and accuse him of abandoning her, he would plead beguilingly, "Can I help it if she took the relationship more seriously than I did? I never told her I loved her and I never said we were any more than passionate friends.") He appeared devoted to Kitty. In response, she had a sense of confidence in herself that I had never seen before—it was both delightful to see her happy and scary to see her invest nearly all of her self-esteem in having "won" this man from women she considered more attractive and dynamic than herself. She would laugh that "If he wants me, then I'm hotter stuff than I thought!" As the relationship progressed, it seemed more and more solid. He told her he loved her, they lived together for two years and then married, to Kitty's absolute joy. He stopped leaving town as often so that they could spend more time together; maybe there were also fewer parts to audition for now that he was over thirty-five. He considered going back to take a few classes in arts management, and Kitty handed over the tuition money with pleasure. He stopped looking for work altogether, so that he could "think without diversion about how I really want to shape my life."

Gradually he became increasingly wrapped up in the local arts scene, and grew disdainful of Kitty's "corporate lifestyle," as he dubbed it. He wanted his wife to "stop acting so middle-aged and middle-class"—this after she showed up at a gallery opening straight from work, dressed in a suit and high heels when every other woman was wearing Betsy Johnson leggings and Arche shoes. She tried to meet both his requirements—that she be hip, on the cutting edge, and keep up the payments on their co-op, his tuition, and most daily expenses—but it took everything out of her. Like a constant drain on a battery, she had no energy left.

He accused Kitty of nagging him when she wanted him to escort her to business parties, and he started taking more and more money out of the account they shared—first without asking her and then without telling her, so that she found out how much money he'd spent only after the monthly bank statement arrived. But he was no less handsome, no less sexy, no less the center of attraction than he ever was, and Kitty believed that she would never find anyone like him. Other women flirted with him at parties, and Kitty left every event swearing that she wouldn't lose him. As you can imagine, her concerned friends watched with mounting horror as she poured her time, love, and money into this man who believed that he was entitled to all of it without repayment. It didn't seem as if this would ever end, and while we all knew better than to say anything directly, we encouraged Kitty to make sure that she knew whether this man was really right for her.

On her thirty-seventh birthday, Kitty waited at work for a mid-morning call (around the time he would awake) to wish her a happy birthday. No call came. When Kitty got home from work at six, he was watching the news and reading *Interview*. "Well," she asked hopefully, "you have anything to say to me?" She figured, by this point, that he'd actually forgotten her birthday and would be horrified to realize it, and they could laugh and celebrate. Instead he said, "Yes, happy birthday, kiddo," and smiled. She just stood there, he smiled a little longer, and went back to the TV and magazine. "That's it?" she exclaimed, her voice rising. "No gift, no kiss, not even a card?" He sighed with exaggerated patience and said, "What do you want from me? I'm here, aren't I?"

That was the moment Kitty knew the relationship was over. By this point she'd so encouraged him to think that he was the best thing that ever happened to her that he believed it in its most essential form. Without really changing his personality, and only altering his behavior slightly, this man had gone from being a reasonable companion to an unreasonable one. He felt a sense of entitlement to everything in Kitty's life, for which he would repay her by remaining her husband. His extreme dependence on her was coupled with a lack of respect that bordered on contempt: She had to *work* to be worthy of him, he just had to *be* to deserve her love and support. Kitty knew, after that exchange, that she deserved better. "It was like cutting off my own hand," as she put it, "but there was no alternative. I would have ended up killing him or myself, and frankly, I worried that it might be me. I felt no sense of worry when I thought it might be him."

She asked him to leave. He tried to woo her back, but his attempts were unsuccessful because Kitty recognized that the patterns engraved

in the relationship were unlikely to change; the acid of his disrespect
for her had gone too deep. He left after tears and promises never to
forget her, and soon moved in with the daughter of one of his
professors. Kitty is still getting over the relationship, saying that she
sees herself "not so much as an Ex-Wife. I think of myself as a
'Recovering Wife' because this is an ongoing process." What would
she tell women about the exotic man? "Tell them to think of the word
exotic as in 'exotic diseases.' Tell them to think of the word *exotic* not
as it applies to Tahiti or snow leopards but as it applies to ice caves in
Antarctica and vultures. Sometimes the exotic shouldn't appeal to us
but instead should appall us. Tell them that he's rare because of the
effects of natural selection—Nature knows that there should not be
more of his kind, and so prevents him from settling in one place for
very long."

CHAPTER TWELVE

NICE WORK IF YOU CAN GET IT

Work, Money, and Questions of Value

"A STARTLING THOUGHT this, that a woman could handle business matters as well as or better than a man," thinks Scarlett O'Hara, who had been reared in the tradition that "men were omniscient and women none too bright. Of course, she had discovered that this was not altogether true but the pleasant fiction still stuck in her mind." Scarlett is surprised to find that she is capable of working as hard and as well as any man. Scarlett recognizes that she can achieve the same success in business as she did in the social arena, and this irrevocably changes her ideas about relationships between men and women.

Though the inner life of even a good husband can remain an exotic landscape or a ledger of hidden accounts, the social script demands that his public life be strictly open to audit. Many studies suggest that the primary role of the husband as provider of food and shelter is strikingly cross-cultural and surprisingly unchanging, given the rapidly evolving role of the wife, which is most apparent when framed in economic terms: Most wives now work outside the home and significantly shape the financial profile of the family. How has this changed the role of the husband—or has it changed it at all? Women as well as men continue to believe, according to no less than three recently published surveys, that a husband should make more money than his wife, be able to support the family on the basis of his income alone if need be, and, presumably as a reward for these pressures, have his career regarded by both spouses as the more important of the two.

Marriage has always been grounded in economics; this is not news. What needs attention, however, is the tension between the growing impact of a woman's relationship to her working life and a man's relationship to his life as provider. Most men in America list the need to support their wives and families among the primary reasons to hold full-time employment. Is business still the primary business of being a husband?

Discovering that they can be good providers, able financial planners, stable heads of households, strong and compassionate adults, full of self-reliance and self-esteem, women no longer have to rely on men to provide them with a public identity or a meal ticket. But the legacy inherited by Scarlett O'Hara is one many women are still trying to shake: Many of us were encouraged to see men as absolutely instrumental in terms of our survival instead of as simply important in our intimate lives. Like Scarlett, I'd certainly "been brought up to believe that a woman alone would accomplish nothing," only to discover not only the possibility that a woman can manage very well on her own, but also the pleasure derived from that realization.

In a moment of epiphany that Margaret Mitchell took great pains to document, Scarlett realizes that she had "managed a planatation without men to help her . . . Why, why, her miund stuttered, I believe women could manage everything in the world without men's help." With the knowledge that she is as capable as a man comes new difficulties. Rearranging old information is always problematic: We have to shuffle around existing beliefs and make room for fresh insights. Scarlett feels "a sudden rush of pride and a violent longing to prove it, to make money for herself as men made money. Money which would be her own, which she would neither have to ask for nor account for to any man." As we've seen, Scarlett forfeits the right to be considered a truly "good girl" because she is both driven by passion and unable to disguise her deepest wishes and fears—although, as a consequence, she becomes expert at confronting them. At this moment, however, Scarlett sees for the first time that she can control her life in an entirely new way: by earning her own money.

The right and ability to control one's own money has always been an issue for women. When, for example, Virginia Woolf writes about the necessity of having "a room of one's own" in order for a woman to be able to be both autonomous and creative, she insists that a woman must also have her own income. Woolf gives her readers the figure of "five hundred pounds a year," but the amount is less significant than the idea: Even if the amount of money a woman earns is small, she has nevertheless earned the right to control her own life without asking permission from someone else. A woman cannot be bound to ask, beg, or cheat money from her husband and still maintain an adequate sense of herself.

I suspect that one reason I feel as strongly as I do about this point is because I grew up watching women spend much of their time trying to figure out ways of getting a little extra cash from their husbands. My mother did not learn to write a check until she was in her late thirties. I remember being with her at a local store when an older lady behind the counter explained that the store would accept a check written on my father's account; I don't think she had even considered the possibility of writing a check before that moment. Like many other women of her generation, she was given a certain amount of cash every week as a household allowance and was expected to meet all expenses with that small fund.

Anything "extra" had to be asked for specially. I remember eavesdropping guiltily when the "extra" item was something I wanted: a new doll, a new dress, or money for the movies. My mother would do my pleading for me when I was a kid, and we waited, like members of some guerrilla force, to ambush my father when he was "in a good mood." My mother would instruct me to help prepare his favorite meal and be cheerful until he was sufficiently relaxed. Then we pounced, giving all the good reasons for this unplanned expenditure. Sometimes it worked, and sometimes it didn't: I grieved for months after being denied a pair of fringed go-go boots, which had seemed crucial to my emotional well-being in fourth grade. I won't say that I felt like Scarlett O'Hara lifting her fist to the sky and swearing, "With God as my witness—I shall never be hungry again!" but I promised myself that when I grew up, I wouldn't have to play tricks on somebody to get them to buy me what I wanted. It didn't even occur to me then that I might grow up and have the financial ability to buy myself what I wanted.

My father worked hard—twelve hours a day, six days a week at a family business—and money was always tight. But neither of my parents thought my mother should work. She believed strongly that a married woman should be at home, keeping house and waiting for her children and husband to return from school and work. What she paid for not working outside the home was, I think, a great price: She was conflicted in the lessons she taught me, her youngest child and only daughter. I heard that I, too, should be a "feminine" woman who wasn't out there scrambling in the rat race, tough and wisecracking with the men. But I also knew that she wished there had been a way for her talents and intelligence to be recognized, and for her to have more economic independence than her life allowed her. Work outside the home would have given her an opportunity for both, as well as provided a community of people who knew her in a capacity apart from that of wife and mother. As it was, she was known only as my father's wife or our mother; there were times, I am sure, when she would have liked to have been known for her own abilities and interests.

I mentioned earlier that as a child I had hoped and planned for a wedding along with the best of them, but at a certain point I decided that I had ambitions other than marriage. Thinking back on it, there was a certain point at which my *own* life became the source of fantasy for me, and replaced the fantasy of who I would marry as my greatest obsession. When I began to imagine what I could *do*, rather than who I could *meet*, I knew that marriage would be a part of the picture but not the whole picture of my life. In deciding to earn my own keep, I was placing marriage in a new light.

I never wanted to have to ask anybody to foot the bill for my rent, my food, my clothes, or my education. Gifts could be accepted gracefully, of course, but an occasional present couldn't be relied upon to insure the needs of the future. I put myself through college and graduate school, and entered the work force as an assistant professor just after the age of thirty, having held a series of part-time jobs for ten years. I have come to respect work for the psychological and emotional payoffs it provides and not just for the paycheck. And I worry about women who think that by marrying for money they're not working for a living. It's clear to me that it's better to marry a man who will be your soul support rather than your sole support.

ECONOMIC SECURITY

Yet there is a tradition of women's marrying for two basic reasons: to provide a "name" for their children and for economic security. Helen Rowland once quipped, "When you see what some girls marry, you realize how they must hate to work for a living." But of course marrying a man who will provide you with economic security *is* working for a living: your job, then, is to be the wife he wants you to be. That can be, in some cases, more complex than the old adage has it—not only is a woman's work never done, it's not even regarded as work.

Taking care of a house, even taking care of a number of children, is regarded by many men as "fun" for a woman, an easy way out of having to do "real work," even if they don't put it into such definite terms. In *American Couples,* researchers—examining the responses of more than 18,000 couples—found that "a wife who is not employed outside the home is at a disadvantage. But this is only partly because she earns no money. We think it is the simple fact that she has a job that gives a wife clout. Men respect paid employment outside the home more than they respect housework." It is a simple equation, but unnerving nonetheless. What the research indicates is that men say one thing— that they respect work inside the home as much as they respect work outside the home—but that this, finally, is not true. "Men's own self-respect is in part derived from their success in the world of work and while they may say they have as much respect for a wife who stays at home, they in fact do not," argue Blumstein and Schwartz.

Their findings are perhaps best illustrated by a recent letter to an advice columnist concerning one man's frustration at the traditional economic arrangement. "Dear Ann Landers," wrote the disgruntled Chicago husband in 1992.

> Allow me to let you in on a little secret: Homemakers have it made. What other job allows a woman so much control over her work day? What other job frees her from true accountability? . . . What other job allows you to have the TV on all day while you're working, and if something interesting comes on, you can watch it and do the household chores later. Homemakers wish they were compensated for the true value of their services. Well, so do police, nurses, fire fighters and teachers. Like most everyone else, they get the going rate, and it's never enough . . . They will never get the respect they deserve until they stop pretending that their lives are so much more miserable than everyone else's. I would be forever grateful if I could stay at home with my boys and opt out of this stinking rat race called "the world of commerce."

He signed himself "Take This Career and Shove It." Ann Landers's response? "Dear Shove it: Well, well, well, there you are. I thought your brand of male chauvinism was dead and buried. Me thinks your basic problem is that you are unhappy with your own job, and perhaps that's what needs fixing in your life." Her response seems to be right on the money: The husband is resentful of what he perceives as the "easy" work given to his wife while he is being frustrated by the narrowness and misery of his own position.

Clearly, being a full-time homemaker is not an easy job, but it is *perceived* by men as easier than full-time work outside the home—and that's where some of the trouble lies. It should be mentioned that for some women and men, needs, desires, fantasies, and ambitions all dovetail perfectly, and there is no reason to fault any arrangement that works for them. But for many women, they fight the battle on both fronts: They work like hell all day, only to have their husbands ask, "So what did you do while I was gone?" as if they imagine their wives have been watching soap operas and eating bonbons since they left that morning.

Many women enter or return to the workplace with a sense of enormous relief after having been at home for a while: Working eight hours a day with people who treat you like an adult and pay you for what you do seems a bonus after living the life of a full-time homemaker. In a recent *New York Times* series on "The Good Mother," women describe trying to combine—as 58 percent of all women now do—a work life with a home life. They found that working has "brought unexpected benefits: a new sense of identity, a role in a broader community, pride in their independence, a temporary escape from children that may allow them to be better mothers in the time they share."

But the fantasy of the "Donna Reed" life is difficult to shake. "I make the cookies, the homemade costumes for Halloween," asserts a thirty-four-year-old mother of two who also works a full day at a local factory. "I volunteer for everything, just to make up for not being here. When I do all that, I get so tired that they lose a happy and cheerful mom, and then I'm cheating them again. It's hard when you were raised with Donna Reed and the Beav's mom." The Cleaver family, as one of my friends put it, was probably named that because they put our identities on the cutting board: "What? You *don't* wear pearls and high heels at breakfast?! (Wham) You don't make a three-course breakfast for the whole family? (Wham) You don't have a family? (Wham) You tend to stay up until two and don't eat breakfast? (Wham)." These women presented homemaking as a constant joy and, given that they were well "taken care of" by their successful spouses (Reed's husband was a physician, remember), there were no apparent difficulties.

There's a good deal of class-based reasoning behind this: Certainly I was brought up to believe that a man should be able to "take care of you" financially, although I abandoned that idea in my teens. Women who are assured of education and encouraged from childhood onward to see themselves as self-supporting no doubt had a greater sense of autonomy than women in my position, and yet even among the upper classes we see women seeking men who will be able to keep them in the style to which they have become accustomed. (I recall hearing a man declare that when he asked his prospective son-in-law whether he'd be able to keep his daughter "in the lifestyle to which she'd become accustomed," the fiancé unhesitatingly replied, "Sure. We're moving in with you.")

That women used to marry almost exclusively for money is not a surprise or a scandal. There were very few ways for women to go through life without being dependent on their fathers or their husbands because they were not permitted by law to have property of their own. George Gissing chronicles, in *The Odd Women,* Monica's decision to marry a much older, dour, and possessive man in order to free herself from the stress of working in a factory, despite the fact that "a year or two ago the image of such a man would have repelled her."

Young girls like Monica, who could barely support themselves, much less their families (women were often expected to make money enough to support unemployable relatives), had no alternative but to marry—or so they consoled themselves. Like George Babbit, in Sinclair Lewis's novel, who marries his weepy girlfriend, Monica marries because she can't think of a good enough reason *not* to marry. "As things went in the marriage war," Monica thinks, "she might esteem herself a most fortunate young woman. It seemed that he had really fallen in love with her; he might prove a devoted husband. She felt no love in return; but between the prospect of a marriage of esteem and that of no marriage at all there was little room for hesitation." Monica feels bound to accept his offer so that she will not have to face the alternatives of being a burden to her family, working herself to death for a pittance in a factory, or taking to the streets as a prostitute.

That she might be able to lead a life of dignity and self-respect while remaining unmarried is unthinkable for a woman in her position. We might be tempted to cluck our tongues at such a dreadful age, but I would argue that many uneducated, lower middle-class and poverty-level women live in such a world today. Given the choice of working fifty-five or sixty-five hours a week at two or more poorly paying jobs that offer no benefits and no hope of improvement *or* marrying a man they don't love but who seems "decent," many women would pick marriage. This is especially true of women who cannot accept responsibility for securing their own rights in the workplace. An old cartoon shows a neatly groomed woman sitting at a typewriter, wearing a button that reads, "Stop the Equal Rights Amendment." The cartoon declares, "This is Mary . . . She's underpaid, sexually harassed, passed over for promotion and stuck in a stereotyped role . . . She's also against the ERA . . . Why? She likes being treated special . . ."

There should be no surprise in this: If women are systematically paid less than men, they will depend on men financially. They will look for a life for themselves and their children that promises to remove them from the shadow of public assistance. They will marry to get out of the economic trap they're in; we have not come as far from Monica's plight as we might wish to think. Women and men, for the most part, continue to believe that it is a husband's job to provide for the family and assure them of a certain respectability of the world. "When married couples are disappointed with the amount of money they make, what they usually mean is that they are displeased with the husband's income," according to Blumstein and Schwartz in *American Couples*. "We infer this because we find that no matter how much or how little a wife earns, her income has much less impact on how each of them feels about the family income. It is up to the man to make the *couple's* mark in the world."

Humorist Carolyn Wells wrote in the early part of the century that "a fool and his money are soon married," and while we can chuckle over such a remark, the bottom line is that it's women putting their bottoms on the line when it comes to marrying for economic security. However, women who are self-supporting and financially independent, while wanting a man who will pay his share, no longer expect him to foot the bill. Many a CEO would gladly keep company with a man who kept regular hours, made a reasonable living, and had the self-confidence to fall in love with her.

THE "SOFT MAN"

Yet many, if not most, men still think women marry for money and economic security. Suspicious when women claim to want a man for reasons other than their financial acumen, many men are bitterly cynical. Warren Farrell snidely comments that "many men hear women saying they'd like a man who shares the housework. 'Is this true?' the men ask. Yes. Women do want men who share the housework, but only if it is in addition to being successful enough to buy the wardrobe and diamond." In a special 1991 issue of *Time* magazine devoted to women's issues, Farrell continues his battle with what he identifies as women's desire for a successful man, exclusive of any other needs.

"We have never worshiped the soft man. If Mel Gibson were a nursery school teacher, women wouldn't want him. Can you imagine a cover of *Time* featuring a sensitive musician who drives a cab on the side?" Personally I believe that women would continue to want Mel Gibson whether he was a nursery school teacher, a bankrupt used-car salesman, or a transvestite flamenco dancer, but I want to argue that it is *Farrell,* not his mythical "women," who cannot shake the old definitions. Tellingly, therefore, Farrell's statement is at best only partly true. Women *do* want men to share the housework, but they also want men to retain their integrity. Women place "companionship" as their primary reason for marrying, not money.

But it is also true that, speaking globally, men control governments, money, education—that, in short, men retain almost every shred of power offered by the world. Barbara Ehrenreich explains the way that this has been justified throughout history and passed off as "natural": "In the crudest antifeminist biologisms, it is the unequal distribution of reproductive functions from which all else follows. Since women bear children they must stay at home with them; God gave women uteruses and men wallets."

"THE CEO'S SECOND WIFE"

When *Fortune* magazine published its August 28 issue in 1989, Time-Warner was astonished by the response—it was the single largest-selling issue in the history of the publication. The cover story? Investments, stocks, bonds? Well, only metaphorically. A photograph of an attractive fortyish woman is framed by the title: "THE CEO'S SECOND WIFE." That women are encouraged to marry in order to achieve a certain status in the world, we have already seen. That a marriage is still inextricably entwined with a financial arrangement is, however, something we admit only with reservations.

Addressing issues ranging from the first wife's vision of the new wife ("first wives invariably think their husbands were lured away by hot

tomatoes proficient at the kind of sex formerly banned in most states")
to the ways in which men change during their second (or third or
fourth) marriages, this article brought the already-coined phrase "tro-
phy wife" into wide circulation. It emphasized that rich and powerful
men often choose to marry the most attractive, most polished, and
usually the youngest woman they can manage to be seen with (without
looking ridiculous), and they often achieve this second marriage by
discarding a first wife who no longer "met their needs."

In such a case, meeting "their needs" translates into being an
attractive, polished, and young woman, and this set of requirements
rules out the wife of their youth, the mother of their grown children.
"Why do men divorce their wives and marry younger women?" I asked
that of a friend who could have been interviewed for the *Fortune* cover
story. His reply? Without even stopping to think, he announced,
"Because they can." When I asked him to elaborate, he explained that
"they feel they have earned the right to have an expensive and
desirable ornament in their lives. A man who has spent most of his life
working to put together a business feels he's paid his dues by the time
he hits fifty-five or sixty. He probably feels like he's handed over his
best years to somebody else—the firm or his family. Now he wants
something for himself. And what he wants for himself is literally a
living doll. As long as women want a wealthy, well-placed man, such
men will be able to choose from among the most adorable and
slavishly devoted women."

Do women, in fact, still want to marry "wealthy, well-placed men"?
We are getting mixed signals about this issue. On one hand, many
women realize that they can support themselves and are no longer
bound to find a man with a prestigious job in order to make sure that
they are "taken care of" in financial terms. Yet some women also
continue to see financial success as sexy, and the men who most
capture women's attentions are the ones who achieve a certain measure of success in their high-paying careers. In the fifties, Phyllis Diller
could get away with saying a line like "I've been asked to say a couple
of words about my husband, Fang. How about 'short' and 'cheap'?" but
the joke now seems anachronistic. To disparage a man about his
height and his ability to earn was the equivalant of doubting his
virility. But there is still a connection between being thought of as a

"good earner" and a "good husband" in the minds of many men and
women. This schizophrenic division between knowing that you don't
need a man to support you and wanting a man who will be a good
earner is clearly spelled out in *Smart Women, Foolish Choices*, where
the writers emphasize the need for women to seek out men who are
"diamonds in the rough."

Now, it would appear at first glance that the male authors are
encouraging women to revise their requirements and take a second
look at men who do not fit the traditional definition of a "good catch."
Fine, you think, it's good to see some of the old shibboleths swept
away. But then they go on to provide examples of men they consider
"diamonds in the rough," and they all have gold-plated professions.
Without exception, as far as I can tell, the men presented as "wise
choices" by Connell Cowan and Melvyn Kinder in *Smart Women,
Foolish Choices* are men with high-earning, high-status jobs. These
"diamonds in the rough" can actually buy enough diamonds to smooth
over any possible difficulties.

Consider the men they see as good "potential" partners, ones
women might have overlooked, and see if you notice any pattern. We
hear about a woman who was ready to dump Dr. Ned, until the fateful
moment when she sees how good a guy a physician can be: "She'd
been encouraged by the 'best friend' to take the time to get to know
Ned but she knew she would never agree to a second date. Even before
his beeper went off, she had been trying to figure out a way to get him
to take her home directly after dinner." Everything changes, however,
when she sees that he can be authorative on his own turf. "After the
house call, they went to an all-night diner for coffee. What she had
seen allowed her to focus on Ned's passion, the kids he takes care of,"
the doctor/authors tell us. They also describe other men women might
pass up if they weren't trained to look carefully at possible partners:
"Chris is not trendy. But then, that is one of his strong points. He is
an attorney in an office which has a lot of flashy, dynamic go-getters.
Chris isn't the one who gets the most clients, but he is the one who
keeps them. He is a brilliant trial lawyer who wins over juries" and
"Freddy, a rather nondescript young attorney . . ."

It's hard to separate the men from the money here; most of the men
in *Smart Women, Foolish Choices* appear to be gold mines along the

lines of Nelson, a forty-three-year-old divorced physician, who is generally considered a "catch," despite the fact that he can be "pretty obnoxious—particularly on the first date when he is uncomfortable. On that first date, he's likely to be loud and boisterous and brag about money, possessions, vacations, and so on. Women find him insufferable." Why is Nelson desirable? Because he doesn't really mean to be a boastful creep. "What they don't know is that in spite of outward appearance, Nelson has always been rather shy and insecure about women." It would be tough to see Nelson as a "diamond in the rough" if he were insufferable *and* unemployed. No wonder many men feel like they are valued only for their ability to earn well. Many men were brought up to think that their main function as a husband was to provide a house so that their wives could stay at home. The resentments of the past several generations of men have left their imprint on the men of today, many of whom still live in the shadow of the "masculine mystique."

PUTTING ON THE GRAY FLANNEL SUIT

In one of the most popular novels depicting the "masculine mystique" of the 1950s, *The Man in the Gray Flannel Suit*, one of the main characters worries about the difference between the fantasy of marriage and actual married life. Sloan Wilson's 1955 novel describes a "typical" family living for "seven years in the little house on Greentree Avenue in Westport, Connecticut," which husband and wife both "detest," for "many reasons, none of them logical, but all of them compelling." The crux of Wilson's argument seems to be summed up by the line "Nothing's wrong with our marriage, or at least nothing permanent . . . We can't be like a couple of children . . . playing house forever." By telling themselves that they can't expect to play house forever, the couple in Sloan's novel is trying to account for the loss of pleasure they experienced after the first few years of marriage. They do not confront the deep nature of their misery but instead blame the system. They regard themselves as the victims of a world bent on destroying the integrity of the individual; they do not see that there could be something wrong with them as a couple. Tellingly,

Sloan's 1984 novel, *The Man in the Gray Flannel Suit II,* has the couple divorce and shows each making new lives of their own.

But there is no hint of that split in the earlier book—unless one is to look at the author's acknowledgments. This document, which is not part of the novel itself but is instead part of the nonfiction prefatory material, declares of the author's wife that while "many of the thoughts on which this book is based are hers," for two years she also "mowed the lawn, took care of the children, and managed the family finances" so that Sloan could find time to write. Perhaps she grew tired of all her ideas being penned under someone else's name while she did all the background work to make it possible?

The wife as volunteer muse/amanuensis/typist/editor/proofreader is not an unusual series of roles for a woman to assume. What is unusual for the wife in such a situation is getting any acknowledgment for her contributions, aside from a few words in the front of the book, which can be altered with each edition. Being supportive of a spouse in his or her work is, surely, what one expects. When that support translates into doing another person's work as if it were one's own, however, the dynamic changes drastically. The male author does not see his wife as a coauthor, even is she positions herself in such a manner. The dust jacket will be emblazoned with his name, the check will arrive with his social security number, and all fame will be awarded to him.

It is not true that behind every famous man stands a good woman, but it is true that anyone standing behind someone else is necessarily overshadowed by them. I have heard tale after tale of academic wives, wives of writers, wives of musicians, wives of painters—wives of any sort of "creative" man—who are driven to fury by the position they find themselves in after years of doing someone else's work instead of their own. Women who in their own right could have written, composed, painted canvases, or sculpted steel find themselves discarded by their husbands or at least written off rather than written about.

What do these husbands have to say about the situation? Confessed one aging colleague in genuine repentance:

"She became a functionary in my life. I swear that if I had learned to use a computer ten years earlier, I probably never would have married her. God forgive me, but I knew that I couldn't make it through graduate school without somebody like her. But, you see, it didn't have to be *her* exactly—anyone like her would have been just as good. I saw her, at first, as a lovely woman who was my helpmate. Then I began to regard her as a collection of the tasks she performed—typist, cook, social organizer—and I stopped seeing her as a full person. She became valuable not for who she was but because of what she *did* for me. I despised myself for what I felt. I left her when my own self-loathing became too difficult to live with." No doubt by the end of her marriage this woman felt that the quickest way to a man's heart is a knife through his back. Such a wife is a causality of the sort of response savored by many artistic men. For example, when Ernest Hemingway, was asked how he could leave his devoted wife and young children, he replied, "Because I am a bastard."

Such a woman might feel like the shrewish, nightmarish wife in Philip Roth's novel *My Life as a Man,* in which the novelist hero's wife considers herself an "editor," since she works with her husband on his manuscript. Roth's hero, Peter, is increasingly frustrated by his wife's insistence that she is as responsible for his work as he is; he resents her absorption of his talents. At a publishing party, Peter is asked by a young woman about his editor. He names a man at the publishing house, and suddenly his wife provokes a hideous scene. "What about me?" she shrieks, "I'm your editor—you know very well I am! Only you refuse to admit it! I read every word you write, Peter. I make suggestions. I correct your spelling." Peter pleads with her, "Those are typos, Maureen," to which his wife, at once pathetic and terrifying, cries, "But I correct them!"

The exchange here damns both husband and wife. If the husband gives his wife credit for being indispensable, he should not then be surprised that she considers herself exactly that—especially if, as often happens in traditional male-female divisions of labor, his work is the only work that is formally recognized by the world as important. She makes herself indispensable, and he relies on her; they do a duet. If she had her own work and her own definition of herself, she would not have a stranglehold on his life; if he insisted on doing his own work without her assumption of the "small and menial" tasks, then he could resist such scenes without guilt. As it stands, they have trapped one another, like two cars mangled in a wreck.

Both partners in such relationships are in an untenable position. If they are going to make his work "their" work, and by doing so, make his life "their" life, then the repercussions are going to echo through the rest of their life together—or apart. Certainly many couples have worked through various ways of sharing such matters with love and respect, and there is no reason to assume that any one pattern will work for all marriages. The problems arise when either spouse sees the marriage as imposing roles that are inherited but not chosen, or pushing ideas that are conventionally acceptable but personally repulsive. If a man feels, for example, that he should not have to assume the financial support of another able adult, he'll resent the burden and perhaps he will suggest that they work out a different way of dividing up fiscal responsibility. If, instead, he starts to feel like he's living a life as circumscribed and pressured as his father's, he might well balk at the prospect of continuing it. He probably does not want to be what Robert Bly calls a "fifties male."

THE PROMISE OF THE GOOD LIFE

In *Iron John*, Robert Bly describes "the fifties male" as a man who "got to work early, labored responsibly, supported his wife and children, and admired discipline." Sound promising? It comes as a package deal, and the rest of the package isn't appealing, given that "this sort of man didn't see women's souls well, but he appreciated their bodies," and that "underneath the charm and bluff there was, and there remains, much isolation, deprivation, and passivity." These men liked girls, in other words, but hated women, whom they feared and for whom they had deep-seated contempt. They were positive and optimistic on the surface, but chilly and resentful inside. Such men saw marriage as a sort of prison sentence imposed for the crime of lust and referred to their wives as "the ball and chain." They hoped, at best, to get into a minimum-security marriage, one that permitted temporary escapes and offered time off for good behavior. Many "fifties males" married because they were "caught" by a woman or merely ran out of reasons to run away.

Gore Vidal has been quoted as arguing that "the thing that makes

an economic system like ours work is to maintain control over people
and make them do jobs they hate . . . Make sure they marry young,
make sure they have a wife and children very early. Once a man has a
wife and two young children, he will do what you tell him to. He will
obey you. And that is the aim of the entire masculine role." Barbara
Ehrenreich develops the argument in *The Hearts and Lives of Men*
when she discusses the "Playboy phenomenon." Ehrenreich argues
convincingly that the "real message" Hugh Hefner was sending out in
the mid-fifties was not eroticism "but escape—literal escape, from the
bondage of breadwinning. For that, the breasts and bottoms were
necessary not just to sell the magazine, but to protect it. When, in the
first issue, Hefner talked about staying in his apartment, listening to
music and discussing Picasso, there was the Marilyn Monroe centerfold to let you know there was nothing queer about these urbane and
indoor pleasures . . . In every issue, every month, there was a
Playmate to prove that a playboy didn't have to be a husband to be a
man."

The idea that the ordinary man will in fact work hard only if he has
a family depending on him is paradoxical in relationship to the
received wisdom that to achieve greatness, however, a man is better
off alone. Pioneers in every field are seen as having to light out for the
territories on their own. A young businessman of some brilliance told
me recently that "as much as I would love to marry and settle down, I
won't do it until I make some kind of name for myself first—I want
everybody who's anybody in my field to know who I am. I'm sorry if
that doesn't sound humble enough these days, but if you want the
truth, that's the truth. Right now, I want to be able to pick up and go
where I need to be without clearing it with anybody besides my staff."

What does this philosophy do to his relationships? "My girlfriend
keeps trying to get me to say where we'll spend Christmas and whether
we'll go on vacation this winter, whether I think I'll want to go to the
beach in July, and whether I might want to go bowling in 1995. She
figures that if I keep saying 'yes' to all these dates, then she'll have me
sown up until I'm six feet under. She has her own life, and she needs
to make plans in advance. Fair enough, but she cannot push me to
make them with her."

In *American Couples*, Blumstein and Schwartz quote one of their male subjects on the question of economic dependence. His remarks are representative of a range of male anger at some women's expectations that they will be supported financially by their husbands. "I don't ever want to be in the situation again where some woman expects me to set her up for life. It's like having another child. Except there are a lot fewer rewards. I don't want to be around the kind of woman anymore who thinks the world owes her a living." But they also quote another young man who, when his wife started to achieve a measure of financial independence, became equally resentful: "She started selling these soap products which I thought was a good way to use up spare time . . . But you know, she's so much better than most of these ladies that they keep promoting her and giving her more responsibility and more territory. I think it's gone a little too far now because they want her to do more hours and be a trainer and I think it's gotten out of hand." It is clear that men are as conflicted as women when it comes to deciding what they want in a spouse: They don't want to support a woman, but neither do they want a woman who will have no need of them. They are resentful of women's dependence and fearful of their independence. In part, these problems arise out of the traditional basis of marriage as a system of exchanges—a system which no longer reflects the way we live.

A FAULTY EXCHANGE SYSTEM

By examining the cultural formats for the exchange of goods between men and women, we have seen the link between economics and erotics. Women have traditionally offered virginity for a wedding ring; the hymen was her proof that she had not been "used" by other men and his offer of an equally new, purely decorative yet expensive object was proof of his ability to provide material goods. This ritualized exchange also served to establish that the wife was a woman without a sexual past and that the husband will now be a man without a sexual future outside marriage. The insistence that the married woman will also be faithful is a remarkably recent development; it would have been heretical to say such a thing aloud one hundred years ago because the assumption was that women would no more desire to have nonprocreative, or "recreational," sex than they would wish to do an extra load of laundry. It was a wife's job to provide sex and she had to do it as dutifully as if she were working nine to five. Enjoying it almost seemed like not keeping part of the bargain.

If men sell themselves as providers, then women do the same—they simply provide differently and meet different needs. If men provide the money, then women provide the sex. Such a bargain is, in part, what is at work in "The Short, Happy Life of Francis Macomber" by Ernest Hemingway, a short story about a wealthy couple out for a hunt in Africa. Beautiful, seductive, manipulative, and impervious to her husband's vulnerabilities, Mrs. Macomber is dismissive of her rich and weak husband. She is "simply enameled in . . . American female cruelty," according to the guide with whom she has an affair. Why does the Macomber marriage stay together? The husband is valuable to his wife because he has money, is from an aristocratic family, and because she believes that he will never be able to leave her. "He was very wealthy, and would be much wealthier . . . If he had been better with women she would probably have started to worry about him getting another new, beautiful wife; but she knew too much about him to worry about him either."

Because of this mutual dependence, Hemingway tells us, "they had a sound basis of union. Margot was too beautiful for Macomber to divorce her and Macomber had too much money for Margot ever to leave him." Macomber is emotionally castrated by his wife, who sleeps openly with men and flaunts her cruelty to her husband the way a hunter might flaunt his kill. There are no illusions between them: Both husband and wife know that their marriage is based on a bad bargain.

But one day Macomber stumbles on his long-buried self-confidence and he is suddenly and profoundly elated by a sense of his own strength. He is successful on a hunt and experiences "more of a change than any loss of virginity. Fear gone like an operation. Something else grew in its place. Main thing a man had. Made him into a man." His wife, however, becomes frightened by her husband's new sense of self. " 'You've gotten awfully brave, awfully suddenly,' his wife said contemptuously, but her contempt was not secure. She was very afraid of something . . . Macomber laughed, a very natural hearty laugh. 'You know I have,' he said. 'I really have.' . . . 'Isn't it sort of late?' Margot said bitterly . . . 'Not for me,' said Macomber."

Fearing that, having earned his manhood, her husband would now be able to leave her, his wife kills him. She makes it look like an accident, and despite the fact that her lover witnesses the scene, she is clearly victorious over her husband. She will have to keep her lover appeased in order to secure her freedom, but she could not bear the thought that her husband might have ceased to support her. Having lived by her pretty face, she had to kill to preserve the right to continue living in such a way. To have a person too dependent on you cannot be, in the end, a healthy thing for anyone.

THE DIFFERENCE BETWEEN "HUSBAND MATERIAL" AND "WIFE MATERIAL"

Accordingly to the folk wisdom pervading our culture, women use their sexuality as bait and material for barter; women are themselves the commodity created and perfected in the "ideal feminine." A beautiful woman, traditionally, need not offer anything apart from herself to secure a husband, and from this assumption develops a framework that makes it seem perfectly natural that a physicist should marry his pretty lab assistant, that a CEO should marry an attractive flight attendant, or that a philosophy professor should marry a cute student. As long as the woman offers physical attractiveness coupled with sexual desirability, very few onlookers would question the man's motive for wishing to become the husband of such a woman; the sexually desirable, physically attractive, and socially acceptable woman becomes an object worthy of possession. The strong, successful, mature man is not questioned when he chooses a weak, un-directed, or childish woman so long as she is considered desirable by other men.

It is significant, however, that to be considered fit "husband materi-al," a man must possess an entirely different set of equally confining attributes: The commodification of men assumes that they will be ambitious, assertive, and successful. Although attractiveness and de-sirability are considered valuable bonuses, a man will be assessed in terms of his sexuality insofar as his sexuality is manifest in public, not private terms. A woman who married for looks or sex would be considered foolish. If a *female* CEO married the twenty-year-old who works in the mailroom she would be subject not to good-natured, vaguely envious joking but to ridicule. The projection of sexuality and that ill-defined but powerful force—"virility"—onto the social, economic, and cultural scripts for husbands still affects our most intimate relationships today. Some men need to make sure that their wives will look up to them and never look anywhere else.

FINDING AN OLD-FASHIONED GIRL

There are ways of finding women who will submit to the assigned script without a murmur, even in today's world. A man can choose a partner who is completely dependent upon him, a woman who will seek him out to fill her every need. Where to secure such a wife? "American Men Find Asian Brides Fill the Unliberated Bill," declared *The Wall Street Journal* on January 25, 1984.

> John Line's matrimonial specifications were very precise. As the 43-year-old Baldwin Park, California, cabinetmaker tells it, "I wanted a wife who isn't career-oriented, who participates very little in the world outside, who doesn't have high aspirations, who is useful, whose life revolves around me." He pauses, then adds: "And yes, she had to be a virgin." A tall order. But after a long search, the oft-married and oft-divorced Mr. Line found his ideal woman—in a remote rural hamlet in the Philippines. After spotting a picture of 23-year-old Felina Lamosa in a catalog of Asian women seeking American husbands.

Presumably even the most insecure of men would be able to deal with a woman whose need for the basic necessities of life might outweigh any desire to flee from a man who has purchased her right to live in his world.

Whoopi Goldberg, playing a Jamaican woman in her Broadway show, did a routine about the way such a woman might feel about her "sponsor": "Now I tell you, this man, he ask me, come to the United States of America. He all wrinkled, I say, you look like de old raisin.

He want me to clean and cook and have a little nooky . . . A while later now de old raisin come upstairs and he was naked and wrinkled, wrinkled, *wrinkled,* all I want to do is *iron* him." Goldberg's monologue provides a humorous response to the assertions put forth by the men seeking mail-order brides that the girls are thrilled to be married to older, unknown men in a foreign country.

And it's impossible to ignore the sort of joke made by one of my otherwise well-behaved aunts, who tells a story (which I believe she heard Bette Midler tell on television) about an older man who calls up a female friend on his eightieth birthday to announce his impending marriage to a twenty-year-old girl. "She says to him," this diminutive woman dressed in a housecoat says with a smile, "when I am eighty I'm gonna marry me a twenty-year-old boy. And let me tell you something: Twenty goes into eighty a helluva lot more than eighty goes into twenty!"

Finally, while the world does not revile relationships between older men and much younger women, it does regard them with a mildly cynical disdain. One account of a wedding in England between a lord and a woman nearly forty years his senior was announced in the London *Times,* which just happened to mention that "the bride-groom's gift to the bride was an antique pendant."

Is it unfair to ask whether the men who wish to buy a poor and disenfranchised woman's way into their world do so because they are so distrustful of the relationship between men and women that they have to purchase the right to a woman's body and, perhaps in the bargain, her heart? The gentlemen who were interviewed for the *Journal*'s article have an enormous amount of undisguised anger toward women. " 'American women put themselves on a pedestal and are neglecting U.S. men,' says Americus Mitchell, a 67-year-old retired patent attorney from Kilmarnock, Virginia. 'It's the same thing as when Ford and General Motors keep turning out bad products. You turn to the Japanese.' Or, in Mr. Mitchell's case, the Filipinos. A year ago, he was married for the third time, to [a] 21-year-old . . . from Quezon City near Manila." For the men described here at least, anger and fear of women who have *not* met their required levels of humility and subservience appear to be the motivating factors in their choices. "I won't buy American"—the product no longer meets their specifications. Rage and frustration appear, sadly, to outweigh the love of possibility—or the possibility of love for these men.

"SHE WHO LIVES BY THE PRETTY FACE, DIES BY THE PRETTY FACE"

In a cartoon by Charles Schultz, we see Peanuts characters Lucy and Schroeder in their usual positions: The blond boy is playing Beethoven on his toy piano and the dark-haired girl is leaning on the edge of the piano and talking about their eventual marriage. Lucy assumes they will marry; Schroeder does not seem remotely interested in the prospect. Undaunted by his persistent lack of interest, Lucy continually brings up the subject of their future lives together and often concentrates on what kind of living he can expect to make as a "piano player" (he considers himself a musician). In this particular scenario, Lucy begins by saying, "Let's just say you and I are married, see . . ." and then describes Schroeder's working as a piano player in some country club until he can "get a real job." Lucy imagines that he'll hate doing this for a living, but will consider it worth all the strain when his "beautiful wife" greets him at the door. In response, Schroeder picks up the piano and Lucy ends up on the floor, having lost her visible means of support. Still lying on the floor, she tells herself that "she who lives by the pretty face, dies by the pretty face." Leaving aside that Charlie Brown pursues the little red-haired girl without asking her what she'll do for a living, we can see that the cartoon (published in 1992) works on the assumption that little girls want to trade their charms for a man's financial security, and the punchline works on the realization that this is, at best, a tenuous arrangement.

FROM ROMANCE TO REALITY

THE QUESTION FACING us in the 1990s isn't whether people will pair off—there have always been couples and there will continue to be—but the question is: What *kinds* of partnerships do we expect? What kinds of romance do we want? What kinds of marriages should we enter—and what kinds should we leave? And, most important, what kinds of relationships—and what kinds of love—will we create for ourselves in the long run?

Our models for love are problematic. The definitions handed to us by poets, parents, and pop songs indicate that love is a combination of the following: an aching and/or itching in the heart, a ravaging hunger of the soul, an addiction, an infection, a drug, a wound, a bleeding heart, a fluttering tummy, and a weeping eye? Writer and comedian Rita Rudner wryly notes that "it's a good thing love is so painful. Otherwise, all the songs on the radio would have to be about root canal." Maybe if we didn't envision our need for love as a sickness, we could stop looking for a lover to cure us. We might then be able to find a husband who will be a partner rather than a miracle worker.

If women were encouraged from an early age to look at marriage as a long journey rather than a point of arrival, perhaps we would prepare more fully and more appropriately for the venture. I've known women to enter into long-term relationships in less time than it took them to decide on a winter coat, and with less attention to detail simply because they believed that if they didn't "fall" in love suddenly then they weren't in love at all. More than two hundred years ago Jane Austen argued that "a lady's imagination is very rapid; it jumps from admiration to love, from love to matrimony, in a moment." Austen's two-hundred-year-old observation is still powerful; it's one we need to respect—and reconsider. Maybe if we rewrite the script dictating that true love will be sudden, shocking, devastating, and unchangeable, our expectations for marriage would stop sounding as if we'd need a driver's-side air bag to survive the accident of meeting a potential mate.

Women and men need to move from romance to reality without sacrificing a sense of humor or a sense of self-esteem—and do it without throwing our hands up in frustration at what seems like the impossible task of revising three hundred years of cultural history. We cannot ignore the differences between how women and men are encouraged to look at marriage. A 1993 televised car advertisement, for example, declared that "if cars were men, you'd want your daughter to marry this one," with the implication that the car was safe, steady, and would last for years. My first response was to write to the ad agency behind the campaign and declare that if *this* woman were a car, she'd run them down. I can't imagine anyone selling a car by saying "if cars were women, you'd want your son to marry this one." (A man might like the idea of dating a car, but not marrying one, and he certainly wouldn't want one his parents to chose for him.) Such an ad simply wouldn't play well, because parents are still not in the business of marrying off their sons to women, no matter how low their mileage. The ideas of marriage has a long way to go before it catches up to how we really live.

Women and men both have to bridge with the gap between fantasy and reality. Women have argued for the past twenty years that we can't be expected to look like Christie Brinkley, think like Marie Curie, joke like Elayne Boosler, make money like Dolly Parton, and still be the sweet girl next door. We need to be aware of those times when we project equivilent fantasies onto men. It is simply not reasonable to expect a husband to have the perseverance of Prince Charming and Romeo, the mysteriously silent gallantry of Heathcliff and Clint Eastwood, the sexy brashness of Rhett Butler and Dennis Quaid, all the while unhesitatingly proffering comfort foods like a combination of the Keebler Elves and the Pillsbury Doughboy. The odds are that your husband won't both cook like Dom DeLuise and dance like Fred Astaire; it's rare to find a man who will show the compassion of Al Gore while exhibiting the wildness of Mel Gibson in *Mad Max.* If women reduce men to "husband material," they risk losing sight of the man as an individual. Nobody wins in such a situation because what you have is a woman searching through the remnants of a childhood fairy tale looking for a real-life partner. How far will we risk falling in order to fall in love?

I grew up falling—falling down, falling in love, falling apart. The scene I remember best from my first movie—*The Snow Queen*—was falling down right outside the theater, ripping my white tights and tearing up my knee. I went down on my knees a lot as a kid. Some of that has to do with growing up Catholic (always afraid of taking The Big Fall), but most of my spills had to do with not paying attention to where I was going. My scarred knees, which remain an embarrassment to this day, apparently illustrated my family's insistence that if I tried to run too fast I would end up not being able to go anywhere at all. The same dynamics pretty much applied to falling in love: If you didn't pay sufficient attention to where you were headed or if you tried to move too fast, you wound up down on your knees, maybe asking for forgiveness, or approval, or, most terrifyingly, love. Falling apart was more complicated because, by definition, you flew off in all directions at once, spinning and spattering yourself against all surfaces, the way a mixer removed too quickly from the cake batter causes chocolate to fly across the kitchen, or, less domestically, the way a bird randomly smashes against indoor windows, desperate for release. Free falls, delicious in their promise of chaos, turn out never to be for free. You pay most easily with a scar, or a divorce. Or you pay through the process of cleaning up the mess: blood, paperwork, chocolate, broken glass, a sense of self.

Romance promises but reality teaches. Sometimes it can seem as if you've fallen into a featherbed of love, but like the Princess and the Pea, you gradually discover the gritty details of your life that lie beneath the layers of insulation and which cannot, after a certain grace period, be ignored. You can't fall so far into love that you leave yourself behind. Perhaps at some point you realize that Prince Charming appears, rather suspiciously, as the hero in quite a number of fairy tales: Doesn't he rescue both Snow White *and* Cinderella? Is Prince Charming playing around, rescuing any old heroine who comes along and leaving his former conquests alone in their castles waiting for his call? Do you kiss a frog hoping he'll turn into a prince, only to find yourself turning into a frog? This is not a good sign.

Growing up, we often imagine that a special event or day will suddenly change our lives and make us into the girl we always wanted to be. We look to ritual and romance to change us, rather than seeing that we make and remake ourselves. We think that maybe on our sixteenth birthday we'll become the sweetheart of the school, or maybe it'll happen the day that our braces are removed, or when our skin clears up, or when we lost fifteen pounds, or when we finally figure out precisely what shape our face is so that we can get the right haircut. Later on we might think that if we could only choose the right college, choose the right job, or choose the right man and make the right marriage, that we somehow, magically, will be transformed into the right kind of woman, the heroine of the story we've pieced together from fairy tales, parental expectations, and social custom. Inconsolable over the loss of what was never really achievable—the perfect self or the perfect man—we mourn and pine for an illusion, often at the expense of our own real lives.

Remarkable and eccentric and imperfect as they are, our days and our nights are the only things we fully own, the only things over which we have any measure of control, and we all too often betray and abandon these days to longing, misery, anger, or disappointment. I think of afternoons spent waiting for a phone call that never came, or evenings spent in hurricanes of tears; I think of crying through days of college when I should have been contentedly bundled up in an overstuffed library chair, or evenings in London when I stayed home to be good instead of going out to enjoy myself as I should have done at twenty-two. I felt that I needed permission to be happy, and *I* knew that permission wasn't forthcoming. I didn't know then that I had to give it to *myself*: No one would be able to make me happy without my consent.

Not until my early thirties did I realize that I was fully responsible for my own choices and decisions and happiness; healthy and able, I had no business trafficking in misery. I was not cut out to be a tragic heroine, and I had to accept the fact that being drawn to men with whom I would be unhappy went back to the elementary school idea that if a boy liked you he teased you, tossed snowballs at your head, or left toads in your lunchbox. "Ooooh," your girlfriends would chant as you cleaned off the bugs he left on your desk. "He must *really* like you a lot." I didn't need advice to change my mind; I needed experience. There are moments of pleasure, laughter, and unity, but whole lives cannot exist in a state of perfection; some days will be boring, some will be difficult, some will be tense and full of impossible pressures. After too many painfully wasted afternoons and evenings, I realized that I was going to keep hurting myself if I kept expecting happy endings in the middle; my life was not going to be any one thing until it was inscribed on my headstone. Until then, I told myself, I shouldn't confuse happiness with stagnation. Life doesn't guarantee that anything will remain the same "forever after," but is instead synonymous with change, adaptation, and mobility.

What is alive can grow and move toward—or away—from any place it has once found itself. It is enraging and invigorating to think that nothing remains the same, however we try to pretend that we can close the book on change once we've achieved a certain goal. Certainly, and despite any fairy tale, no woman's life ends once she is married. For better or for worse, we all make and remake our own lives on a daily basis because no one day bears the burden of the future. No one page tells the whole story, not even the one that ends with "And they lived happily ever after." Whole days can be perfect, but whole lives cannot. And yet these good days should not be under-estimated.

When I was nervously greeting guests at my wedding a few years ago, I was eager for everything to go as well as possible. Surrounded by those people we loved and respected, my future husband and I were busy putting the finishing touches on our new house (putting up curtains, for example, until about two hours before the ceremony). Everything was set. The weather, a gray and rainy in the morning, had cleared to late-afternoon October sunshine. Friends were in the kitchen preparing food as I got dressed. Down to the last moments, it all went terrifically. Then there was some commotion about not being able to get the flower attached to Michael's lapel; with the best of intentions, some family members had ground the rose into the suit's fabric in their urgency to make it secure. The resulting patch of green undercut, to put it mildly, the dark blue suit's formality. Then as I was coming down the stairs, music playing, everyone expectant, the smoke alarm rang out from the kitchen, prompting one guest to say that surely this was a new ritual: "The alarm goes off, and the bride enters?" I sat on the steps until the noise stopped and finally went downstairs. By that time, the ribbon had dropped off my bouquet and was trailing behind me. The minister, a young woman who had prepared a lovely ceremony, began by saying that marriage was not an easy task, not meant for the cowardly since it was bound to be difficult at moments. "No marriage is perfect, but when they need your support, you should remind them of the perfection of this day." She paused, we paused, and the room was filled with applause and good-natured laughter. This day, with all its imperfections, was indeed as perfect as any day could have been. It was perfect because it contained within the possibility of making over the old rules and old scripts; it was perfect, not because it met any preconceived notions or fanta-sies—if a small fire in the kitchen had interrupted my plans fifteen years earlier I would have burst into tears rather than laughter—but because we had, with the community of people around us, made it—the day, our marriage—*our own*. It was as close to perfect as life allows because it was a celebration of change, and because the very imperfections of the ceremony and the day made it truly ours. Our signatures were there, in that green stain, tangled white ribbon, and in the laughter.

There are no perfect endings, but there are good, reasonable chances to create a future that includes room enough for *life* as well as for love. Married life does not, after all, have to be a contradiction in terms.

NOTES

CHAPTER ONE

Page 4   "If I were a man . . .": Cynthia Heimel, *If You Can't Live Without Me, Why Aren't You Dead Yet?* (New York: Harper-Collins, 1991), 75.

Page 6   "I think, therefore . . .": Lizz Winstead, 1989 performance.

Page 7   "I want a man in my life . . .": Joy Behar, 1989 performance.

Page 11   "every schoolchild understands . . .": Philip Blumstein, Ph.D., and Pepper Schwartz, Ph.D., *American Couples: Money, Work, Sex* (New York: William Morrow and Company, Inc., 1983), 319.

Page 13   "The boy of six wants . . .": James Thurber, "Claustrophobia, or What Every Young Wife Should Know." In *Tales for Males*, ed. Edward Fitzgerald (New York: Cadillac Publishing, 1945), 93.

Page 14   "While all children are . . .": Alexandra Symonds, "Neurotic Dependency in Successful Women," *Journal of the American Academy of Psychoanalysis* vol. 4 (January 1976): 96.

Page 16   "Have you any notion . . ." and "Life for both sexes": Virginia Woolf, *A Room of One's Own* (New York and London: Harcourt Brace Jovanovich, 1957), 26, 35.

CHAPTER TWO

Page 21   "For women, talk . . .": Deborah Tannen, "Sex, Lies, and Conversation." *The Washington Post* (Sunday, June 14, 1990): C3.

Page 21   "women speak because they wish . . .": Jean Kerr, *Please Don't Eat the Daisies* (New York: Fawcett, 1979).

Page 27   "female eccentricities . . .": Ellen Moers, *Literary Women* (New York: Oxford University Press, 1963; 1977), 100.

Page 29   "lusts after innumerable women . . ." and "resides in a large . . .": Albert Ellis, "Healthy and Disturbed Reasons for Having an Extramarital Affair." In *Current Issues in Marriage and the Family*, ed. J. Gibson Wells (New York: Macmillan Publishing Co., Inc., 1983), 276.

Page 29   "I noticed her in a corner . . .": Ninki Hart Burger, *The Executive's Wife* (New York: Macmillan, 1968), 144.

Page 30   "being an older unmarried girl . . . " and "if . . . you balk . . .": Lee Tidball, "This Is Why." *Good Housekeeping* vol. 137, no. 4 (October 1953): 62+.

Page 32   "Women do not wish . . .": Marilyn Quayle, speaking at the 1992 Republican Convention.

Page 32   "She has a very major cause . . .": Dan Quayle, quoted in *New Woman*.

Page 33   "postpones marriage even into . . .": Barbara Ehrenreich, *The Hearts of Men* (New York: Anchor/Doubleday, 1983), 12.

Page 34   "for both parties marriage is . . .": Simone de Beauvoir, *The Second Sex*, trans. H. M. Parshley (New York: Penguin, 1977), 447.

Page 34   "a girl must, a man may . . ." and "been bored all the afternoon . . .": Edith Wharton, *The House of Mirth* (New York: Penguin, 1985), 12, 22, 25.

Page 35   "Marriage promises to turn . . .": Maxine Hong Kingston, *The Woman Warrior—Memories of a Girlhood Among Ghosts* (New York: Vintage, 1977), 14.

Page 36   "an added number of friends . . .": Lee Tidball, "This Is Why." *Good Housekeeping* vol. 137, no. 4 (October 1953): 62+.

Page 37   "These women were as though . . .": Karen Horney, "The Overvaluation of Love: A Study of a Common Present-Day Feminine Type." *Psychoanalytic Quarterly* vol. 3 (1934): 608.

Page 37   "These women feel they have . . ." and "From childhood on . . .": Alexandra Symonds, "Neurotic Dependency in Successful Women." *Journal of the American Academy of Psychoanalysis* vol. 4 (January 1976): 101.

CHAPTER THREE

Page 42   "when marriages closed in . . .": John Updike, "A Month of Sundays" (New York: Fawcett, 1985).

Page 42   "When Sunday morning came . . .": John O'Hara, *Butterfield 8* (New York: Bantam, 1935), 14.

Page 43   "I sit in the sun . . .": John Cheever, "The Fourth Alarm." *The Stories of John Cheever* (New York: Knopf, 1978).

Page 43   "to watch the cycle . . .": Philip Roth, *My Life as a Man* (New York: Holt, Rinehart, and Winston, 1970), 78.

Page 43   "She wondered how Ernest . . .": Dorothy Parker, "Too Bad." *The Portable Dorothy Parker*, ed. Brendan Gill (New York: Viking Press, 1973), 175.

Page 45   "sitting there, quite alone . . .": D. H. Lawrence, *Sons and Lovers* (London: Penguin, 1913), 47.

Page 45   "I deal with problems . . .": Richard Meth and Robert Pasick, *Men in Therapy—The Challenge of Change* (New York: Guilford Press, 1990), 66.

Page 46   "Of the ten . . .": Leslie Koempel, "Why Get Married?" *The Saturday Evening Post* (February 14, 1965).

Page 48   "the shining-haired, the starry-eyed . . ." and "the bearing of children . . .": Philip Wylie, *A Generation of Vipers* (New York: Rinehart & Co. Inc., 1942; 1955), 184, 185.

Page 49   "wicked heart wandering . . .": Thomas Hardy, *Far From the Madding Crowd* (New York: Signet, 1960), 66.

Page 50   "the most common representations . . .": Richard Meth and Robert Pasick, *Men in Therapy—The Challenge of Change* (New York: Guilford Press, 1990), 59.

Page 51   "Feminism was established . . ." and "love is the only human emotion . . .": Rush Limbaugh, *The Way Things*

Ought to Be, ed. Judith Regan (New York: Penguin, 1992), 24, 25.

Page 52   "Male chauvanist pigs who . . . out there . . .": Herb Goldberg, "In Harness, the Male Condition." In *The Gender Reader,* ed. Evelyn Ashton-Jones and Gary A. Olson (Boston: Simon & Schuster, 1991), 65.

Page 53   "men married to working women . . .": Arlie Hochschild and Anne Machung, *Second Shift: Inside the Two-Job Marriage* (New York: Viking Penguin, 1989).

Page 54   "it was as if [men] had got used to . . ." and "This was a way . . .": Victor Seidler, *Rediscovering Masculinity— Reason, Language and Sexuality* (London: Routledge, 1989), 61.

Page 54   "I don't think women understand . . ." and "An 18-year-old virgin . . .": Anthony Pietropinto, M.D., and Jacqueline Simenauer, *Beyond the Male Myth—What Women Want to Know About Men's Sexuality* (Canada: Optimum, 1977), 139, 326.

Page 56   "Misogyny has deep cultural roots . . .": Victor Seidler, *Rediscovering Masculinity—Reason, Language and Sexuality* (London: Routledge, 1989), 48.

Page 56   "Men seem less complex . . .": Anthony Pietropinto, M.D., and Jacqueline Simenauer, *Beyond the Male Myth— What Women Want to Know About Men's Sexuality* (Canada: Optimum, 1977), 6.

Page 57   "a womb, an ovary . . .": Simone de Beauvoir, *The Second Sex,* trans. H. M. Parshley (New York: Penguin, 1977), 35.

Page 57   "Oh, good Lord, what's the matter . . .": Dorothy Parker, "Dusk Before Fireworks." *The Portable Dorothy Parker,* ed. Brendan Gill (New York: Viking Press, 1973), 141.

Page 57   "Man has succeeded in enslaving . . .": Simone de Beauvoir, *The Second Sex,* trans. H. M. Parshley (New York: Penguin, 1977), 219.

Page 58   "Why couldn't he [being a Master] . . ." and "Still a very good-looking woman . . .": Tom Wolfe, *Bonfire of the Vanities* (New York: Bantam, 1988), 11, 13.

Page 59   "a man of about thirty . . ." and "libido has taken up . . .": Sigmund Freud, *New Introductory Lectures on Psychoanalysis,* trans. James Strachey (London: The Hogart Press and the Institute of Psychoanalysis, 1984), 134–35.

Page 60   "whatever they may say . . .": Heather Jenner and Muriel Segal, *Men and Marriage* (New York: G. P. Putnam's Sons, 1970), 72.

Page 60   "a single Man has not nearly the Value . . .": Benjamin
          Franklin, letter to a friend, 1745. *American Families: A
          Documentary History,* ed. Donald M. Scott and Bernard
          Wishy (New York: Harper & Row, 1982), 55.

Page 61   "She had become so dully habituated . . .": Sinclair Lewis,
          Babbitt (New York: Signet, 1922), 10.

Page 61   "All her life Emily had been looking . . .": John O'Hara,
          Butterfield 8 (New York: Bantam, 1935), 138.

Page 62   "To precipitate a crisis . . .": Joan Wexler and John Steidl,
          "Marriage and the Capacity to Be Alone." *The Psychoanaly-
          tic Review* 41 (February 1978): 73.

Page 62   "I don't even know if I'm . . .": John O'Hara, *Butterfield 8*
          (New York: Bantam, 1935), 172.

Page 62   "I am a good man . . .": Sloan Wilson, *The Man in the Gray
          Flannel Suit* (New York: Pocket Books, 1955), 79.

Page 63   "It was coming to him . . .": Sinclair Lewis, *Babbitt* (New
          York: Signet, 1922), 221.

Page 63   "I'm dying . . .": John Updike, *Couples* (New York: Fawcett
          Crest, 1968), 217.

CHAPTER FOUR

Page 64   "as fun as tennis . . ." and "Today's Frigid Male . . .": Skip
          Hollandsworth, "Zipper Control—A Lesson Men Are
          Struggling to Learn." *Glamour* (July 1992): 122.

Page 65   "it is not uncommon to encounter . . .": Anthony Pietro-
          pinto, M.D., and Jacqueline Simenauer, *Beyond the Male
          Myth—What Women Want to Know About Men's Sexuality*
          (Canada: Optimum, 1977), 75.

Page 65   "Where these men desire . . .": Sigmund Freud, "The Most
          Prevalent Form of Degradation in Erotic Life." *The Col-
          lected Papers of Sigmund Freud,* vol. 1, ed. Ernest Jones
          (New York: Basic Books, 1959), 502.

Page 66   "confronted . . . with that female openness . . .": John
          Updike, "Baby's First Steps." *The New Yorker* 27 (July
          1992): 27.

Page 67   "Oh my America! . . .": John Donne, "Elegy on Going to
          Bed." *The Complete English Poems of John Donne,* ed.
          C. H. Patrides (London: Everyman's Classic Library,
          1991).

Page 68   "she bent and breathed . . ." and "You don't want to
          love . . .": D. H. Lawrence, *Sons and Lovers* (London:
          Penguin, 1913), 173, 218.

Page 68   "growing body of opinion which . . .": Philip Roth, *My Life as a Man* (New York: Holt, Rinehart, and Winston, 1970), 173.

Page 69   "an institution is a way of life . . .": Philip Blumstein, Ph.D., and Pepper Schwartz, Ph.D., *American Couples: Money, Work, Sex* (New York: William Morrow and Company, Inc., 1983), 318.

Page 70   "there is by now a very considerable . . .": Jessie Bernard, *The Future of Marriage* (New York: Bantam Books, 1972), 4.

Page 71   "there are still real dangers . . ." and "A man in that position . . .": Stephen Fried, " 'Thirtysomething': A Fun House Mirror on American Men." *GQ* (April 1989), 317.

Page 72   "as boys, we are brought up . . . " and "From an early age we learn . . .": Victor Seidler, *Rediscovering Masculinity— Reason, Language and Sexuality* (London: Routledge, 1989), 47, 157.

Page 74   "a man's social status has a sexual . . . " and "economic equilibrium, then . . .": G. V. Hamilton and Kenneth Macgowan, " 'What Is Wrong with My Marriage?': The Verdict of 100 Women." In *Men: The Variety and Meaning of Their Sexual Experience*, ed. A. M. Krich (New York: Dell Publishing, Co., Inc., 1954), 258, 269.

Page 75   "fewer than a quarter of the wives . . .": Philip Blumstein, Ph.D., and Pepper Schwartz, Ph.D., *American Couples: Money, Work, Sex* (New York: William Morrow and Company, Inc., 1983), 52.

Page 76   "Marriage is sometimes advised . . .": Rubin Blanck and Gertrude Blanck, *Marriage and Personal Development* (New York: Columbia University Press, 1968), 23.

Page 78   "P.O.W.s": Norman Mailer, *The Prisoner of Sex*, intro. Pete Hamill (New York: D. I. Fine, 1985).

Page 79   "It appears that ordinary men . . .": Thomas Hardy, *Far From the Madding Crowd* (New York: Signet, 1960), 127.

Page 79   "willingness to give up a lifetime's . . .": Walter Farrell, *Why Men Are the Way They Are* (New York: McGraw-Hill, 1986), 364.

Page 80   "the only thing about marriage . . .": Florence King, *Lump It or Leave It* (New York: St. Martin's Press, 1990).

Page 80   " 'Don't worry, darling . . .' ": Florence Moriarty, ed. *True Confessions—Sixty Years of Sin, Suffering, and Sorrow* (New York: Simon & Schuster, 1979), 61.

Page 81   "those who insist on believing . . ." and "We American males . . .": Allan Sherman, *The Rape of the APE—The Official History of the Sex Revolution 1945–1973* (Chicago: Playboy Press, 1973), 367, 394.

Page 84   "is suddenly faced with the realization . . .": Herb Goldberg, *The New Male: From Macho to Sensitive but Still All Male* (New York: Signet Books, 1979), 167.

Page 85   "We're all in this together . . .": Jane Wagner, *The Search for Signs of Intelligent Life in the Universe* (New York: Harper & Row, 1986).

Page 85   "became particularly uncomfortable . . .": Herb Goldberg, *The New Male: From Macho to Sensitive but Still All Male* (New York: Signet Books, 1979).

Page 85   "it was just beginning to dawn . . .": John O'Hara, *Butterfield 8* (New York: Bantam, 1935), 137.

Page 86   "men in their twenties . . .": Andrew Postman, "5 Ways Women Are Wrong About Men." *Glamour* (July 1992): 187.

Page 87   "we do the world's will . . .": George Bernard Shaw, *Man and Superman* (England: Penguin, 1957), 207.

Page 88   "no great virtues or rewards . . .": Anthony Pietropinto, M.D., and Jacqueline Simenauer, *Beyond the Male Myth— What Women Want to Know About Men's Sexuality* (Canada: Optimum, 1977), 91.

CHAPTER FIVE

Page 89   "likes to be able . . .": James Thurber, "Claustrophobia, or What Every Young Wife Should Know." In *Tales for Males*, ed. Edward Fitzgerald (New York: Cadillac Publishing, 1945), 94.

Page 90   "Prefer steady girl . . .": Anthony Pietropinto, M.D., and Jacqueline Simenauer, *Beyond the Male Myth—What Women Want to Know About Men's Sexuality* (Canada: Optimum, 1977), 99.

Page 95   "I shall decay . . ." and "There are two tragedies . . .": George Bernard Shaw, *Man and Superman* (London: Penguin, 1957), 203.

Page 97   "I know I did not . . .": Ernest Hemingway, *A Farewell to Arms* (New York: P. F. Collier & Son Corporation Publication, 1929), 32.

Page 98   "Even if luck . . .": Scott Turow, *Presumed Innocent* (New York: Warner Books, 1987), 398.

Page 98   "One evening when . . .": Sinclair Lewis, *Babbitt* (New York: Signet, 1922), 76.

Page 98   "who reached their . . ." and "unattached and on her": Philip Roth, *My Life as a Man* (New York: Holt, Rinehart, and Winston, 1970), 169.

Page 99   "until recently . . .": Herb Goldberg, *The New Male: From Macho to Sensitive but Still All Male* (New York: Signet Books, 1979), 185.

Page 101   "90 percent say . . .": Carl Arrington, "A Generation of Men Grows Up." *Men's Life* (October/November 1990): 65.

CHAPTER SIX

Page 107   "Married. It was . . .": Erma Bombeck, *Motherhood: The Second Oldest Profession.* (New York: Dell, 1985).

Page 107   "We think heterosexual . . ." and "Men are less . . .": Philip Blumstein, Ph.D., and Pepper Schwartz, Ph.D., *American Couples: Money, Work, Sex* (New York: William Morrow and Company, Inc., 1983), 253.

Page 108   "Among men, homicides . . .": "Odds and Trends." *Time* (Special Issue Fall 1991): 26.

Page 108   "though possibly thou . . .": Benjamin Wadsworth, *The Well-Ordered Family, or Relative Duties* (Boston, 1712).

Page 109   "the man is the . . ." and "the same false . . .": Pope Pius XI, "On Christian Marriage." In *The Gender Reader*, ed. Evelyn Ashton-Jones and Gary A. Olson (Boston: Simon & Schuster, 1991), 165.

Page 109   "He for God . . .": John Milton, *Paradise Lost*, ed. Scott Elledge (New York: Simon & Schuster, 1979).

Page 110   "adapt to his . . .": Marabel Morgan, *The Total Woman* (New York: Pocket Books, 1973), 81.

Page 110   "For God is always . . .": Cynthia Heimel, *But Enough About You* (New York: Simon & Schuster, 1986), 70.

Page 112   "desire [that] you . . ." and "letter was the . . .": Abigail and John Adams, letters to each other. In *American Families: A Documentary History*, eds. Donald M. Scott and Bernard Wishy (New York: Harper & Row, 1982), 106.

Page 115   "Your friend (or wife) . . ." and "your secretaries at work . . .": Joanna Russ, "Dear Colleague: I Am Not an Honorary Male." In *Pulling Our Own Strings*, ed. Gloria Kaufman and Mary Kay Blake (Bloomington: Indiana University Press, 1980).

Page 116   "The Husband must . . .": *Marriage Manual*, 1891.

Page 116   "rationalist philosophy . . .": Victor Seidler, *Rediscovering Masculinity—Reason, Language and Sexuality* (London: Routledge, 1989), 46.

Page 117   "obvious that the values . . ." and "these values are . . .": Virginia Woolf, *A Room of One's Own* (New York and London: Harcourt Brace Jovanovich, 1957), 26.

Page 118   "In conversations . . .": Marc Feigen Festeau, "Friendship Among Men." In *The Gender Reader*, ed. Evelyn Ashton-Jones and Gary A. Olson (Boston: Simon & Schuster, 1991), 75.

Page 119   "since it has been masculinity . . .": Victor Seidler, *Rediscovering Masculinity—Reason, Language and Sexuality* (London: Routledge, 1989), 47.

Page 120   "Someone who understands . . .": Cynthia Heimel, *But Enough About You* (New York: Simon & Schuster, 1986), 69.

Page 120   "the costs associated . . .": Cooper Thompson, "New Visions of Masculinity." In *Gender Images—Readings for Composition*, ed. Melita Schaum and Connie Flanagan (New York: Houghton Mifflin, 1992), 79.

Page 120   "The communication problems . . .": Deborah Tannen, "Sex, Lies, and Conversations." *The Washington Post* (Sunday, June 14, 1990): C3

Page 122   "Women should let . . .": Anthony Pietropinto, M.D., and Jacqueline Simenauer, *Beyond the Male Myth—What Women Want to Know About Men's Sexuality* (Canada: Optimum, 1977), 141.

Chapter Seven

Page 128   "romance is a lovely . . .": Sonya Friedman, *Men Are Just Desserts* (New York: Warner Books, 1983), 19.

Page 130   "by remembering that men . . .": John Grey, *Men Are From Mars, Women Are From Venus* (New York: HarperCollins, 1992), 33.

Page 131   "perpetuation of the family . . ." and "male culture seems . . .": Barbara Ehrenreich, *The Hearts of Men* (New York: Anchor/Doubleday, 1983), 8, 182.

Page 134   "But you were . . .": Terry McMillan, *Waiting to Exhale* (New York: Viking, 1992), 31.

Page 135   "Bennett and his colleagues . . ." and "found that marriage was . . .": Susan Faludi, *Backlash* (New York: Crown Publishers, Inc., 1991), 10.

Page 137   "single women over thirty . . .": Caroline Bird, "Why
            Women Should Stay Single." In *Current Issues in Marriage
            and the Family*, ed. J. Gibson Wells (New York: Macmillan
            Publishing Co., Inc., 1983).

Page 137   "research literature reaching . . .": Jessie Bernard, *The
            Future of Marriage* (New York: Bantam Books, 1972), 28.

Page 138   "Our home has only . . .": Henrik Ibsen, *A Doll's House*,
            trans. Fay Weldon, unpublished manuscript.

Page 141   "I told the operator . . ." and "It was as if . . .": Nancy
            Cobb, *How They Met* (New York: Turtle Bay Books/
            Random House, 1992).

Page 141   "I do not wish [women] . . .": Mary Wollstonecraft, *A
            Vindication of the Rights of Women* (Troy, N.Y.: Whitson
            Publishing Co., 1982).

Page 142   "I like men . . .": Ellen Currie, *Available Light* (New York:
            WSP, 1986), 90.

CHAPTER EIGHT

Page 144   "seek out states . . .": Connell Cowan and Melvyn Kinder,
            Smart Women, Foolish Choices (New York: Signet Books,
            1985), 103.

Page 144   "could enjoy all . . .": Ellen Moers, *Literary Women* (New
            York: Oxford University Press, 1963; 1977), 126.

Page 145   "lived alone, worked hard . . .": Alexandra Symonds,
            "Neurotic Dependency in Successful Women." *Journal of
            the American Academy of Psychoanalysis* vol. 1, no. 1 (January 1976): 101.

Page 146   "every woman adores . . .": Sylvia Plath, "Daddy." In *The
            Heath Introduction to Poetry*, ed. Joseph DeRoche (Lexington, Mass.: D. C. Heath, 1992), 419.

Page 146   "hook and eye . . .": Margaret Atwood, "You Fit Into Me."
            In *Responding to Literature*, ed. Judith A. Stanford (Mountain View, Calif.: Mayfield Publishing Co., 1992), 1180.

Page 147   "I blame Campion . . .": Margaret Drabble, *The Waterfall*
            (New York: Signet/Plume, 1969), 102.

Page 147   "women never tire of . . .": Thomas Hardy, *Far From the
            Madding Crowd* (New York: Signet, 1960), 154.

Page 148   "Peaceful, noncontentious living . . .": Jules Masserman,
            Individual and Familial Dynamics (New York: Grune &
            Stratton, 1959), 5.

Page 148   "Ashley was only . . ." and "I loved you so . . .": Margaret
            Mitchell, *Gone With the Wind* (New York: Avon Books,
            1979), 1016, 1029–30.

Page 149   "when these women . . .": Karen Horney, "The Over-
            valuation of Love: A Study of a Common Present-Day
            Feminine Type." *Psychoanalytic Quarterly* vol. 3 (1934):
            605–38.

Page 150   "since women do not . . .": Anthony Pietropinto, M.D.,
            and Jacqueline Simenauer, *Beyond the Male Myth—What
            Women Want to Know About Men's Sexuality* (Canada:
            Optimum, 1977), 299.

Page 151   "Did it never strike . . ." and "What do you talk . . .": Emily
            Brontë, *Wuthering Heights* (New York: Penguin, 1965),
            122.

Page 152   "How was I to know . . .": Erica Jong, *Fear of Flying* (New
            York: Holt, Rinehart, and Winston, 1973), 35.

Page 152   "He is handsome . . ." and "it would degrade . . .": Emily
            Brontë, *Wuthering Heights* (New York: Penguin, 1965),
            118, 121.

Page 153   "the oddity is that . . .": preface Albert Guerard, *Twentieth
            Century Interpretation of Wuthering Heights*, ed. Thomas
            Vogler (Englewood Cliffs, N.J.: Prentice Hall, 1968),
            65.

Page 154   " 'I wish I were a girl . . .' " and "if I cannot keep Heath-
            cliff . . .": Emily Brontë, *Wuthering Heights* (New York:
            Penguin, 1965), 155, 163.

Page 155   "back in say, 1807 . . ." and "If you really want . . .":
            Cynthia Heimel, *Sex Tips for Girls* (New York: Simon &
            Schuster, 1983), 200.

Page 155   "dark, handsome, and great . . ." and "most girls
            dream . . .": Barbara Cartland, *Barbara Cartland's Book of
            Love and Lovers* (Canada: Thomas Nelson & Sons Ltd.,
            1978), 46, 69.

Page 156   "It is a curious business . . ." and "I thought [while marry-
            ing]": Margaret Drabble, *The Waterfall* (New York: Signet/
            Plume, 1969), 115, 149.

Page 159   "A former police chief . . .": Herb Goldberg, *The New
            Male: From Macho to Sensitive but Still All Male* (New York:
            Signet Books, 1979), 10.

Page 160   "once a woman has . . ." and "by the distance . . .": Warren
            Farrell, *Why Men Are the Way They Are—The Male-Female
            Dynamic* (New York: McGraw-Hill, 1986), 59.

Page 160   "centerfold is sexual comfort . . .": Eric Goodman, "Men
            and Their Porn Pleasures." *Glamour* (July 1992): 92.

Page 161   "Professional Girls . . ." and "Professional Girls are desper-
            ate . . .": Cynthia Heimel, *If You Can't Live Without Me*,

Why Aren't You Dead Yet? (New York: HarperCollins, 1991), 114.

Page 162   "It's an accomplishment . . .": Ray Raphael, *The Men from the Boys: The Rites of Passage in Male America* (Omaha: University of Nebraska Press, 1988), 72.

Page 163   "women have always . . .": Barbara Cartland, *Barbara Cartland's Book of Love and Lovers* (Canada: Thomas Nelson & Sons Ltd., 1978), 43.

CHAPTER NINE

Page 167   "dat's de very prong . . ." and "gradually, she pressed . . .": Zora Neale Hurston, *Their Eyes Were Watching God* (New York: HarperCollins, 1990), 22, 67.

Page 169   "And if I married . . ." and "Why not take this . . .": Margaret Mitchell, *Gone With the Wind* (New York: Avon Books, 1979), 125.

Page 170   "choice of mate . . .": David Freedman, "On Women Who Hate Their Husbands." *Psychoanalysis and Female Sexuality* (New Haven, Conn.: College and University Press, 1966), 234.

Page 170   "when it comes to . . .": Philip Blumstein, Ph.D., and Pepper Schwartz, Ph.D., *American Couples: Money, Work, Sex* (New York: William Morrow and Company, Inc., 1983), 266.

Page 172   "All girls will haggle . . .": Paul Clemens and Pat Nerney, "The Little Black Book." In *Reading for Men*, ed. Alan Le May (New York: Nelson & Doubleday, 1958), 35.

Page 172   "Now, for God's sake . . .": Anita Brookner, *The Debut* (New York: Vintage Contemporaries, 1981), 117–18.

Page 172   "how valuable a woman . . .": *Marriage: Myth and Institution* (New York), 220.

Page 172   "Your first step . . .": Connell Cowan and Melvyn Kinder, *Smart Women, Foolish Choices* (New York: Signet Books, 1985), 60.

Page 173   "Here I am all of . . .": Terry McMillan, *Waiting to Exhale* (New York: Viking, 1992), 94.

Page 175   "Power is the ability . . .": Philip Blumstein, Ph.D., and Pepper Schwartz, Ph.D., *American Couples: Money, Work, Sex* (New York: William Morrow and Company, Inc., 1983), 283.

Page 176   "they don't like you . . .": Dorothy Parker, "A Telephone Call." *The Portable Dorothy Parker*, ed. Brendan Gill (New York: Viking Press, 1973), 121.

Page 176   "Many women are taught . . .": Dr. Cynthia Adams, personal interview.

Page 179   "mere passing academic . . ." and "This is how I fell . . .": Fay Weldon, "Ind. Aff., or Falling Out of Love in Sarajevo." *Moon Over Minneapolis* (London: HarperCollins, 1991), 43.

Page 183   "You can become . . ." and "With true masculine wiles . . .": Sinclair Lewis, *Babbitt* (New York: Signet, 1922), 295.

Page 184   "likely to have a . . ." and "our data tell us . . .": Philip Blumstein, Ph.D., and Pepper Schwartz, Ph.D., *American Couples: Money, Work, Sex* (New York: William Morrow and Company, Inc., 1983), 262, 264.

Page 186   "in a family . . .": Judith L. Alpert, *Psychoanalysis and Women: Contemporary Reappraisals* (N.J.: Analytic Press, 1986).

Page 187   "the bribe offered . . .": Alexandra Symonds, "Neurotic Dependency in Successful Women." *Journal of the American Academy of Psychoanalysis* vol. 4, no. 1 (January 1976): 97.

Page 188   "Knowing one is valued . . .": Judith L. Alpert, *Psychoanalysis and Women: Contemporary Reappraisals* (N.J.: Analytic Press, 1986).

Page 188   "a woman, dissatisfied . . .": Louise J. Kaplan, *Female Perversions—The Temptations of Emma Bovary* (New York: Doubleday, 1991), 527.

Page 189   "not allowed to fight . . .": Alexandra Symonds, "Neurotic Dependency in Successful Women." *Journal of the American Academy of Psychoanalysis* vol. 4, no. 1 (January 1976): 99.

Page 189   "told me of her . . .": Martin Symonds, "Psychodynamics of Aggression in Women." *The American Journal of Psychoanalysis* vol. 36, no. 3 (1976): 195.

CHAPTER TEN

Page 192   "Charles [is] rather . . ." and "all about love . . .": Gustave Flaubert, *Madame Bovary—A Story of Provincial Life* (New York: Penguin, 1950), 37, 47, 50, 53, 54.

Page 194   "put . . . down to her faulty . . .": Anita Brookner, *The Debut* (New York: Vintage Companies, 1981), 7–8.

Page 195   "Making life means . . .": George Bernard Shaw, *Pygmalian* (England: Penguin, 1957), 128.

Page 196   "there are a half . . ." and "if every novelist . . .": George Gissing, *The Odd Women* (New York: W. W. Norton & Co., 1977), 58.

Page 197   "in the past . . .": Margaret Drabble, *The Waterfall* (New
                York: Signet/Plume, 1969), 290.
Page 198   "That was the end . . .": Virginia Woolf, "Lapin and
                Lapinova." In *Women of the Century: Thirty Modern Short
                Stories,* ed. Regina Barreca (New York: St. Martin's Press,
                1983), 62.
Page 200   "the litany of the good wife . . .": Fay Weldon, *The Life and
                Loves of a She-Devil* (New York: Ballantine Books, 1983),
                26.
Page 201   "finding out how much . . .": "Companionship." *Brides*
                (April/May 1991): 369.
Page 203   "She would have . . .": Gustave Flaubert, *Madame Bovary—
                A Story of Provincial Life* (New York: Penguin, 1950), 53.
Page 203   "Whereas man is . . .": Simone de Beauvoir, *The Second
                Sex,* trans. H. M. Parshley (New York: Penguin, 1977).
Page 204   "no other road . . .": Betty Friedan, *The Feminine Mystique*
                (New York: Dell Publishing Co., Inc., 1963), 21.
Page 204   "deep sense of isolation . . ." and "the trivialization of
                life . . .": Elizabeth Janeway, *The Powers of the Weak* (New
                York: Knopf, 1980).
Page 205   "After months of planning . . .": Donna Hoke Kahwaty,
                "Postwedding Blues—Understand Your Depression." *Brides*
                (April/May 1991): 240.
Page 206   "Courtship is usually . . .": Philip Blumstein, Ph.D., and
                Pepper Schwartz, Ph.D., *American Couples: Money, Work,
                Sex* (New York: William Morrow and Company, Inc.,
                1983), 176.
Page 206   "too often, the bride . . ." and "look at your depression
                . . .": Donna Hoke Kahwaty, "Postwedding Blues—Under-
                stand Your Depression." *Brides* (April/May 1991): 240.

CHAPTER ELEVEN

Page 209   "a husband is . . .": Helen Rowland, *The Rubaiyat of a
                Bachelor.* (New York: Dodge Publication Co., Inc., 1915).
Page 211   "married because I . . .": Lou Saathoff, "Lovers and Other
                Husbands." *Lear's* (June 1991): 40.
Page 211   "a marriage would be . . ." and "Bathsheba loved Troy . . .":
                Thomas Hardy, *Far From the Madding Crowd* (New York:
                Signet, 1960), 38, 39, 156, 161, 179.
Page 215   "I should like to see . . .": Oliver Wendell Holmes, *The
                Professor at the Breakfast Table* (Boston: Tickner & Fields,
                1960).

Page 215   "without thinking . . ." and "I am convinced . . .": Jane
            Austen, *Pride and Prejudice* (London: Penguin, 1972).

Page 221   "not without a collection . . ." and "I'm extremely . . .":
            Henry James, *Portrait of a Lady* (New York: Penguin,
            1984), 106, 116, 162, 203, 214, 249, 252, 312, 475, 549.

Chapter Twelve

Page 227   "A startling thought . . ." and "a sudden rush . . .":
            Margaret Mitchell, *Gone With the Wind* (New York: Avon
            Books, 1973), 620.

Page 231   "When you see . . .": Helen Rowland, *The Rubaiyat of the
            Bachelor.* (New York: Dodge Publications, Co., Inc.,
            1915).

Page 231   "a wife who is not . . ." and "Men's own self-respect . . .":
            Philip Blumstein, Ph.D., and Pepper Schwartz, Ph.D.,
            American Couples: Money, Work, Sex (New York: William
            Morrow and Company, Inc., 1983), 139.

Page 233   "brought unexpected . . .": Susan Chira, "New Realities
            Fight Old Images of Mother." *New York Times* (October 4,
            1992): 1.

Page 234   "a year or two . . ." and "As things went . . .": George
            Gissing, *The Odd Women* (New York: W. W. Norton &
            Co., 1977), 68.

Page 235   "When married couples . . .": Philip Blumstein, Ph.D., and
            Pepper Schwartz, Ph.D., *American Couples: Money, Work,
            Sex* (New York: William Morrow and Company, Inc.,
            1983), 71.

Page 235   "many men hear . . ." and "We have never . . .": Sam Allis,
            "What Do Men Really Want?" *Time* (Special Issue Fall
            1991): 81.

Page 236   "In the crudest antifeminist . . .": Barbara Ehrenreich, *The
            Hearts of Men* (New York: Anchor/Doubleday, 1983), 69.

Page 236   "first wives invariably . . .": Julie Connelly, "The CEO's
            Second Wife." *Fortune* (August 28, 1989): 54.

Page 238   "She'd been encouraged . . ." and "pretty obnoxious . . .":
            Connell Cowan and Melvyn Kinder, *Smart Women, Foolish
            Choices* (New York: Signet Books, 1985), 208, 210, 219.

Page 239   "seven years . . ." and "Nothing's wrong with . . .": Sloan
            Wilson, *The Man in the Gray Flannel Suit* (New York:
            Pocket Books, Inc., 1955), 1, 114.

Page 241   "What about me?": Philip Roth, *My Life as a Man* (New
            York: Holt, Rinehart, and Winston, 1970), 120.

Page 242   "got to work early . . .": Robert Bly, *Iron John: A Book About Men* (Reading, Mass.: Addison-Wesley, 1990).

Page 242   "the thing that makes . . ." and "but escape—literal escape . . .": Barbara Ehrenreich, *The Hearts and Lives of Men* (New York: Anchor/Doubleday, 1983), 29, 51.

Page 244   "I don't ever want . . ." and "She started selling these . . .": Philip Blumstein, Ph.D., and Pepper Schwartz, Ph.D., *American Couples: Money, Work, Sex* (New York: William Morrow and Company, Inc., 1983), 88, 134.

Page 245   "simply enameled . . ." and " 'You've gotten awfully . . .' ": Ernest Hemingway, "The Short, Happy Life of Francis Macomber." In *Anthology of American Literature*, ed. George Michael (New York: Macmillan, 1989), 1458, 1465, 1472.

Page 247   "John Line's matrimonial . . ." and " 'American women put . . .' ": "American Men Find Asian Brides Fill the Unliberated Bill." *Wall Street Journal* (January 25, 1984): 1.

BIBLIOGRAPHY

Adams, Abigail, and John Adams. Letters to each other, 1776. *American Families: A Documentary History,* edited by Donald M. Scott and Bernard Wishy, 106–7. New York: Harper & Row, 1982.

Adams, Cynthia, and Paul Haskew. *When Food Is a Four Letter Word.* Englewood Cliffs, N.J.: Prentice Hall, 1984.

Alda, Alan. "Masculinity in Transition—What Every Woman Should Know About Men." In *The Gender Reader,* edited by Evelyn Ashton-Jones and Gary A. Olson, 56–59. Boston: Simon & Schuster, 1991.

Al-Issa, Ihsan. *The Psychopathology of Women.* Englewood Cliffs, N.J.: Prentice Hall, 1980.

Allis, Sam. "What Do Men Really Want?" *Time* (Special Issue Fall 1991): 80–82.

Alpert, Judith L. *Psychoanalysis and Women: Contemporary Reappraisals.* N.J.: Analytic Press, 1986.

"American Men Find Asian Brides Fill the Unliberated Bill." *Wall Street Journal* (January 25, 1984): 1, 22.

Arrington, Carl. "A Generation of Men Grows Up." *Men's Life* (October/ November 1990): 64–70.

Arond, Miriam. "Companionship." *Brides* (April/May 1991): 368–69.

Auden, W. H., and Louis Kronenburger, eds. *The Faber Book of Aphorisms.* England: Viking, 1964.

Austen, Jane. *Pride and Prejudice.* London: Penguin, 1972.

Atwood, Margaret. "You Fit Into Me." In *Responding to Literature,* edited by Judith A. Stanford, 1180. Mountain View, Calif.: Mayfield Publishing Co., 1992.

Barreca, Regina. *They Used to Call Me Snow White . . . But I Drifted: Women's Strategic Use of Humor.* New York: Viking/Penguin, 1991.

Benjamin, Jessica. *The Bonds of Love: Psychoanalysis, Feminism, and the Problem of Domination.* New York: Pantheon, 1988.

Bernard, Jessie. *The Future of Marriage.* New York: Bantam Books, 1972.

Bird, Caroline. "Why Women Should Stay Single." In *Current Issues in Marriage and the Family,* edited by J. Gibson Wells, 27–35. New York: Macmillan Publishing Co., 1983.

Blanck, Rubin, and Gertrude Blanck. *Marriage and Personal Development.* New York: Columbia University Press, 1968.

Blumstein, Philip, Ph.D., and Pepper Schwartz, Ph.D. *American Couples: Money, Work, Sex.* New York: William Morrow and Company, Inc., 1983.

Bly, Robert. *Iron John: A Book About Men.* Reading, Mass.: Addison-Wesley, 1990.

Bradstreet, Anne. "To My Dear and Loving Husband." In *The Works of Anne Bradstreet in Prose and Verse,* edited by John W. Ellis. Boston, 1867.

Brontë, Emily. *Wuthering Heights.* New York: Penguin, 1965.

Brookner, Anita. *The Debut.* New York: Vintage Contemporaries, 1981.

Brown, Michelle, and Ann O'Conner, eds. *Hammer and Tongues—A Dictionary of Women's Wit and Humour.* London: Grafton, 1988.

Burger, Ninki Hart. *The Executive's Wife.* New York: Macmillan, 1968.

Cartland, Barbara. *Barbara Cartland's Book of Love and Lovers.* Canada: Thomas Nelson & Sons Ltd., 1978.

Castro, Janice. "Get Set: Here They Come." *Time* (Special Issue Fall 1991): 50–52.

Caws, Mary Ann. "Realizing Fictions." Centential Residential Address of Publication of Modern Language Association, vol. 99, no. 3, May 1984: 312–21.

Cheever, John. "The Fourth Alarm." *The Stories of John Cheever.* New York: Knopf, 1978.

Chira, Susan. "New Realities Fight Old Images of Mother." *New York Times* (October 4, 1992): 1, 32.

Clemens, Paul, and Pat Nerney. "The Little Black Book." In *Reading for*

Men, edited by Alan Le May, 5–49. New York: Nelson & Doubleday, 1958.

Cobb, Nancy. *How They Met.* New York: Turtle Bay Books/Random House, 1992.

Cole, Wendy. "To Each Her Own." *Time* (Special Issue Fall 1991): 46–49.

Connelly, Julie. "The CEO's Second Wife." *Fortune* 28 (August 1989): 53+.

Cowan, Connell, and Melvyn Kinder. *Smart Women, Foolish Choices.* New York: Signet Books, 1985.

Currie, Ellen. *Available Light.* New York: WSP, 1986.

De Beauvoir, Simone. *The Second Sex.* Translated by H. M. Parshley. New York: Penguin, 1977.

Donne, John. "Elegy on Going to Bed." *The Complete English Poems of John Donne,* edited by C. H. Patrides. London: Everyman's Classic Library, 1991.

Drabble, Margaret. *The Waterfall.* New York: Signet/Plume, 1969.

Ehrenreich, Barbara. *The Hearts of Men.* New York: Anchor/Doubleday, 1983.

———. "The Wretched of the Hearth." *The New Republic* (April 2, 1990): 304+.

Ellis, Albert. "Healthy and Disturbed Reasons for Having an Extramarital Affair." In *Current Issues in Marriage and the Family,* edited by J. Gibson Wells, 275–83. New York: Macmillan Publishing Co., 1983.

Faludi, Susan. *Backlash: The Undeclared War Against American Women.* New York: Crown Publishers, Inc., 1991.

Farrell, Warren, Ph.D. *Why Men Are the Way They Are—The Male-Female Dynamic.* New York: McGraw-Hill, 1986.

Festeau, Marc Feigen "Friendship Among Men." In *The Gender Reader,* edited by Evelyn Ashton-Jones and Gary A. Olson, 74–85. Boston: Simon & Schuster, 1991.

Flaubert, Gustave. *Madame Bovary—A Story of Provincial Life.* New York: Penguin, 1950.

Franklin, Benjamin. Letter to a friend, 1745. In *American Families: A Documentary History,* edited by Donald M. Scott and Bernard Wishy, 55. New York: Harper & Row, 1982.

Freedman, David. "On Women Who Hate Their Husbands." *Psychoanalysis and Female Sexuality,* 221–37. New Haven, Conn.: University and College Press, 1966.

Freud, Sigmund. "The Most Prevalent Form of Degradation in Erotic Life." In *The Collected Papers of Sigmund Freud,* vol. 1, edited by Ernest Jones, 203–26. New York: Basic Books, 1959.

———. *New Introductory Lectures on Psychoanalysis,* translated and edited by James Strachey. London: The Hogarth Press and Institute of Psychoanalysis, 1974.

Fried, Stephen. " 'Thirtysomething': A Fun House Mirror on American Men." *GQ* (April 1989).

Friedan, Betty. *The Feminine Mystique*. New York: Dell Publishing Co., Inc., 1963.

Friedman, Sonya. *Men Are Just Desserts*. New York: Warner Books, 1983.

Gibbs, Nancy. "The Dreams of Youth." *Time* (Special Issue Fall 1990): 10–14.

Gissing, George. *The Odd Women*. New York: W. W. Norton & Co., 1977.

Gittelson, Natalie. "Marriage: What Women Expect and What They Get." *McCall's* 107 (January 1980): 87+.

Goldberg, Herb. *The New Male: From Macho to Sensitive but Still All Male*. New York: Signet Books, 1979.

———. "In Harness, the Male Condition." In *The Gender Reader*, edited by Evelyn Ashton-Jones and Gary A. Olson, 60–67. Boston: Simon & Schuster, 1991.

Goodman, Eric. "Men and Their Porn Pleasures." *Glamour* (July 1992): 92.

Goodman, Jack, and Alan Green. "Love, or How to Woo and Win a Woman." In *Tales for Males*, edited by Ed Fitzgerald, 31–38. New York: Cadillac Publishing, 1945.

Gray, John, Ph.D. *Men Are From Mars, Women Are From Venus*. New York: HarperCollins, 1992.

Guerard, Albert. Preface to *Wuthering Heights*. *Twentieth Century Interpretations of Wuthering Heights*, edited by Thomas Vogler. Englewood Cliffs, N.J.: Prentice Hall, 1968: 63–68.

Hamilton, G. V., M. D., and Kenneth Macgowan. " 'What Is Wrong with My Marriage?': The Verdict of 100 Women." In *Men: The Variety and Meaning of Sexual Experience*, edited by A. M. Krich, 115–32. New York: Dell Publishing Co., Inc., 1954.

Hardy, Thomas. *Far From the Madding Crowd*. New York: Signet, 1960.

Heimel, Cynthia. *Sex Tips for Girls*. New York: Simon & Schuster, 1983.

———. *But Enough About You*. New York: Simon & Schuster, 1986.

———. *If You Can't Live Without Me, Why Aren't You Dead Yet?* New York: HarperCollins, 1991.

Hemingway, Ernest. *A Farewell to Arms*. New York: P. F. Collier & Son Corporation Publication, 1929.

———. "The Short, Happy Life of Francis Macomber." In *Anthology of American Literature*, edited by George Michael. New York: Macmillan, 1989.

Hollandsworth, Skip. "Zipper Control—A Lesson Men Are Struggling to Learn." *Glamour* (July 1992): 122

Holmes, Oliver Wendall. *The Professor at the Breakfast Table*. Boston: Tickner & Fields, 1960.

Hochschild, Arlie, and Anne Machung. *Second Shift: Inside the Two-Job Marriage*. New York: Viking Penguin, 1989.

Horney, Karen. "The Overvaluation of Love: A Study of a Common Present-Day Feminine Type." *Psychoanalytic Quarterly* vol. 3 (1934): 605–38.

Hurston, Zora Neale. *Their Eyes Were Watching God*. New York: HarperCollins, 1990.

Ibsen, Henrik. *A Doll's House*. Translated by Fay Weldon, unpublished.

"Jake: A Man's Opinion. 'Take Control of the Breakup.' " *Glamour* (August 1992).

James, Henry. *Portrait of a Lady*. New York: Penguin, 1984.

Janeway, Elizabeth. *The Powers of the Weak*. New York: Knopf, 1980.

Jenner, Heather, and Muriel Segal. *Men and Marriage*. New York: G. P. Putnam's Sons, 1970.

Jong, Erica. *Fear of Flying*. New York: Holt, Rinehart, and Winston, 1973.

Joyce, James. *Ulysses*. New York: Random House, 1990.

Kahwaty, Donna Hoke. "Postwedding Blues—Understand Your Depression." *Brides* (April/May 1991): 240+.

Kaplan, Louise J. *Female Perversions—The Temptations of Emma Bovary*. New York: Doubleday, 1991.

Kelly, Mike. "Good Riddance to the New Man." *Men's Life* (October/November 1990): 35.

Kerr, Jean. *Please Don't Eat the Daisies*. New York: Fawcett, 1979.

King, Florence. *Lump It or Leave It*. New York: St. Martin's Press, 1990.

Kingston, Maxine Hong. *The Woman Warrior—Memories of a Girlhood Among Ghosts*. New York: Vintage, 1977.

Koempel, Leslie. "Why Get Married?" *The Saturday Evening Post* (February 14, 1965).

Lawrence, D. H. *Sons and Lovers*. London: Penguin, 1913.

Lawson, Annette. *Adultery—An Analysis of Love and Betrayal*. New York: Basic Books, Inc., 1988.

Legman, G. *Rationale of the Dirty Joke—An Analysis of Sexual Humor*. New York: Grove Press, 1968.

Lewis, Sinclair. *Babbitt*. New York: Signet, 1922.

Limbaugh, Rush. *The Way Things Ought to Be*. Edited by Judith Regan. New York: Penguin, 1992.

McMillan, Terry. *Waiting to Exhale*. New York: Viking, 1992.

Mailer, Norman. *The Prisoner of Sex*. Introduction by Pete Hamill. New York: D. I. Fine, 1985.

Masserman, Jules H., M.D., ed. *Individual and Familial Dynamics*. New York: Grune & Stratton, 1959.

Mead, Margaret. "Introduction." In *Men: The Variety and Meaning of Sexual*

Experience, edited by A. M. Krich, 9–25. New York: Dell Publishing Co., Inc., 1954.

Menninger, Karl A., M.D. "Impotence and Frigidity." In *Men: The Variety and Meaning of Sexual Experience,* edited by A. M. Krich, 99–114. New York: Dell Publishing Co. Inc., 1954.

Meth, Richard L., and Robert S. Pasick. *Men in Therapy—The Challenge of Change.* New York: Guilford Press, 1990.

Milton, John. *Paradise Lost.* Edited by Scott Elledge. New York: Simon & Schuster, 1979.

Mitchell, Margaret. *Gone With the Wind.* New York: Avon Books, 1979.

Moers, Ellen. *Literary Women.* New York: Oxford University Press, 1963; 1977.

Morgan, Marabel. *The Total Woman.* New York: Pocket Books, 1973.

Moriarty, Florence, ed. *True Confessions—Sixty Years of Sin, Suffering, and Sorrow.* New York: Simon & Schuster, 1979.

Morrison, Toni. *Beloved.* New York: Alfred A Knopf, 1987.

O'Hara, John. *Butterfield 8.* New York: Bantam, 1935.

"Odds and Trends," *Time* (Special Issue Fall 1991): 26.

Osborne, John. *Look Back in Anger.* New York: Penguin, 1957.

"The Outrageous Things Some People Say!" *Cosmopolitan* (September 1986): 152.

Parker, Dorothy. "Dusk Before Fireworks." In *The Portable Dorothy Parker,* edited by Brendan Gill, 135–50. New York: Viking Press, 1973.

———. "Here We Are." In *The Portable Dorothy Parker,* edited by Brendan Gill, 125–34. New York: Viking Press, 1973.

———. "A Telephone Call." In *The Portable Dorothy Parker,* edited by Brendan Gill, 119–24. New York: Viking Press, 1973.

———. "Too Bad." In *The Portable Dorothy Parker,* edited by Brendan Gill, 170–81. New York: Viking Press, 1973.

Pietropinto, Anthony, M.D., and Jacqueline Simenauer. *Beyond the Male Myth—What Women Want to Know About Men's Sexuality.* Canada: Optimum, 1977.

Plath, Sylvia. "Daddy." In *The Heath Introduction to Poetry,* edited by Joseph DeRoche, 419. Lexington, Mass.: D. C. Heath, 1992.

Pope Pius XI. "On Christian Marriage." In *The Gender Reader,* edited by Evelyn Ashton-Jones and Gary A. Olson, 163–67. Boston: Simon & Schuster, 1991.

Postman, Andrew. "5 Ways Women Are Wrong About Men." *Glamour* (July 1992): 132+.

Raphael, Ray. *The Men from the Boys: Rites of Passage in Male America.* Omaha: University of Nebraska Press, 1988.

Roth, Philip. *My Life as a Man.* New York: Holt, Rinehart, and Winston, 1970.

Rowland, Helen. *The Rubaiyat of a Bachelor*. New York: Dodge Publishing Company, 1915.

Russ, Joanna. "Dear Colleague: I Am Not an Honorary Male." In *Pulling Our Own Strings*, edited by Gloria Kaufman and Mary Kay Blakely. Bloomington: Indiana University Press, 1980.

Saathoff, Lou. "Lovers and Other Husbands." *Lear's* (June 1991): 40

Sayers, Dorothy. "Are Women Human?" *Unpopular Opinions*. London: Victor Gollancz Ltd., 1946.

Schaum, Melita, and Connie Flanagan. *Gender Images—Readings for Composition*. New York: Houghton Mifflin, 1992.

Schreiber, Lee. "Women—Counterespionage: What the Women's Magazines Are Saying About Us." *Men's Life* (October/November 1990): 20.

Scott, Donald M., and Bernard Wishy, eds. *America's Families—A Documentary History*. New York: Harper and Row, 1982.

Seidenberg, Robert. "The Trauma of Eventlessness." *The Psychoanalytic Review* vol. 59, no. 1 (1972): 95–109.

Seidler, Victor J. *Rediscovering Masculinity—Reason, Language and Sexuality*. London: Routledge, 1989.

Shaw, George Bernard. *Man and Superman*. England: Penguin, 1957.

———. *Pygmalian*. England: Penguin, 1957.

Sherman, Allan. *The Rape of the APE—The Official History of the Sex Revolution 1945–1973*. Chicago: Playboy Press, 1973.

Shultz, Charles. "Peanuts." *The Hartford Courant* (September 27, 1992).

Skolnick, Arlene. *The Intimate Environment—Exploring Marriage and the Family*. Boston: Little, Brown & Co., 1978.

Syfers, Judy. "I Want a Wife." In *The Gender Reader*, edited by Evelyn Ashton-Jones and Gary A. Olson, 341–44. Boston: Simon & Schuster, 1991.

Symonds, Alexandra. "Neurotic Dependency in Successful Women." *Journal of the American Academy of Psychoanalysis* vol. 4, no. 1 (January 1976).

Symonds, Martin. "Psychodynamics of Aggression in Women." *The American Journal of Psychoanalysis* vol. 36, no. 3 (1976): 195–203.

Tannen, Deborah. "Sex, Lies, and Conversations." *The Washington Post* (June 14, 1990): C3.

Thompson, Cooper. "New Visions of Masculinity." In *Gender Images—Readings for Composition*, edited by Melita Schaum and Connie Flanagan, 77–83. New York: Houghton Mifflin, 1992.

Thurber, James. "Claustrophobia, or What Every Young Wife Should Know." In *Tales for Males*, edited by Edward Fitzgerald, 93–104. New York: Cadillac Publishing, 1945.

——— "Courtship Through the Ages." *Tales for Males*, edited by Ed Fitzgerald, 9–13. New York: Cadillac Publishing, 1945.

Tidball, Lee. "This Is Why." *Good Housekeeping* vol. 137, no. 4 (October 1953): 62+.

"To Predict Divorce, Ask 125 Questions." *New York Times* (August 11, 1992).

Turow, Scott. *Presumed Innocent.* New York: Warner Books, 1987.

Updike, John. *Couples.* New York: Fawcett Crest, 1968.

———. "A Month of Sundays." New York: Fawcett, 1975.

———. "Baby's First Steps." *The New Yorker* (July 27, 1992): 24–27.

Wadsworth, Benjamin. *The Well-Ordered Family, or Relative Duties.* Boston, 1712.

Wagner, Jane. *The Search for Signs of Intelligent Life in the Universe.* New York: Harper & Row, 1986.

Weldon, Fay. "Ind. Aff." *Moon Over Minneapolis.* London: HarperCollins, 1991: 35–45.

———. *The Life and Loves of a She-Devil.* New York: Ballantine Books, 1983.

Wells, J. Gipson. *Current Issues in Marriage and the Family.* 3rd. ed. New York: Macmillan, 1983.

Wells, S. R. *Wedlock: Or the Right Relations of the Sexes: Disclosing the Laws of Conjugal Selection and Showing Who May and Who May Not Marry.* New York: Fowler & Wells Co., 1888.

Wexler, Joan, and John Steidl. "Marriage and the Capacity to Be Alone." *The Psychoanalytic Review* 41 (February 1978): 72–82.

Wharton, Edith. *The House of Mirth.* New York: Penguin Books, 1985.

"What Are the Odds?" *Men's Life* (October/November 1990): 8.

Wilson, Sloan. *The Man in the Gray Flannel Suit.* New York: Pocket Books, Inc., 1955.

Wolfe, Tom. *Bonfire of the Vanities.* New York: Bantam, 1988.

Wollstonecraft, Mary. *A Vindication of the Rights of Women.* Troy, N.Y.: Whitson Publishing Co., 1982.

Women pro & con. New York: Peter Pauper Press, 1958.

Woolf, Virginia. *A Room of One's Own.* New York and London: Harcourt Brace Jovanovich, 1957.

———. "Lapin and Lapinova." In *Women of the Century: Thirty Modern Short Stories,* edited by Regina Barreca, 55–62. New York: St. Martin's Press, 1993.

Wylie, Philip. *A Generation of Vipers.* New York: Rinehart & Co. Inc., 1942; 1955.